ORGANIZATIONAL BEHAVIOUR

THE 360 DEGREE SERIES

Series Editor: Paul E. Smith, University of Hertfordshire

Other titles in The 360 Degree series include:

Financial Accounting (forthcoming)
Parminder Johal & Beverly Vickerstaffe
ISBN 978 1 444 17041 2

Business Economics (forthcoming)
Rob Dransfield
ISBN 978 1 444 17045 0

ORGANIZATIONAL BEHAVIOUR

PAUL E. SMITH
WENDY YELLOWLEY
MARILYN FARMER

HODDER EDUCATION
AN HACHETTE UK COMPANY

Orders: please contact Bookpoint Ltd, 130 Milton Park, Abingdon, Oxon OX14 4SB. *Telephone:* (44) 01235 827720. Fax: (44) 01235 400454. Lines are open from 9.00 – 5.00, Monday to Saturday, with a 24-hour message answering service. You can also order through our website **www.hoddereducation.co.uk**.

British Library Cataloguing in Publication Data
A catalogue entry for this book is available from the British Library

ISBN: 978 1 44413 533 6

First Published 2012
Impression number   1 2 3 4 5 6 7 8 9 10
Year   2012 2013 2014 2015 2016

The advice and information in this book are believed to be true and accurate at the date of going to press, but neither the authors nor the publisher can accept any legal responsibility or liability for any errors or omissions.

Cover photo: Electric fan © cynoclub/iStockphoto
Typeset by Datapage India Pvt Ltd
Printed and bound in Italy

What do you think about this book? Or any other Hodder Education title?
Please send your comments to the feedback section at
www.hoddereducation.co.uk

CONTENTS

ACKNOWLEDGEMENTS

The authors and publishers would like to thank the following for their help and permission in writing this book:

Steven Borthwick

Ed Blisset

Gregor Gall

Elizabeth Kubler-Ross

Derek Pugh

Len Ryder

Every effort has been made to trace and acknowledge the owners of copyright. The publishers will be glad to make suitable arrangements with any copyright holders whom it has not been possible is contact.

SERIES PREFACE

The *360 Degree Series* is an exciting new range of textbooks that provides students with a clear introduction to business and management at undergraduate level. The books are very much written with the university and college student in mind, including those who are relatively unfamiliar with this particular field of study and are seeking a clear and accessible text to help them get up to speed with the subject quickly.

The *360 Degree Series* aims to inspire students' interest in the subject and to motivate them to explore further by setting out the key topics, important ideas and essential debates required for study. Relevant theories and concepts are clearly explained and applied to practice using case studies and real-life examples. Current trends are outlined and up-to-date material provided.

Within each book, chapters include an outline and objectives and are clearly structured with headings and sub-headings, so they are easy to follow and can readily be applied to lectures and seminars. Key terms are defined and case study boxes and activity questions include real-life examples that help to put learning into context. Students are encouraged to check their understanding at regular intervals throughout via a number of reflective questions, reinforcing the point being made and creating a solid basis for further learning. For revision, review questions and a key ideas table are included at the end of each chapter, together with recommended reading, useful websites and references to encourage further exploration of the subject. All this, together with the free online support materials, combine to make titles in The *360 Degree Series* essential companions for students studying the dynamic and exciting world of business today.

As editor of The *360 Degree Series*, I hope the books will help to boost your understanding and enjoyment of the subject, and thus lead to success in your studies.

Paul E. Smith
University of Hertfordshire
Series Editor

SERIES PREFACE

PREFACE

Organizational Behaviour (OB) is concerned with the design and functioning of organizations and the behaviour of individuals and groups within these organizations. It is therefore of crucial importance to students of business and management as well as to managers and employees. Some of the key questions include: What motivates people at work? What makes for effective leadership? What influence does our personality have on us at work? What is meant by 'emotional intelligence'? How can high-performance teams be formed? How can organizations be designed to ensure greater flexibility and responsiveness? The text also includes a review of new trends and contemporary issues in the workplace, including work-life balance, happiness at work, the value of soft skills, diversity, technology at work, and globalization. An understanding of such current and emerging issues will be of importance whatever your future career path and will help you to be better equipped to face the challenges of a rapidly changing and inter-dependent world.

One of the challenges of studying OB is that there are so many different views and perspectives on the subject, with a range of often competing ideas and theories. This book clearly sets out and explains such theories and perspectives through the key themes boxes and illustrates their application through the use of case studies, many based on real-life interviews. Once the initial ideas have been introduced and explained, you are encouraged to reflect and evaluate these for yourself. Questions that reinforce your understanding and help you to ensure that you have understood the concepts are provided throughout the book. At the end of each chapter review questions and a key ideas table are included for revision, together with recommended reading, useful websites and references to encourage you to develop your own understanding of OB with confidence. Also, to support you in your learning further, there are online resources, including extra case studies, sample essay questions and suggested answers – to access these, simply go to **www.hodderplus.com/360**. Registration is free and will take only a couple of minutes.

Paul E. Smith
University of Hertfordshire

Wendy Yellowley
University of Hertfordshire

Marilyn Farmer
University of Hertfordshire

GUIDE TO THE BOOK

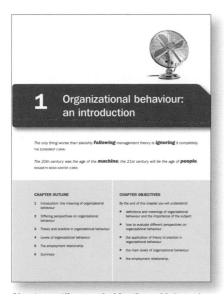

Chapter outlines and objectives Main topics and ideas are listed clearly at the start of each chapter to guide you carefully through the subject

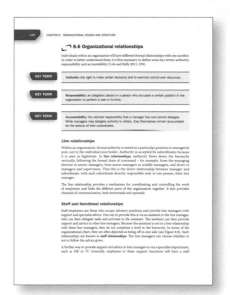

Key terms Terminology is both explained as you need it and gathered together as a glossary at the back of the book for reference

Case studies Relevant, real-world case studies highlight the key principles of organizational behaviour, bringing theory to life

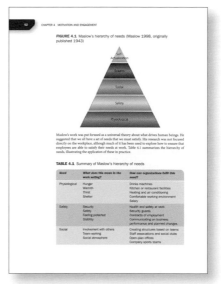

Tables and figures Carefully selected tables and figures illustrate essential concepts and complex ideas

Key themes These boxes provide different perspectives and a more rounded view of particular topics

Activities Activities are located throughout each chapter to facilitate comprehension

Reflective questions Frequent and challenging questions help you apply, analyse and evaluate what you've read to reinforce your understanding and promote critical thinking skills

Revision support Chapter summaries, review questions, recommended reading lists and references are provided to help you revise, and additional support materials are available at www.hodderplus.com/360

1 Organizational behaviour: an introduction

*The only thing worse than slavishly **following** management theory is **ignoring** it completely.*
THE ECONOMIST (1994)

*The 20th century was the age of the **machine**; the 21st century will be the age of **people**.*
ROSABETH MOSS KANTER (1989)

CHAPTER OUTLINE

1   Introduction: the meaning of organizational behaviour

2   Differing perspectives on organizational behaviour

3   Theory and practice in organizational behaviour

4   Levels of organizational behaviour

5   The employment relationship

6   Summary

CHAPTER OBJECTIVES

By the end of this chapter you will understand:

● definitions and meanings of organizational behaviour and the importance of the subject

● how to evaluate different perspectives on organizational behaviour

● the application of theory to practice in organizational behaviour

● the main levels of organizational behaviour

● the employment relationship.

1.1 Introduction: the meaning of organizational behaviour

Organizational behaviour (OB) is a popular subject on many business school degree programmes. It is also taught on a wide range of business and management postgraduate programmes and courses aimed at the practising manager. Yet organizations do not have 'organizational behaviour departments' in the same way that they have marketing, HR or accounting departments. What is OB? What does the subject cover? And why might it be considered important? These are some of the questions that will be considered in this chapter, and in the rest of the book.

OB can be defined in terms of the study of individuals and groups in organizations. As the second word suggests, one of its principal concerns is *behaviour*, of individuals and of groups, while the first word suggests that it also has something to do with the study of organizations. Thus, as a starting point, it can be suggested that OB is concerned with the behaviour of individuals and groups in an organizational context. For this, an understanding of psychology will be important.

KEY TERM

> **Organizational behaviour (OB):** can be defined in various ways, but, in general, OB is concerned with the behaviour of individuals and groups in an organizational context.

Exploring the organizational part of the term a bit further, OB is also concerned with how organizations are designed and structured, and how they function. Organizations will also be influenced by the external environment or context in which they operate. So here, some understanding of sociology will undoubtedly be important, and of organizational studies, politics and economics.

Combining the elements, however, reminds us that each will have an influence on the other: thus, how organizations are designed and run will affect individuals and groups within them, while, of course, 'organizations' themselves and how they are run are an outcome of individuals and groups of individuals.

ACTIVITY

> ### Definitions and meanings
>
> Here are a number of, and views about, OB:
>
> ❝ *that aspect of theory and practice concerned with the behaviour of individuals and groups in organizational contexts*
> (MARTIN AND FELLENZ 2010: 14)
>
> ❝ *the study of the structure, functioning and performance of organizations, and the behaviour of groups and individuals within them*
> (PUGH 1971: 9)
>
> ❝ *the study and understanding of individual and group behaviour and patterns of structure in order to help improve organizational performance and effectiveness*
> (MULLINS 2010: 3)

> " *a field of study that investigates the impact that individuals, groups, and structure have on behaviour within organizations for the purpose of applying such knowledge toward improving an organization's effectiveness*
> (ROBBINS *et al.* 2010: 7)

> " *a multidisciplinary field of enquiry, concerned with the systematic study of formal organizations, the behaviour of people within organizations, and important features of the social context, that structures all the activities that occur inside the organization*
> (BRATTON *et al.* 2010: 9)

> " *in leading textbooks, OB tends to be presented as largely cut-and-dried and settled, thus lacking any controversy, conflict or contest, yet such appearances are deceptive. There are fundamental differences of view – cultural, political and ethical – about how organizations are organized, how they should be organized and how they can be studied. To some extent, these mirror and amplify differences of opinion and preference among people working in organizations (between factions of senior managers for example) about how to organize and manage their operation.* "
> (KNIGHTS AND WILLMOTT 2007: 13)

Q   What are the similarities between the different definitions of OB outlined above? And how do they differ? Consider these views.

The importance of organizational behaviour

The definitions in the case study remind us to consider what the study of OB is *for* – that is, what is our purpose? For example, one purpose could be simply to improve our understanding: of ourselves and our behaviour, and that of others, and of organizations – that is, knowledge for knowledge's sake. Another would be to enable people to be better managers, and a related one would be to improve organizational effectiveness – that is, to enable organizations to run better. Lastly, it could be in order to improve understanding, not just for its own sake, but to challenge how things are perceived and done now – that is, the status quo – and to try to bring about change.

Reflective question

Why might an understanding of OB be considered of relevance to the practising manager?

1.2 Differing perspectives on organizational behaviour

People have differing views on a whole host of areas: politics and how best to run the country, art, sport, and so on, and they are often keen to express these – for example, on Internet blogs and networking sites, in letters to newspapers, on TV chat shows and on talk radio. It is no different in OB. If we look at the definitions of OB by the different authors in the case study in Section 1.1, we can see this: the first one stresses the behaviour of individuals and groups, and suggests a more *psychological* perspective. In the second, the stress is more on organizations and their structure and functioning, which could perhaps be termed an *organizational* perspective. The next two highlight organizational effectiveness and a more *managerial* perspective. Bratton *et al.*'s definition points to the multidisciplinary nature of the subject and emphasizes the social context – that is, a more *sociological perspective*; this and the last definition also adopt a more *critical* view.

One way that academics, managers and consultants can express their views is to write textbooks or articles. Of course, any one textbook does not have to adopt a single perspective to the exclusion of all others; many OB books are both multidisciplinary and cover multiple perspectives, as this one attempts to do. Similarly, just because a particular book takes a more *psychological* perspective on the subject, or a *critical* one, does not mean that it cannot also aim to be useful to the practising manager. It is just that books taking a more *managerial* perspective have a tendency towards seeing various approaches towards the management of employees, or the interaction between different managers or departments, as relatively unproblematic, while more *critical* perspectives point out that management decisions may be contested by employees and representative bodies such as trade unions, or that different managers may fight for political influence. Books written from this perspective therefore tend to put a greater emphasis on issues such as *power* and *control*.

1.3 Theory and practice in organizational behaviour

The study of OB is *multidisciplinary* – that is, it draws from a range of other subject disciplines, such as psychology, sociology, anthropology, economics and political science. Why should this be the case? The reason lies in the fact that any one situation at work is subject to a number of interconnecting influences. Consider, for example, a meeting between senior managers of a department and employee representatives to discuss and begin negotiations on next year's pay deal. The interactions will be influenced by the personalities, attitudes and behaviours of the individuals involved (psychology), as well as by the structure and the power relations in the organization (sociology), and the ability of the firm to pay (economics). To try to understand what is going on, therefore, we need to draw on these different disciplines. It could also be argued that a manager would increase his or her understanding and benefit from knowledge of such perspectives.

In studying OB you will be introduced to a range of different *theories*. This may give rise to questions about their relevance – that is, why study theory? Why not just look at practical examples of management in action in different organizational settings? To answer this question it is useful to look at an explanation of the meaning of theory:

> Theory helps in building generalized models applicable to a range of organizations or situations. It provides a conceptual framework and gives a perspective for the practical study of the subject. (Mullins 2010: 4)

Almost any management action or decision (on how best to motivate employees, for example) is based on some sort of idea or model about what the outcome will be, even if it is just a hunch. The advantage of such a manager being aware of various theories (of motivation in this case) is that it leads to a more in-depth understanding of the situation and, hopefully, a better decision and outcome. One could therefore argue that the test of a good theory is its usefulness – that is, the extent to which it can be applied in practice. This brings us on to another useful tool for managers: data and statistics that can be used to provide evidence-based arguments. This could be *quantitative* data (in the form of numbers or figures) or *qualitative* data (in the form of attitudes and opinions).

CASE STUDY The application of theory to practice

Joe is a production manager who has the belief that money is the key motivator. He therefore wants to introduce a simple, individual payment-by-results system: the more each individual worker has produced at the end of the week, the bigger bonus they will get and, Joe reasons, the more motivated they will be. But how can he test his belief?

What Joe has created is a model or theory: that the workers will be motivated by the chance to earn a bigger bonus and will therefore put in more effort, and also that this effort will lead to higher productivity. These ideas are not new; F.W. Taylor suggested something very similar in the early 1900s (see Section 2.3). How can Joe test his theory? One way would be to try it out in practice and measure the results. So he introduces strict measurement of what each individual produces and he tells his workers that, at the end of the week, he will give a bonus to those who have produced the most. But when he measures production at the end of the week, overall it has gone down. What can have gone wrong?

To try to find an answer to this question, Joe switches from quantitative data (measuring the amount produced) to qualitative data. He gathers a group of employees together to ask them for their opinions. What he finds surprises him: they feel that the new system puts them in competition with each other and they worry that this will threaten their friendships. In addition, much of the work requires them to collaborate with each other. Also, they do not like the strict supervision and measurement that have been brought in. In fact, they feel angry and are threatening strike action. What can Joe do now?

By looking at management and organizational theories of motivation, Joe finds that it is rather more complicated than he thought: although money can be one of the key motivators for many people, there are others, such as social and psychological factors (being part of a group, enjoying your job, having some responsibility). After considering this, and reading case studies of similar organizational situations, Joe resolves to consult with the workers first. As a result of this, team-based working is introduced, whereby each team has a certain amount of responsibility for how the work is carried out and who does what. Joe also introduces a team-based bonus. He finds that not only is productivity up, but so are staff satisfaction and morale. The new theory appears to be working!

Q Why is it considered important to study theory as well as practical application in OB?

1.4 Levels of organizational behaviour

OB can be looked at from a number of different *levels*, each of which interacts with the others. These levels are set out below.

The individual

Organizations are made up of a collection of different individuals, each with his or her own background, personality, attitudes, skills and attributes. Understanding the behaviour of individuals requires an appreciation of these differences, which is where psychology is important.

This is what makes the study of OB both interesting and at times complex and unpredictable. Different individual employees may react to the same situation in different ways. Thus any theory or model that suggests 'one best way' is likely to be flawed. Any management initiative may also need to take this into account. Consider an organization in which each member of staff has traditionally worked in his or her own individual office. As a result of reorganization, management are proposing to bring in open-plan offices, with many staff sharing one large space. How will staff react to this? The answer is likely to be that they will do so in different ways, some staff welcoming the change with its promise of increased connectivity and sociability, others bemoaning the fact that they will lose their sense of quiet and privacy. One of the key roles of management is to coordinate and integrate the individual members of staff in order to meet organizational goals, while at the same time being aware of such individual differences and needs. Matching the two is not always easy and this is sometimes referred to as 'the organizational dilemma'.

KEY TERM

The organizational dilemma: refers to the difficulty that may be experienced in reconciling individual goals with organizational goals.

One could easily argue that organizational goals will and should take priority, but it could also be suggested that there is a danger that this might be at the expense of employee morale and commitment. Equally, such goals may be contested. As Mullins (2010: 6) points out, where the needs of the individual and the demands of the organization are incompatible, this can result in frustration. This can lead to conflict and other consequences, such as labour turnover and industrial unrest.

Such differences may be unavoidable in a competitive environment, but there may be steps that management can take to improve such situations: if there is a culture of trust, for example, this will provide a more positive climate for when difficult decisions have to be made. Management processes, such as communication and involvement, may also help, as will demonstrating that alternative options have at least been considered before a decision was made.

The group

Much work is done in groups or teams and these are essential to the workings of organizations. Group working brings many advantages – different expertise and roles, ideas, support – but it may also bring challenges. Group members will influence each other in ways that may or may not be beneficial to the organization. As well as the formal groups set up in organizations, informal groups are likely to arise. Just as we need to understand the psychology of individual behaviour, we need to understand group structure, functioning and behaviour.

The organization

Individual behaviour and interaction, as well as group functioning, take place within, and are influenced by, the context of the organization. Organizations have formal *structures* that set out the different levels and job roles in the organization and the relationships between these. Structures can be formal and hierarchical or more flexible and flat. The behaviour of individuals and groups will be influenced by such structures, as well as by the *culture*, *technology* and *management style* of the organization.

KEY TERM

Organization: 'a social arrangement for achieving controlled performance in pursuit of collective goals' (Buchanan and Huczynski 2010: 8).

The environment

Organizations operate within the wider environment – local, national and global – and changes and trends in this environment will influence the activities of organizations. For example, individual employees come from this environment, so demographic and population trends, as well as societal changes, will impact on the internal workings of the organization.

One way of categorizing the external environment is via a PESTLE analysis – that is, to outline and consider the influence of political, economic, social, technological, legal and environmental factors and trends. All these will affect the functioning of organizations and the behaviour of individuals and groups within them.

KEY THEMES Metaphors of organizational life

In his book, *Images of Organization*, Gareth Morgan (1997) suggests that metaphors can enhance our understanding of organizational life. When we use a metaphor, such as 'this man is lion-hearted', we get an image in our minds of a lion and this helps us to focus on and imagine a particular feature or quality of the subject we are referring to, in this case, the man's courage and strength.

Metaphors are particularly relevant to organizations and management because organizations are such complex entities. By using different metaphors, we are able to better understand organizations and how to manage them. Morgan uses eight organizational metaphors:

1 Thinking of organizations as **machines** helps us to focus on the efficient and orderly relation between the different parts of the organization, just as a machine operates in a predictable and reliable way. We can see this focus in the writings of classical management theorists, such as Fayol and Weber. It also helps us to understand the possible negative consequences of this – for example, if managers focus too much on orderly and efficient operation, then the human element may be lost.

2 If we think of organizations as living **organisms** – that is, in biological terms – we start to think about how organizations depend on, and need to adapt to, their environment, just as an animal or a plant needs to adapt.

3 Viewing organizations as **brains** helps us to focus on the inventive and creative aspects. It may help managers to organize things in such a way that enhances flexibility and creative action.

4 Focusing on **cultures** emphasizes the values, beliefs and day-to-day rituals found in organizations. The culture of an organization shows itself in many different ways, and at different levels – for example, how people dress and speak to each other, or the organization's mission statement. Shared values stress a culture common to all in the organization, yet there may be subcultures that challenge this.

5 Political behaviour is part of organizational life, yet it is not often discussed openly. Viewing organizations as **political systems** reminds us of the power relations, the negotiating, dealing and influencing that go on every day in organizations.

6 Using the metaphor of **psychic prisons**, Morgan encourages us to see the darker side of organizational life. He argues that people in everyday life are trapped by illusions, and hence the way they understand reality is at best partial, and the same applies to people in organizations. This metaphor also encourages us to dig beneath the surface and consider the unconscious processes and patterns that exert a strong influence on us.

7   Staying with the darker side, the metaphor of **instruments of domination** focuses on how organizations can lead to the few dominating the many. Using this metaphor, we see how organizations can use and exploit their employees. Work hazards, industrial accidents and stress can lead to work being detrimental to the physical and psychological health of workers. Cheap labour in the developing world can be used by multinationals to provide cheap goods in sweatshop conditions. Such multinationals may be major forces in the world economy. Examples of abuse include the 1984 disaster at the Union Carbide plant in Bhopal, India, in which thousands died, and the role of certain banks prior to the financial crisis in the first decade of the 21st century.

8   Just as the universe is in a state of constant **flux and transformation**, so are organizations. Flux and transformation embody characteristics of both permanence and change. Using this metaphor encourages us to view organizations as having the ability to change and to play an active role – for example, in influencing their environment. Thus, if organizations are currently polluting the planet and creating greenhouse gases, they have the potential to transform and become environmentally friendly.

Q   How might the use of metaphors increase our understanding of the workings of organizations?

1.5 The employment relationship

In the previous section we outlined how OB could be viewed at a number of different levels: individual, group, organizational and the wider context – that is, the local, national and global environment. Bratton *et al.* (2010) and others have argued that any one aspect or level cannot usefully be examined in isolation, since each interacts with, is influenced by and in turn influences the others. Thus we need to adopt a *multidimensional approach* to studying OB. Individual employees are not passive robots that employers, or their agents (that is, managers), can simply influence and control as they wish. Individual employees differ on a number of levels, such as age, personality, education, background and life experiences, and they bring these with them into the workplace. They also bring with them their expectations, beliefs and attitudes. All these factors combine to influence organizations and their managers. Not only that, but individuals form groups, both formal and informal, in the workplace and outside, and these may challenge the management prerogative. Of course, employers and managers are also individuals with their own backgrounds and beliefs, and they in turn form groups.

KEY TERM

> **Technology:** how an organization transfers its inputs into outputs.

At an organizational level, the *strategy, technology, structure, culture* and *management processes* of the organization exert an influence on and are also formed and influenced by individual managers and employees, as well as groups.

Finally, the external context both exerts an influence on and is in turn influenced by organizations and the individuals and groups that make up these organizations. Thus, for example, legislation, economic activity and technological developments all affect organizations, as do the activities of competitor organizations, of course. Increasingly, *globalization* means that these influences have a global reach. European Union regulations, international trade agreements and competition from organizations in other countries are all examples of this.

Globalization: the process in which organizations extend their activities beyond purely national boundaries to participate and compete around the world.

1 | Think of an organization you are familiar with. What are and what have been the key external influences on this organization, now and in the recent past? How have these external factors influenced this organization?

2 | Look through a current copy of the *Financial Times* or the business pages of any quality newspaper. What are the key external influences impacting on organizations mentioned in these pages?

The different actors, processes and influences introduced above can be summarized and analysed in terms of the *employment relationship*. This relationship is set out in Figure 1.1.

FIGURE 1.1 The employment relationship

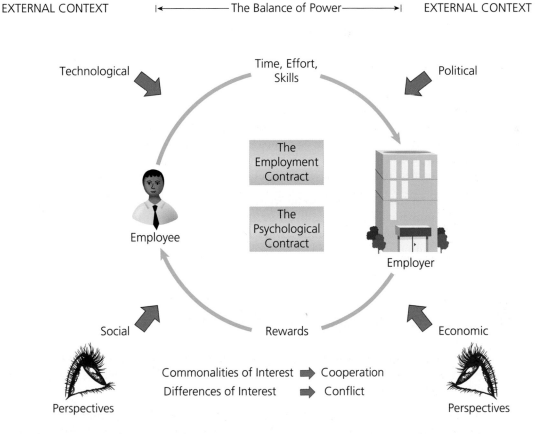

EXTERNAL CONTEXT |◄──────The Balance of Power──────►| EXTERNAL CONTEXT

Technological

Time, Effort, Skills

Political

The Employment Contract

The Psychological Contract

Employee

Employer

Social

Rewards

Economic

Commonalities of Interest ➡ Cooperation
Differences of Interest ➡ Conflict

Perspectives

Perspectives

The employee and employer

At the centre of the employment relationship are the employee and the employer. In economic terms, the employee sells his or her time and effort, and, in return, receives rewards or remuneration. These rewards could be *extrinsic*, such as pay and benefits, or *intrinsic*, such as job satisfaction and responsibility. The formal arrangements between the two parties are set out in the *employment contract*, but there is also likely to be a more implicit unwritten contract, known as the *psychological contract*, which is made up of the unwritten expectations of each party.

> **Psychological contract:** the mutual and unwritten expectations arising from the people–organization relationship.

The balance of power

Another useful concept with regard to the employment relationship is *the balance of power*. This relates to the relative power that each party has over the other. If viewed on a spectrum, the balance would normally be more with the employer than the employee. After all, employers have the power to hire and fire and to set out terms and conditions. However, there are certain influencing factors that can shift the balance of power at least somewhat in the other direction. One factor would be the relative rarity of the skills and abilities that the employee has – that is, whether these are in short supply. A gifted footballer, for example, can have considerable power to set his own terms and conditions with the football club that employs him. Other factors may be external, such as legislation and trade unions. Legislation acts to constrain the power of the employer – that is, in decisions on hiring and firing and pay (equal opportunities, equal pay, minimum wage, redundancy and dismissal legislation, for example). Trade unions offer strength in numbers and allow members to negotiate terms and conditions of employment that they may not have been able to achieve individually.

Commonalities and differences of interest

It could be argued that employee and employer have interests in common – that is, that they would both benefit from the success of the organization (through increased profits, promotion and development opportunities, for example). Such commonalities should lead to *cooperation*.

On the other hand, it could also be argued that the parties have differences of interest: thus the individual employee is likely to seek to maximize his or her pay rates and seek favourable employment conditions, while the employer has a vested interest in keeping costs, including employment costs, down. Such differences of interest can lead to *conflict*. Conflict can show itself in a variety of forms, from the more obvious, such as strikes, to more subtle manifestations, such as disengagement, absence and labour turnover. It can be argued that management's role is to reduce conflict and enhance cooperation.

The extent to which we subscribe to either view will depend in part on what *perspective* we take, on OB and on the employment relationship (see Section 1.2). One perspective on the employment relationship is the *unitary* perspective, which stresses common goals and an absence of conflict. This equates to a particular managerial philosophy, which seeks to promote a common culture and high commitment.

A second perspective is known as *pluralist*, which suggests a number of different interest groups, each with differing goals. Thus management may have differing goals to employees, and different departments in an organization may also have competing goals. This is seen as natural and inevitable. Conflict is also seen as natural, but to be managed through communication, negotiation and compromise.

Finally, the *radical* perspective equates to the critical perspective outlined in Section 1.2. This perspective sees the capitalist economic system and the work organizations within such systems as leading inevitably to exploitation of employees and their alienation (Bratton *et al.* 2010).

FIGURE 1.2 Professor Gregor Gall

Gregor Gall is Professor of Industrial Relations and Director of the Work and Employment Research Unit (which looks at the fundamentals of the employment relationship) at the University of Hertfordshire. Here is his response to the question: What single thing would you change about Human Resource Management?

❝ *If I could change one thing about HR … it would be to strip away the verbiage that mystifies what the employment relationship is actually about.*

Leafing through the pages of People Management *and the Guardian's* Saturday Work Supplement, *or clicking around* personneltoday. com, *you'd be hard pressed to find analysis which identifies the quintessential features and dynamics of the employment relationship.*

What we have instead are endless portrayals of endless attempts by the HR profession, dressed up in all manner of garb, to find the pot of gold at the end of the rainbow. The pot is a contented and committed workforce which gives the employer a competitive advantage.

But if the quintessential nature of the employment relationship was identified, we'd all understand why the endless attempts will always come unstuck and yet, perversely, why they will also always still keep coming.

We live in a capitalist society where the raison d'être of capital (employers) is to generate profit – and ever-increasing profit at that – in a

dog-eat-dog world. We know too that the public sector is being forced to skip to this beat as well, whether through backdoor privatization or marketization. This means the employment relationship is a capitalist employment relationship.

So in any workplace and in any sector you care to name, with or without unions, the relationship between employer and workers is an unequal one. The very fact of using the terms 'employer' and 'worker' signifies this. The inequality comprises an inequality in power and resources. Yes, employers are dependent upon workers for labour, but workers are far more dependent upon employers for economic survival.

Following from this, the two sides of the relationship have, when all is said and done, different and conflicting interests. The interest of the employer is to get more work out of the worker for less wage and the interest of the worker is to get more wage out of the employer for less work.

But there is more than that to the employment relationship. While the discipline of the labour market – essentially the threat of the dole – is always there, the employer needs to impose structures and beliefs to control workers in order to achieve its goal. Labour time must be turned into labour power for ends the employer deems necessary.

Added to this is that employers, in their search for profit, compete against each other in a cut-throat and unregulated manner. At the same time, the economy goes through booms and slumps.

This means that the anarchy of the market leads to despotism of the workplace because employers seek to shield themselves from competitors – and the impact these competitors have on their profits – by making workers the shock absorbers.

*In other words, employers use workers'
terms and conditions of work as something
they can control to deal with the market
they cannot control. To protect themselves,
workers often organize themselves
collectively into unions.*

Put all this together, and we have:

● **alienation:** the fruits of the workers' labour
is taken away from them

● **exploitation:** workers are paid less than the
value of their labour – this is the definition
of profit

● **conflict and instability (and not cooperation and stability):** not only
within organizations but also between
organizations.

*As long as these constitute the quintessential
features and dynamics of the employment
relationship, all the attempts to create the
contented and committed workforce will come
unstuck. If the world of HR could comprehend
this, it could then see the wood and not the trees.*

**(www.xperthr.co.uk/blogs/employment-intelligence /2010/09/
professor-gregor-gall-if-i-cou.html)**

**Q   What does Professor Gall's response tell us about his perspective on the employment relationship
and OB?**

Internal context and processes

The relationship between employee and employer takes place in the context of the
particular organization, and this particular internal context will have a strong influence
on this relationship – for example, employment in a car factory is very different from
employment in an investment bank or a research laboratory. The structure and culture of
the organization, together with the technology used, will exert an influence.

Within the organization, employees and managers will also form groups, both formal
and informal, which in turn will influence individual behaviour and organizational
outcomes. There may also be representative bodies, such as trade unions and employers'
associations.

Lastly, various processes will be in evidence, such as communication, consultation and
involvement, which will lead to particular outcomes – for example, in terms of agreements
on pay and conditions. These outcomes will reflect the balance of bargaining power between
the two parties (employee and employer).

External context

The employment relationship and the behaviour of individuals and groups are not
only influenced by (and have an influence on) the internal context of the particular
organization in question (organizations do not operate in a vacuum); the external
context in terms of political, economic, social, technological, legal and environmental
factors also needs to be considered, and this will form an important theme in this book.
Thus in a recession (economic factor) employees will tend to have less bargaining
power and are likely to fear losing their jobs, while in a boom time unemployment is
likely to be low and job prospects good. Changes of government (political factor) and
the resultant policies of the political party in power will also affect the employment
relationship.

Reflective question

Why may there be both differences and commonalities of interest in the employment relationship? Give examples of each.

 ## 1.6 Summary

This chapter has provided an introduction to OB. There are different definitions of OB, and a number of these were compared and contrasted, and differing perspectives on the subject outlined. The importance of theory and its application to practice was also set out. OB can be viewed from a number of levels – the individual, group, organization and wider context – and it has been argued that a multidimensional approach to studying the subject is needed. Finally, the different actors, processes and influences on and in OB can be analysed in terms of the employment relationship, and this was outlined.

KEY THEMES Warren Bennis

In his book, *Geeks and Geezers*, Warren Bennis of Harvard Business School in the United States compares leaders under the age of 35 ('geeks') with those over 70 ('geezers'). His ideas on the various topics below highlight some of the key issues in OB.

On young and old leaders:

  I want to understand human development. I think it's the new challenge. In the future we will see chairs in cognitive psychology and human development in schools of business.

  … when I go out and talk to my students, who are 20-year-olds, and young executives, I'm not sure I really understand how they see the world. These people are visual, digital and virtual. I want to understand what their aspirations are; how they perceive the world; how they define success; what their career goals are. Basically what provides the meaning in their lives. The second group, the 70-plus leaders, are all people who manage to keep their minds open and continuously reinvent themselves. I want to know why these people keep growing and why other people get stuck. I've seen people in their forties who are on a treadmill to oblivion. But these older leaders are still hungry for growth. Why?

  A number of companies, including General Electric, have reverse mentoring, where young people mentor older people to acquaint them with the e-world. There is a lot of ageism which I probably wouldn't be sensitive to except for the fact I am in my seventies. Bridging the gap between the young and old – these will be profound issues for society in general.

On older leaders (geezers):

  Geezers have lived longer and have gone through an awful lot. I think what the geeks haven't experienced are the crucibles like World War Two and the Depression. They have had formative years of almost uninterrupted prosperity, growth and success. They are often children of affluence. So 9/11 was the first collective shock to the world view they grew up with. It was quite a jolt to them.

On 'crucibles' (major life experiences):

  I think they (crucibles) are created all the time. Having to fire people, being fired, being shipped to an office you don't like, thinking that you have been demoted when maybe you haven't. We all experience crucibles, but what do we do at the back end of them? Do we learn from them? Do we extract wisdom from them?

On his experiences in World War Two:

❝ What I learned was discipline and the sense of self-mastery. I was very shy and felt that I was a boring human being, and then in the course of being in the army I felt that I was more interesting to myself. It was a coming of age.

On the young business leaders:

❝ I think they feel that they have more licence to talk about themselves and their inner feelings. Unlike some of the geezers who would never dream about talking about their relationships

with their family and so on. The younger generation are more free with their feelings, aspirations and things like that.

On business school courses:

❝ There is a required course on ethics at Harvard Business School, but not at most business schools. It's a very difficult topic, but we need to think about the purpose of education. We have to ask the question at business schools, is there something more important than money? Do corporations exist for something more than money and the bottom line? Of course they do, but we have to explain it better.

Adapted from 'Warren Bennis: geeks, geezers and beyond', in Crainer and Dearlove 2003

Q   Summarize the key OB issues in the extract above, under the following headings:
- **Individual and group issues**
- **Organizational issues**
- **Wider context issues.**

How do these different issues interrelate and influence each other?

Key ideas

Organizational behaviour (OB):

- OB is a popular subject on undergraduate degree and postgraduate courses.
- OB can be viewed in terms of the study of individual and group behaviour, and the structure and functioning of organizations, but there are various definitions and meanings of the subject.
- There are a number of reasons for studying OB, and the subject can provide important insights for managers.

Perspectives, theory and practice:

- People have differing views on a whole host of subjects and the same is true of OB.
- The study of OB is multidisciplinary: it draws on a range of different disciplines.
- In studying OB, the reader will come across various different theories. Theories help in building generalized models that can be applied in a range of settings.
- Management action or decisions rest on some sort of idea or model. Relevant theories therefore provide useful tools for managers.
- Data and statistics from research studies and reports provide other useful sources of information and decision-making tools for managers.

Levels of organizational behaviour:

- OB can be examined at a number of levels, each of which interacts with the others.

The main levels are: individual, group, organization and wider context.

The employment relationship:

- The different actors in OB (such as managers and employees) are active agents and interact with the other actors. The strategy, structure, culture, technology and processes of an organization exert an influence on, and in turn are influenced by, the people who make up the organization.

- At the centre of the employment relationship are the employee and the employer.

- Each party to the employment relationship is likely to have both differences and commonalities of interest.

- The employment relationship can be viewed and analysed from differing perspectives, including unitary, pluralist and radical perspectives.

- The employment relationship takes place within both an internal and an external context.

Review questions

1. How would you define 'organizational behaviour'?
2. Why might the study of OB be considered important?
3. Why is the study of relevant theory considered important in OB?
4. What are the key levels in OB?
5. What is meant by the 'organizational dilemma'?
6. Why is an appreciation of the external context important to our understanding of OB?
7. In the employment relationship, what is meant by 'the balance of power'? And what factors can help to shift this balance?
8. Compare and contrast the unitary, pluralist and radical perspectives.

Recommended reading

Buchanan, D.A. and Huczynski, A.A. (2010) *Organizational Behaviour* (7th edn). Harlow: Pearson Education.

Butler, M. and Rose, E. (2011) *Introduction to Organizational Behaviour*. London: Chartered Institute of Personnel and Development.

Grey, C. (2009) *A Very Short, Fairly Interesting and Reasonably Cheap Book About Studying Organizations*. London: Sage Publications.

Mullins, L.J. (2010) *Management and Organizational Behaviour* (9th edn). Harlow: Pearson Education.

Useful websites

www.socialpsychology.org/io.htm – provides access to a portal to websites and online resources on organizational psychology

www.thinkers50.com – a listing of the world's top 50 business thinkers; includes videos, book extracts and other links

References

Bratton, J., Sawchuk, P., Forshaw, C., Callinan, M. and Corbett, M. (2010) *Work and Organizational Behaviour* (2nd edn). Basingstoke: Palgrave Macmillan.

Buchanan, D.A. and Huczynski, A.A. (2010) *Organizational Behaviour* (7th edn). Harlow: Pearson Education.

Crainer, S. and Dearlove, D. (2003) *Business, the Universe and Everything. Conversations with the World's Greatest Management Thinkers*. Chichester: Capstone Publishing.

Knights, D. and Willmott, H. (2007) *Introducing Organizational Behaviour and Management*. London: Thomson Learning.

Martin, J. and Fellenz, M. (2010) *Organizational Behaviour and Management* (4th edn). Andover: Cengage Learning.

Morgan, G. (1997) *Images of Organization*. London: Sage.

Mullins, L.J. (2010) *Management and Organizational Behaviour* (9th edn). Harlow: Pearson Education.

Pugh, D.S. (ed.) (1971) *Organization Theory: Selected Readings*. Harmondsworth: Penguin Books.

Robbins, S.P., Judge, T.A. and Campbell, T.T. (2010) *Organizational Behaviour*. Harlow: Pearson Education.

2 Organization and management

To **manage** *is to forecast and plan, to organize, to command, to coordinate and to control.*
(HENRI FAYOL)

If you ask **managers** *what they do, they will most likely tell you that they plan, organize, coordinate and control. Then* **watch** *what they* **do***. Don't be surprised if you can't relate what you see to those four words.* (HENRY MINTZBERG)

CHAPTER OUTLINE

CHAPTER OBJECTIVES

By the end of this chapter you will understand:

- the variety of views on what management is and what managers do

- the main approaches to organization and management

- the importance of historical context to the development of the different approaches

- how to evaluate the applicability of the approaches to organization and management today.

2.1 Introduction

In Chapter 1, definitions of organizational behaviour were reviewed and the importance of the subject discussed. One possible reason for studying OB is to enable people to be better managers, and an associated reason is to enable organizations to be more effective. Of course, what we mean by 'better' and 'more effective' is open to interpretation and depends on our perspective. For example, managers may have different views on these compared with employees. Shareholders' views may differ from those of customers. However, accepting this proviso, it is clear that the subject matter of OB – that is, the structure and functioning of organizations and the behaviour of individuals and groups within these organizations – will be of relevance to managers.

The first chapter also reviewed the application of theory to practice in OB and the importance of such theories. Douglas McGregor, a management writer, summed up this importance very well:

> Every managerial act rests on assumptions, generalizations, and hypotheses – that is to say, on theory. Our assumptions are frequently implicit, sometimes quite unconscious, often conflicting; nevertheless, they determine our predictions that if we do a, b will occur. Theory and practice are inseparable. (McGregor 1987)

Theories are somewhat akin to a road map: they give managers a sense of direction, an idea of how to get to a particular place – how to design and structure an organization in the best way, how to communicate effectively, how to engage staff. Theories are not absolute and do not have to be applied slavishly; managers can compare and contrast different theories, pick those aspects they agree with and discard the rest.

As Crainer and Dearlove (2001: 4) suggest, management is nothing new: for as long as there has been civilization, management has been practised. The building of the temples of ancient Greece or the pyramids in Egypt demanded management. As argued in Chapter 6, on leadership, military leaders had to manage people and resources effectively. Chapter 6 also discusses possible differences between management and leadership. However, although management as an activity has been present for centuries, it is only relatively recently that it has been written about and studied as a discipline and a profession. While medicine and law are ancient professions, it was only in the 20th century that management emerged as such, with the appearance of writers on management and organization, and the establishment of business schools in universities.

Even now, as Crainer and Dearlove point out, there is little agreement as to what management is or what it involves. It is something that is viewed differently in different countries and by different people. It also changes over time. The more firmly you try to grasp its meaning, the more it slips through your fingers. Yet even if an all-encompassing definition and theory of management escape us, there are obviously many different practitioners who are seen as 'managers', and many different views and ideas on the subject. Arguably, this is what management is about: ideas and their application. Managers and management writers are continually searching for new and better ways of doing things and reacting to changes in the environment. This is just one aspect that makes the study of management so fascinating.

 ## 2.2 Approaches to organization and management

As we have suggested above, management as a discipline and a profession really took off in the early 20th century. In essence, organization and management theories sought to shed light on two fundamental questions: first, how best to design and structure organizations and work, and second, how best to manage people within these organizations. Any such theories need to be examined and evaluated with regard to their historical context, as well as their relevance today.

The Industrial Revolution occurred during the eighteenth and nineteenth centuries, beginning in the UK before spreading to the rest of Europe, North America and eventually worldwide. It saw the introduction of steam power and mechanization. Industrialization led to the development of the factory system and the concentration of workers in factories, textile mills and mines. Thus work changed from manual labour on farms and small-scale cottage industries to much larger-scale organizations. This led to a rise in interest in organization and management. The transition was not without its difficulties, including child labour and dirty and dangerous working conditions. Many craft workers lost their jobs or faced work that had been deskilled. Some, who became known as the Luddites, rebelled against these conditions, destroying machines and factories. However, ordinary working people also found increased opportunities for employment in the new factories and mills, although working conditions were often tough and hours long, with the pace of labour set by machines. Trade unions were formed to help advance the interests of working people.

The emergence of large-scale formal organizations, with new technologies of production, and the resulting questions of how to design and structure these organizations and manage the workforce within them, led to more formalized approaches to organization and management being put forward by management writers from the end of the 19th century. These writers and their proposals can be categorized into four main approaches:

- classical, including scientific management and bureaucracy
- human relations
- systems
- contingency.

These four broadly follow a historical timeline, commencing with the classical approach.

Reflective question

What two fundamental questions did organization and management theories seek to address?

2.3 The classical approach

Writers of the classical approach focused on the formal aspects of structure and work organization. As will be seen, they stressed rationality, efficiency and rules and regulations. As with the other approaches, many of the key ideas can still be seen in operation today. Two of the most well-known exponents of classical theories applied to management were Henri Fayol (1841–1925) in France and F.W. Taylor (1856–1915) in the United States. A third writer, German sociologist Max Weber (1864–1924), was more concerned with the structuring of organizations.

Henri Fayol and the principles of management

Fayol was originally a mining engineer. His key work on management was first published in French in 1916 and the English translation in 1949 (Pugh and Hickson 2007). He argued that management plays an important part in the governing of organizations of all types and sizes – industrial, commercial, political and any other. At the core of his contribution to management thinking is his definition of management, which he saw as comprising five elements:

- to forecast and plan
- to organize
- to command
- to coordinate
- to control.

Fayol used this classification to divide up his writings on how to manage. He then used the benefit of his own experience to put forward a number of general principles of management, of which there were 14:

1. Division of work and specialization
2. Authority, the right to issue commands
3. Discipline
4. Unity of command, that each worker should have only one boss
5. Unity of direction, with clear, planned objectives
6. Subordination of individual interests to the general interest
7. Remuneration: pay is an important motivator
8. Centralization or decentralization, depending on the type of business and employees
9. Scaler chain: the need for clear hierarchy as well as lateral communication
10. Order, both material and social
11. Equity: treating employees justly and fairly
12. Stability of tenure: low labour turnover needed, particularly among managerial staff
13. Initiative: allowing all staff to show initiative in some way
14. *Esprit de corps*: management must focus on ways to develop staff morale.

To sum up, Fayol was one of the first to provide a theoretical analysis of management. As well as his 14 principles, he provided a definition of what management is. Both of these still provide a framework for managers today to analyse what they do. Yet it can also be argued that his ideas have certain shortcomings, particularly in the context of management today: as with other classical writers, his focus on the formal ignores the more informal psychological and social aspects of organizations. His definition and principles can also be seen as attempting to provide a 'one best way' of managing, and thus as being inflexible. As can be seen from the Mintzberg quote at the beginning of this chapter, management in practice may be very different from Fayol's precise definition.

F.W. Taylor and scientific management

Frederick Winslow Taylor was also an engineer by training. He joined the Midvale Steel Works and worked his way up, eventually becoming chief engineer. He later worked for the Bethlehem Steel Works and became a consultant. He observed that many tasks were carried out haphazardly and thus inefficiently, and also pointed to 'systematic soldiering' by workers, in which they restricted output in order to protect their interests. In founding scientific management he aimed to overcome these difficulties.

Taylor set about a systematic study of work to discover the most efficient way of performing a particular task. One example was the development of the 'science of shovelling', working out the optimum load that a 'first-class' worker could manage with each shovelful, and making sure the shovel was the correct size and the correct shovelling technique was adopted. He took a rational-economic view of motivation, believing that money was the main motivator and that workers would be willing to work in the most efficient and productive way in order to maximize their earnings. He set out a number of principles of work:

- The development of a true science of work: measuring the most efficient way of working and what would constitute good performance, for which the worker would receive a higher rate of pay.
- The scientific selection and progressive development of the worker: scientifically selecting the right worker for a particular job and systematically training them to ensure the required output.
- The bringing together of the science of work and the scientifically selected and trained workers: Taylor believed that inefficiency was due to poor management and that the application of scientific management by managers would overcome this.
- The constant and intimate cooperation of management and workers: that managers should take on all the duties that they are better suited to, including the continuous supervision and control of the workers. The workers could then concentrate on achieving their targets.

The key to Taylor's approach was maximum specialization and the removal of extraneous tasks, allowing the employee to concentrate on the essential task. Taylor applied these ideas not only to the workers, but to management as well, arguing that their duties should also be separated out and done by different specialists.

Scientific management: an approach to job design based on short, repetitive work cycles, clear definition of the task and motivation based on money.

KEY TERM

Taylor demonstrated that output and efficiency could be dramatically improved if his methods were adopted, but he was also widely criticized for a system that was said to reduce workers to the level of efficiently functioning machines. It was also argued that his methods led to deskilling and workers losing control of their activities, and thus that work became boring and repetitive. His methods led to worker complaints and industrial unrest in some of the factories and plants where his methods had been applied. It can also be argued that his views of human motivation were too simplistic. However, in his scientific measurement of work, and the selection, training and motivation of workers, we can see the forerunner of people management techniques such as time-and-motion studies, job analysis, recruitment and selection, and payment by results. We can also see elements of his approach in the organization of work today in a variety of settings, including call centres and fast-food restaurants.

CASE STUDY Scientific management and fast food

Consider a fast-food hamburger restaurant. Ritzer (2006), in quoting the term 'McDonaldization', argues that everything about it stresses efficiency, measurability, predictability and control. Each final product – a Big Mac, for example – is formed of a number of standardized subparts – the burger, the bun, the lettuce and so on – which can be reproduced to form an outcome that will be the same whichever branch you go into. But it is not only the food that this process applies to; the jobs are also broken down into clearly specified and easily repeatable subtasks. There are clear instructions concerning the positioning of the burger on the grill, cooking times and sequence for turning the burgers. The machine for the fries clearly indicates the required cooking time and when the fries are ready. There is little or no room for discretion or innovation from the staff; these elements have been subsumed by the technology. One does not need to be a skilled chef to produce the food. For the customers, the system provides the fastest way to get from hungry to full.

Henry Ford applied Taylor's thinking to factory production lines in car production, in a process that has become known as Fordism. Each car was made up of a number of standardized and interchangeable parts. On such production lines the pace of work was controlled by the line and not the worker; jobs tended to be routine and repetitive, and have minimal skill requirements. Such mass production techniques were later applied not only to cars, but also to a wide range of other products, including washing machines, refrigerators, vacuum cleaners, radios and, more recently, personal computers and mobile phones. The production methods led to a dramatic fall in the cost of producing such items, which led to mass consumption and a rise in living standards.

KEY TERM

Fordism: a form of work design that applied scientific management principles to production line work and the introduction of single-purpose machine tools.

Reflective questions

What are the main advantages and disadvantages of Fordism techniques?

Weber and bureaucracy

Weber was a German sociologist who was particularly interested in issues of power and authority in organizations, and in the question of why people follow orders in organizations – why they do as they are told (Pugh and Hickson 2007). He outlined three ideal organizational types, according to how authority is legitimized:

- charismatic
- traditional
- rational-legal.

In the first of these, the way authority is exercised is based on the personal qualities of the leader – that is, their charisma. This was most usually associated with religious or political leaders, but, as Chapter 6, on leadership, shows, organizations may have charismatic founders, such as Richard Branson. In simple terms, people in the organization would respect the person's authority and follow their commands because of their inspirational qualities. One of the problems is that of succession – that is, when the leader dies.

The second basis for order and authority is termed 'traditional'. This is based on inheritance and what has been established in the past: the master–servant relationship and feudal systems are examples, but it can also be found in modern organizations where management positions are handed down to members of the same family – as with Rupert Murdoch's business empire, for example. An obvious problem with such an approach is that these individuals may not be the best people for the job– that is, it is not based on rationality or expertise.

The idea of rational analysis led to Weber's third type of authority, rational-legal, which Weber saw as being the dominant one in modern society. In this system, managers are appointed using a rational approach based on their expertise and ability to do the job. Authority is exercised through a system of rules and regulations. Weber used the term 'bureaucracy' to describe such an organization and argued that this would be the most efficient form of organization.

CASE STUDY Rules and procedures

The following is an excerpt from a university's HR policy on recruitment and selection.

‟Recruitment and Selection Policy

1 Aims

1.1 To provide a set of guidelines and standards for the recruitment and selection of employees into and within the University, thereby establishing a consistent approach across all Strategic Business Units (SBUs).

1.2 To ensure that the University is meeting with its legal obligations and is following best practice.

1.3 To give practical guidance to line managers on conducting the recruitment process with the objective of selecting the best candidate and reducing the risk of making mistakes.

1.4 This policy should be read in conjunction with the **Recruitment and Selection Handbook** ('the handbook') which is on the HR website. This contains detailed descriptions of the steps to be taken at each stage of the recruitment process.

2 Key Points

2.1 Basic Principles of Recruitment and Selection (also set out in the University's Equality and Diversity Policy)

In the recruitment and selection of staff, the University aims to:

- attract suitable applicants from within or outside the University by advertising posts and roles, i.e. development opportunities, additional duties etc. with a role description and person specification internally and externally

- ensure that all potential applicants are treated fairly

- select on merit

- appoint the most suitable candidates

- provide that all roles are deemed to be open to applications for part-time and flexible working unless stated otherwise.

All staff with responsibility for recruitment and selection are required to:

- comply with the University's current Recruitment Policy and the procedures laid down in the handbook

- choose media and methods of advertising that communicate the University's commitment to equality and diversity and employ appropriate strategies to attract suitable applicants from groups which are currently under-represented

- ensure that all stages of recruitment and selection are accessible to disabled people, and that any reasonable adjustments are

made where required by disabled applicants in line with the advice in the handbook.

Q 1 Why might the bureaucratic form of organization, based on rational decision-making and clear rules and procedures, be seen as the most efficient?

2 What are the possible downsides or drawbacks of bureaucracy?

As Pugh and Hickson (2007: 7) argue, the reason for the bureaucracy's efficiency lies in its organizational form. Clear goals are identified and the best means will be used to achieve these. Decisions will be made rationally, rather than on the personal whims of the leader. Each role in the organization will have a clear definition and job description, and roles will be arranged in a hierarchy so it is clear who is managing whom. There should also be a set of written rules and procedures for almost any eventuality: staff absence, conduct and performance, the appraisal process, contract and working arrangements, pay and reward, and so on.

The four main features of bureaucracy can be summarized as follows (Stewart 1999):

- *Specialization*, applying more to the job than the person undertaking the job. This makes for continuity, as the job will usually continue after the current post-holder has left.
- *Hierarchy of authority*, making for a sharp distinction between management and workers. Within the management ranks there are clearly defined levels of authority. This stratification is particularly marked in the armed services and civil service.
- *System of rules*, which aims to provide for an efficient and impersonal approach. The system of rules is generally stable, though there may be some modification and updating at times. A knowledge of the rules is essential to holding a job in a bureaucracy.
- *Impersonality*, meaning that allocation of privileges and the exercise of authority should not be arbitrary, but in accordance with the specified system of rules. In more highly developed bureaucracies there tend to be carefully defined procedures for appealing against certain types of decisions.

Criticisms of bureaucracy

As Mullins (2010: 50) points out, Weber's concept of bureaucracy has a number of potential disadvantages and has been subject to criticism:

- Rules, procedures, record-keeping and paperwork may become goals in their own right rather than the means to an end.
- Officials may develop a dependence on bureaucratic status, symbols and rules.
- Initiative may be stifled and a focus on rules and procedures may lead to inflexibility and unresponsiveness.
- The system can lead to officious bureaucratic behaviour on the part of officials.
- Impersonality can lead to a lack of sensitivity or responsiveness to individual incidents or problems.

As we will see in Chapter 8, the growth in bureaucracy has come about as a result of the increasing size and complexity of organizations and the requirement for administrative efficiency. The work of the classical writers has emphasized the need for specialization and formalization, as well as clarity of role and responsibility. This leads to the need for hierarchy and clear rules and procedures. Yet in fast-moving, competitive, turbulent environments, large-scale bureaucracies are unlikely to be able to respond to change quickly enough.

In conclusion, the word 'bureaucracy' today has negative connotations for many people: it is associated with 'red tape', form-filling and unresponsive officials. Bureaucratic organizations may also lack the speed and flexibility to respond adequately to changing conditions. Yet to cast bureaucracy in a totally negative light would be doing Weber a disservice; he saw bureaucracy as an ideal type and as the most efficient form of organization, yet he was also aware of the possible negative consequences of the impersonal approach that it stressed. Not only that, at the time he was writing, large-scale organizations did not face the rapidly changing context found today. If we picture the degree of bureaucratic organization as a continuum, then organizations today may well have to relinquish many of the rigidities associated with conventional bureaucracies, yet it is difficult to imagine any large organization without many elements of bureaucracy, and this is particularly true where accountability has to be clearly demonstrated, such as in public-sector organizations.

> **Bureaucracy:** a structure that emphasizes specialization, formalization, rules and regulations, and centralized authority and decision-making.

KEY TERM

2.4 The human relations approach

As we have seen, classical writers focused on the formal organization of work and on structure. The human relations approach is usually thought of as having its beginnings in the Hawthorne studies conducted in the 1920s and 1930s. Although the initial experiments can be seen to have had a classical management basis, subsequent studies unearthed findings that changed how people think of management.

The Hawthorne studies

The Hawthorne studies took place in the Hawthorne works of the Western Electric Company near Chicago. They are often associated with Elton Mayo (1880–1949), but, while he was among those who wrote about the experiments, there is some doubt as to the actual degree of his involvement (Rose 1988). The studies involved four main phases:

- The illuminations experiments (1924–27)
- The relay assembly test room (1927–33)
- The interviewing programme (1928–30)
- The bank wiring observation room (1931–32).

The illuminations experiments

These set out to measure the effect of changes in lighting on productivity. The results were inconclusive in that no correlation was found between the two (Buchanan and Huczynski

2010). Production increased both when the lighting was reduced and in the control group where lighting stayed the same. Clearly other factors were at work.

The relay assembly test room

The work here involved assembling telephone relays from small parts. Six women workers were transferred from their normal workstations to a separate area, with a researcher to take notes. They had been working a 48-hour six-day week, with no tea breaks. During a total of 13 time periods, changes were made to hours worked, rest pauses and breaks. The results showed an almost continuous increase in output, which began when rest periods, lunches and early finishing times were introduced, but was maintained when these were withdrawn. It was concluded that the reasons for the increase in output were as follows:

- The women felt themselves to be a special group.
- The self-selected nature of the group led to a supportive and cohesive group.
- They were informed and consulted about the experiments.
- A different and more informal type of supervision was introduced.
- The friendliness of the observer/researcher had an influence.

The improved output due to an increase in attention paid to the workers in the study became known as 'the Hawthorne effect'. People behave differently than they normally would when they are observed or are part of an experiment. The effect of the group seemed very important, which led the researchers to set up an employee interviewing programme to explore employee attitudes.

The interviewing programme

The researchers carried out over 20,000 interviews to explore how employees felt about their working conditions and supervision. These interviews can be seen as a precursor of modern employee involvement schemes, attitude surveys and employee counselling. One outcome of the interviews was that informal groups existed in the workplace alongside the formal groups, and this formed the basis of the next study.

The bank wiring observation room

This involved the study of 14 men. It was found that they formed informal groups, with specified 'norms' of behaviour and ways of enforcing these. Although a financial incentive scheme was in operation, the men decided on a level of output that was below what they could have achieved, believing that otherwise management would simply raise the level required. The experiment highlighted that work is a group activity and that people feel the need to be part of a group. Informal groups can have a strong influence on individual behaviour at work and managers need to understand the workings of such groups and collaborate with them.

These conclusions led to the 'human relations approach' to management, which recognized that work has an important social function for employees and is a group activity, and also that how managers and supervisors behave has an important effect on employee motivation and productivity.

Overall, although the Hawthorne studies have been criticized on a number of counts, including the methodology adopted and failure to take account of environmental factors, as well as for adopting a managerial perspective and unitary frame of reference, there is no doubt that they generated a lot of new ideas around management and supervision, motivation, work groups and job design.

Hawthorne effect: the tendency for people to behave differently than they normally would when they are observed or are part of an experiment.

KEY THEMES Differing perspectives on OB – the Hawthorne studies

The Hawthorne studies have achieved a certain renown or fame, at least in management and OB circles. It could be argued that this has been as much for what they were seen to represent and the ideas they subsequently generated, as for the value of the actual studies themselves. Thus, to some, the human relations approach, which originated with the Hawthorne studies, can be characterized as being the triumph of light over darkness, the good guy over the bad, with the latter representative of the scientific management approach. Thus Grey (2009: 45) suggests that in the 'received version' of human relations theory, the Hawthorne researchers, led by a heroic Elton Mayo, identified the 'human factor' in organizations in that, for the first time, workers were recognized as having psychological and social needs and interests; this was very different from Taylor's scientific management view of workers as machines fuelled by money. This discovery of the human factor, so the story goes, ushered in a new era in which employees' needs were acknowledged and steps taken to meet them.

Grey goes on to point out one tiny flaw in this view: it is not strictly true (depending on how we define truth, of course). He points out that interest in workers' needs predated the Hawthorne studies – an example being 19th-century Quaker industrialists, who developed worker housing and other facilities, such as those at Bourneville in the UK. Second, the beginnings of the Hawthorne studies, the desire to investigate how changes in lighting levels affect productivity, can be seen to lie firmly in scientific management traditions. And lastly, Grey argues that Taylor was also aware of the informal side of the organization, in what he identified as the systematic soldiering of the workforce, which he intended his methods to overcome. It can also be argued that the Hawthorne studies and human relations theory have the same sort of formal and instrumental rationality as scientific management, in that both attempted to control workers and increase productivity – they just used different methods.

Q **1 Referring back to the different perspectives on OB outlined in Chapter 1, what sort of perspective can authors such as Grey be seen to be adopting?**

2 Grey argues that the human relations authors have as their goal the control of workers and the enhancement of productivity. What methods would managers adopting this approach use to achieve these aims?

Neo-human relations

The results of the Hawthorne studies and their emphasis on workers' psychological and social needs fed into the work of a number of management writers in the 1950s and 1960s, particularly with regard to motivation. Among these are Maslow, Herzberg and McGregor (see Chapter 4 for more details).

2.5 The systems approach

The classical approach can be seen to emphasize the technical aspects of organizations and work – 'organizations without much concern for people' – while the human relations approach, with its investigation of social and psychological aspects, has sometimes been characterized as a concern for 'people without organizations'.

The systems approach attempts to bring these two elements together, and to examine the interaction between them. Rather than looking at individual elements separately and in isolation, the systems approach encourages us to look at the total work organization and the interrelationships among the different variables, as well as to consider the interactions between the organization and its environment.

KEY TERM

> **System:** something that operates through the interdependence of its component parts.

Systems theory

The biologist Ludwig von Bertalanffy first used the term 'systems theory' in 1951. A system can be defined as 'something that functions through the interdependence of its component parts', with an open system being one that 'interacts in a purposive way with its external environment in order to survive' (Buchanan and Huczynski 2010: 87). A plant or an animal can be seen in this way. We as human beings are made up of a number of interrelating and interdependent parts: skeleton, cardiovascular system, muscular system and so on. A problem in one of these subsystems will affect the whole body. We also depend on and interact with the external environment: we breathe in air for oxygen and breathe out carbon dioxide; we depend on the environment for food and expel waste products.

Although systems approaches were first applied in the natural and physical sciences, authors such as Miller and Rice (1967) also likened organizations to biological systems. An organization is made up of different subparts, which can be viewed as being the different departments, but also in terms of the human element: the people who work there, the physical building, the information flows and so on. An organization also continually interacts with its external environment and is dependent on this environment: for employees, customers, finance and so on. Viewing organizations as systems encourages us to view them in terms of *inputs*, *outputs* and the *transforming processes* in between (see Figure 2.1).

FIGURE 2.1 Organizations as systems

ACTIVITY

> Consider a situation at work: a previously high-performing employee has recently begun to perform poorly and this has been raised in the appraisal interview. In analysing this issue, the classical approach would focus on organizational and structural elements of the job: job design, payment systems, supervision. The human relations approach would consider the employee's social and psychological needs at work – the work group, for example.
>
> How would you analyse this scenario from a systems approach perspective?

KEY THEMES **Systemic thinking in organizational consultancy**

In their book, *Taking Positions in the Organization*, Campbell and Groenbaek (2006) set out their approach to consulting on organizational issues, which involves providing a framework for managing what can be a very complex process. They start by meeting the client to listen to their concerns and the way those concerns are presented: 'We try to observe both content and process. For example, we assume that our client's presentation of the problem represents his or her position among many possible positions, which helps us to think immediately about other positions and stories-not-told' (2006: 126). They use a metaphor of concentric circles to hold the levels of the organization in mind as they talk to the client.

FIGURE 2.2 Levels of the organization

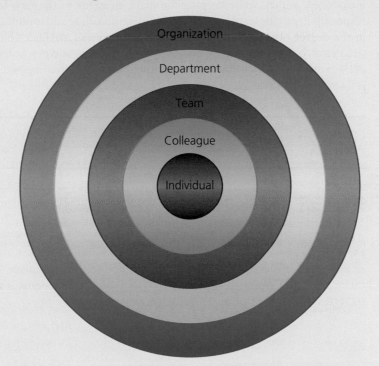

The issue presented by the client will be located in the relevant circle (see Figure 2.2). For example, if the issue involves a staff member who is overly critical when he or she communicates with others, that would be located near the centre of the circle. On the other hand, if the issue is that the organization is struggling between the forces of centralization and localization, this would be located in the outer circles. This allows the consultants to know where to start, but of course, taking a systemic approach means they will want to move back and forth between the levels to view the problem 'systemically'. How will the different levels interact and influence each other in the context of a particular issue or problem?

Socio-technical work systems

The idea of viewing an organization as a system came out of work conducted at the Tavistock Institute of Human Relations (in London), an organization that still exists today. Erik Trist and other researchers at the Institute focused in particular on two components: the technical and the social (Pugh and Hickson 2007). Their ideas came from an investigation of the introduction of new technology in the coal-mining industry. Traditionally, the miners had worked in small, cohesive, self-selected groups on one part of the coal face – the 'shortwall' method – with each group having relative independence and autonomy. The introduction of new technology in the form of mechanical coal-cutters and mechanized conveyor belts fundamentally changed this way of working. Shift working was introduced, with each shift specializing in one operation – preparation, cutting or loading (Mullins 2010), which was known as the 'longwall' method. The new method led to problems – a lack of co-operation between shifts and dissatisfaction among the miners – which meant that the new technological system was not as efficient as it should have been.

The researchers realized that the introduction of such new technology could not be viewed in isolation, but needed to be considered in conjunction with the effects it would have on the social system – that is, a socio-technical approach. A 'composite longwall' method was introduced, which, while keeping the main elements of the new technology, gave more responsibility to the team and reintroduced multiskilling and multitasking, with a reduction in the degree of specialization evident in the longwall method. This new method proved successful, both economically and in terms of meeting the psychological and social needs of the workers. The transition from traditional shortwall to composite via longwall methods is illustrated in Table 2.1.

KEY TERM

Socio-technical system: a system made up of both technology and a social organization (the people aspect).

TABLE 2.1 From shortwall to composite longwall

Approach	Technology	Work organization	Job characteristics
Shortwall	Hand and pneumatic picks	Single place	Composite autonomous miners
Longwall	Mechanized coal cutters, conveyor belts	Longwall cutting, shift work	Task fragmentation and mechanization, mass production
Composite longwall	Electric coal cutters	Composite	Composite, autonomous, self-regulating teams

(Adapted from Buchanan and Huczynski 2010: 89)

As can be seen, the socio-technical systems approach is concerned with the interaction between the structural and technological aspects of an organization on the one hand, and the human element on the other. If we invest in new technology without regard for its effects on employees, then there may well be unintended consequences. This is of prime importance today, with the rapid development and implementation of information communication technologies (ICTs).

The particular example of the work of the Tavistock Institute given above and the development of the socio-technical approach concerned coal miners in the 1940s. What current examples can you give?

2.6 Contingency approaches

As we have seen, the classical and human relations approaches were each rather partial in their coverage and area of focus, as well as attempting to be rather universalistic in their solutions. For example, classical writers such as Fayol attempted to outline general principles of management that would be applicable in all situations. The focus of the classical approach was also on structure and the organization of work. Human relations writers rather neglected these components and focused on group and individual behaviour. Contingency theory has a renewed focus on organizational structure and systems, and on their links to organizational performance, but without adopting a universalistic or 'one best way' approach.

In the contingency approach, which can be seen as a development of the systems approach, it is argued that the most appropriate structure of an organizational system is dependent (or contingent) on a number of factors, including that of the nature of the external environment faced by the firm. These factors could include the size of the organization, the technology adopted, the nature of tasks undertaken, the level of expertise of the employees and the type of market the organization operates in. Using a contingency approach can help explain why a small advertising agency is likely to have a different structure and management style to, say, a large local authority or government department. It can also help to design relevant organizational structures and processes. More detailed examples are contained in Table 2.2.

TABLE 2.2 Examples of the connections between organizational purpose and design

Purpose	Implications for organizational design
Generating ideas (e.g. a PR or advertising agency)	Loose, flexible structure, relatively informal. As it grows in size, however, more formal structures are likely to appear.
Government civil service	Strong formal structures. Strict controls on procedures and authorizations, and stress on policies and procedures to ensure consistency.
Major service company (e.g. a retail bank)	Formal structures, but with some flexibility, so that variations in demand can be met quickly.
Small business attempting to grow	Informal approach. Owner and managers likely to take on several business functions at one time.

(Adapted from Lynch 2006)

The 'if–then' relationship

The contingency approach has been characterized as an 'if–then' relationship (see, for example, Luthans 1985; Mullins 2010). Variables such as size, technology, type of organization and its purpose, characteristics of the members, and environment form the 'if' factors. These variables then impact on the structure and systems of management of the organization (see Figure 2.3).

FIGURE 2.3 The 'if–then' contingency relationship (adapted from Mullins, 2010:588)

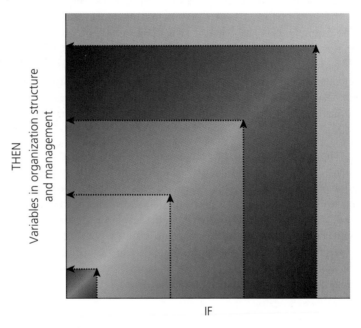

Situational Factors
(e.g. Organization size, Technology, Environment)

Contingency thinking can be applied to decisions on structure, management systems and leadership. These are explored further in Chapters 6 and 8.

2.7 Other approaches to organization and management

A fourfold classification of approaches to organization and management has been set out above, roughly following a sequential timeline, from the early 1900s to the 1980s and 1990s, and continuing into the 21st century. Any such classification is bound to be rather simplistic, but forms a useful basis for better understanding organizations. In addition, within each of the four main categorizations, there are offshoots, some of which have been outlined here. Thus bureaucracy can be seen as an offshoot of the classical approach, and neo-human relations writers form a branch of the human relations approach. To illustrate the diversity of possible views on organizations and management, and to give a flavour of more recent developments, two further approaches will be mentioned briefly: social action and postmodernism.

Social action

Social action can be seen as a sociological approach to the study of organizations. Writers from this tradition attempt to view the organization from the perspective of individual members of that organization, each of whom will have their own goals, beliefs and interpretations. Thus to understand behaviour at work, it is argued that we need to understand the individual's own perceptions of any particular situation. This approach can therefore provide a useful counterpoint to approaches that focus on organizational goals rather than on meeting the needs of the individuals who make up the organization.

Postmodernism

Much of the writings of the four main approaches outlined above concerns the 'modern organization': based around concepts of rationality, efficiency and competitiveness in a capitalist economic system, which is viewed as being supreme. Contingency theory, however, alerts us to the idea that the increasing turbulence and uncertainty in their operating environment will have implications for the structuring and functioning of organizations – towards more organic and flexible forms, for example. This current level of accelerated change has been referred to as 'the postmodern condition' (Clegg 1990). As Johnson and Gill (1993) point out, 'postmodernity' originally developed in an architectural and artistic context, referring to, among other things, randomness, anarchy and fragmentation, in contrast to the solid, monolithic structures and approaches of modernism. In organizational terms, the move from modernism to postmodernism would be characterized by new organizational approaches to coping with an increasingly turbulent and uncertain world, as well as to new ways of thinking. Such ideas are further developed in Chapter 10, which looks at recent and current trends.

2.8 Summary

This chapter began by pointing out that, although management can be defined formally in terms of planning, organizing, coordinating and control, what managers actually do on a day-to-day basis may differ from this, and, because of the variety of practice, it is difficult to arrive at an all-encompassing definition.

The Industrial Revolution brought large numbers of workers together in one organization for the first time. This led to questions about how best to design and structure such organizations, and how best to manage the employees within them. Different management writers have taken different approaches to such questions and these approaches can be classified into four broad groupings: classical, human relations, systems and contingency.

The classical approach focused on the formal aspects of work and stressed rationality and efficiency. Henri Fayol defined management in terms of five elements and proposed a number of general principles of management, while F.W. Taylor put forward the concept of scientific management and Max Weber the concept of bureaucracy. In contrast, writers of the human relations approach were concerned with the informal aspects and the social and psychological needs of workers. The systems approach attempts to bring these two elements together – one example is the work of the Tavistock Institute on socio-technical work systems. Contingency writers argue that the best way to design and structure organizations and manage the people within them is dependent on a number of variables, including size, type of task, type of employees and nature of the external environment.

Key ideas

Introduction:

- The subject matter of OB is of relevance to managers.
- Managerial actions rest on the assumption that if we do a then b will occur. Theory and practice are inseparable and theory is of relevance to managers.
- Management as an activity is nothing new; it has been practised throughout history.
- There are many different views on what management is and what managers do.

Approaches to organization and management:

- Management as a discipline and profession took off in the early part of the 20th century.
- Organization and management theories essentially attempt to shed light on two fundamental questions: how best to design and structure organizations, and how best to organize and manage the people within them.
- The Industrial Revolution, and the resulting work in factories, mills and mines, led to the need for new approaches to the management of employees and the design of organizations.
- Approaches to organization and management can be classified into four broad categories: classical, human relations, systems and contingency.

The classical approach:

- Writers of the classical approach focus on the formal aspects of structure and organization; stress is laid on rationality, efficiency, rules and regulations.
- Henri Fayol defined management in terms of five elements: planning, organizing, commanding, coordinating and controlling. He also put forward a number of general principles of management.
- F.W. Taylor studied work systematically in order to determine and apply the most efficient methods of working. This approach became known as scientific management.
- Weber outlined three ideal organizational types. The third of these, which he termed 'rational-legal', was deemed to be the most efficient, and Weber used the term 'bureaucracy' to describe such an organization.

The human relations approach:

- This approach is thought to have its beginnings in the Hawthorne studies of the 1920s and 1930s.
- The Hawthorne studies were made up of four main elements: the illuminations experiments, the relay assembly test room, the interviewing programme and the bank wiring observation room.
- The studies pointed to the importance of informal aspects of work and group norms of behaviour, as well as the social and psychological needs of workers.

The systems approach:

- This approach attempted to bring together the technical aspects of the classical approach and the people aspects of human relations.

- It saw organizations as systems and likened them to biological systems, stressing the interdependence of component parts and their interaction with the environment.
- The work of Trist and others at the Tavistock Institute brought together the technical and social aspects of work – through their studies of the introduction of new technologies in coal mining, for example.

Contingency approaches:

- The contingency approach moved away from a universalistic or 'one best way' approach.
- It argued that how best to design and structure work organizations, and manage the people within them most effectively, is dependent on a number of variables, including the size of the organization, the types of tasks and employees, and the nature of the external environment in which the organization is operating.
- This can be seen in terms of an 'if–then' contingency relationship.

Other approaches:

- Although the fourfold framework provides a useful basis for classification, there are offshoots to this, including bureaucracy as an offshoot of the classical approach, and neo-human relations as an offshoot of the human relations approach.
- Examples of other more recent developments are the social action and postmodern views of organization.

Review questions

1. List Fayol's five key elements of management.
2. What is meant by a rational-economic view of motivation?
3. What is meant by the term 'Fordism'?
4. What are the chief characteristics of bureaucracy?
5. Outline the key experiments and findings of the Hawthorne studies.
6. What were the key findings of Trist and his colleagues' investigation into coal mining?
7. With reference to organizations, give an example of an 'if–then' contingency relationship.
8. Summarize the social action approach to organization and management.

Recommended reading

Grey, C. (2009) *A Very Short, Fairly Interesting and Reasonably Cheap Book About Studying Organizations*. London: Sage Publications.
Pugh, D.S. and Hickson, D.J. (eds.) (2007) *Writers on Organizations*. London: Penguin Books.

Useful websites

www.hrmguide.co.uk – provides articles, news and surveys, including useful information on history of management; bridges the gap between theory and practice

www.managers.org.uk – site of the Chartered Management Institute with access to useful management news and discussion

References

Buchanan, D.A. and Huczynski, A.A. (2010) *Organizational Behaviour* (7th edn). Harlow: Pearson Education.

Campbell, D. and Groenbaek, M. (2006) *Taking Positions in the Organization*. London: Karnac Books.

Clegg, S.R. (1990) *Modern Organizations: Organization Studies in the Postmodern World*. London: Sage.

Crainer, S. and Dearlove, D. (eds.) (2001) *Financial Times Handbook of Management* (2nd edn). Harlow: Pearson Education.

Grey, C. (2009) *A Very Short, Fairly Interesting and Reasonably Cheap Book About Studying Organizations*. London: Sage Publications.

Johnson, P. and Gill, J. (1993) *Management Control and Organizational Behaviour*. London: Paul Chapman Publishing.

Luthans, F. (1985) *Organizational Behaviour* (4th edn). New York: McGraw-Hill.

Lynch, R. (2006) *Corporate Strategy* (4th edn). Harlow: Pearson Education.

McGregor, D. (1987) *The Human Side of Enterprise*. Harmondsworth: Penguin Books.

Miller, E.J. and Rice, A.K. (1967) *Systems of Organization*. London: Tavistock Publications.

Mullins, L.J. (2010) *Management and Organizational Behaviour* (9th edn). Harlow: Pearson Education.

Pugh, D.S. and Hickson, D.J. (2007) *Writers on Organizations*. London: Penguin Books.

Ritzer, G. (ed.) (2006) *McDonaldization: The Reader* (2nd edn). Thousand Oaks, CA: Pine Forge Press.

Rose, M. (1988) *Industrial Behaviour* (2nd edn). London: Penguin.

Stewart, R. (1999) *The Reality of Management* (3rd edn). Oxford: Butterworth-Heinemann.

3 The individual: personality, perception and attitudes

*Every **person** carries within him or herself **patterns** of thinking, feeling and potential acting which were learned throughout their lifetime.* (GEERT HOFSTEDE)

*Emotional Intelligence is a master **aptitude**, a capacity that profoundly affects all other **abilities**, either facilitating or interfering with them.* (DANIEL GOLEMAN)

CHAPTER OBJECTIVES

By the end of this chapter you will understand:

- the nature/nurture debate about personality

- theories of personality relating to types and traits

- how personality is measured using questionnaires

- the development of the big five personality characteristics

- the emergence of the concept of emotional intelligence

- perception and the link with the psychological contract

- attitude formation and attitude measurement in the workplace.

3.1 Introduction

When we meet someone for the first time, we often form immediate impressions based on very limited information. Perhaps the clothes they are wearing, the way they talk or even the firmness of their handshake will start to form a picture in our mind about what this person might be like. If we continue to get to know the person, it is more likely that we will adapt our first impressions and begin to base our estimation of the person on his or her more consistent and enduring ways of behaving. So personality refers to the unique characteristics that determine and influence how people act and behave.

The sort of experience described above is the focus of this particular chapter; the implications of individual personality, the process of perception and how we form attitudes hold much relevance for organizational life.

 ## 3.2 Individual differences and personality

Personality: the characteristics of an individual that make the individual unique and shape his or her behaviour.

> ### *Reflective questions*
>
> There is much debate centred on whether personality is inherited (nature) or developed in response to environmental conditions (nurture). Which side of the debate would you support, and why?
>
> If you were to ask a friend to use three words to describe you, what do you think they would be? If you were to ask a colleague at work to use three words to describe you, what do you think they would be? Do they differ? If so, why might this be?

All individuals are unique, but although we are all different, we all share several things. Research into personality has provided a fascinating wealth of material about which there remains controversy and debate. This chapter will attempt to provide a snapshot of the varying explanations of personality to whet the reader's appetite.

The study of personality dates back to the Middle Ages, when the first examples of personality theory suggested that personality was linked to our physiological make-up and the balance of our bodily fluids. People were characterized as having a cheerful, energetic and lively personality if they had a greater amount of blood, while those with a higher level of phlegm were said to be typically calm and placid. Those with a lot of 'black bile' were classified as gloomy individuals, and those with more yellow bile were said to be aggressive and hasty. This sort of approach to personality attempted to provide a classification or typology system in which every individual could fit. Since then, other researchers, such as Sheldon (1954), have attempted to produce typologies of personality, using bodily shape as an indicator of personality type, with the mesomorph (athletic, muscular people), endomorph (plump, rounded people) and ectomorph (thin, fragile people) being the main indicators.

Sheldon called this the 'somatotype' theory of personality:

- mesomorphs – energetic, hearty and outgoing, but insensitive
- endomorphs – happy, jolly and easygoing
- ectomorphs – introspective, restrained and shy.

Debate the value of the somatotype explanation of personality. Can you think of any friends or famous people who might seem to fit the types? What are the limitations of just looking at body shape for an explanation of personality and how people might behave at work?

One of the most famous theories about personality derived from the work of Sigmund Freud (1856–1939), who developed his psychodynamic view of personality in the late 19th century. He proposed that our personality develops through the way that we resolve inner conflicts as we mature through childhood. Freud (1938) suggested that our early childhood experiences provide the foundation for our future adult personality, and that there are distinct biological connections to elements of our personality. For the purposes of this book, we do not intend to explore the very interesting work of Freud, but recommend that any student of personality should explore his work in more depth. Freud's work has been much criticized, however, as it has been argued that the sample on which he based his research was limited; this draws into question the degree of scientific rigour of his work. It is also argued that he placed too much emphasis on unconscious sexual desires. As far as organizational behaviour is concerned, Freud's work did not help us to be able to predict an individual's behaviour, as his focus was very much on the resolution of childhood conflicts, rather than on exploring the links between personality and future behaviour.

3.3 Type A and Type B personalities

To review personality, we will focus on more recent theories and start with 'type' explanations of personality, which provide a different perspective. One of the most well-established typologies is known as Type A and Type B personality types, put forward by Friedman and Rosenman (1974); it is an overtly simple system, but one that many of us can probably relate to.

Type A personality

Type A personalities can be defined as having the following characteristics:

- competitive
- excessive need for achievement
- aggressive
- hasty
- impatient – feel the urgency of time
- restless
- need to control
- find their way into more demanding jobs
- more physically reactive
- more likely to suffer heart disease – Type A men aged 39–49 are seven times more likely.

Typical behaviour for people with Type A personality includes the following:

- always moving
- finish other people's sentences
- do two or more things at once
- feel guilty when relaxing
- explosively accentuate key words in speech
- find it difficult to talk about personal issues
- fail to notice lovely things in life
- no time to spare
- busy schedule
- nervous habits.

Type B personality

Type B personalities can be defined as having the following characteristics:

- relaxed and not worried about time
- feel no need to impress others
- play to relax
- relax without guilt
- work calmly
- less need to control
- rate themselves more positively.

Typical behaviour for people with Type B personality includes the following:

- tend to work methodically and do not worry if they do not finish the work
- are happy to get involved, but are not overly competitive and are happy to take a back seat
- are often reflectors rather than doers
- come up with ideas and can be innovative.

Further research by Friedman (1996) found that there may be 'good' and 'bad' Type A and B personalities:

- Type A – healthy and charismatic, or hostile and competitive
- Type B – relaxed and quiet, or tense and inhibited.

Reflective question

Reflect on any organization that you are familiar with, and think of how individuals may be required to exhibit Type A behaviours in the workplace. Organizations often reward Type A behaviour – for example, there may be peer pressure to work late, a culture of 'presenteeism', job overload to meet high performance standards, deadlines set reflecting time urgency, leadership role models demonstrating workaholic tendencies.

Reflective question

The latest statistics from the BBC News Report (5th October 2011) state that the most frequently cited cause of absence from work is stress. Consider which of the two personality types might be more resilient to stress at work, and why (**www. bbc.co.uk/news/health-15179336**).

 ## 3.4 The nomothetic debate and personality testing

KEY TERM

Nomothetic: this approach views personality as inherited and stable, remaining constant as we grow as individuals. Its stability means that it can be measured and tested, and individuals can be assessed against common characteristics.

The big debate on personality is about whether it is inherited (a product of 'nature', the nomothetic approach) or developed in response to environmental conditions (a product of 'nurture', the idiographic approach). Put simply, are you born with your personality or does your personality develop over time and in response to your upbringing and social experiences?

The psychologists who put forward the notion that personality is a product of birth and inherited (Cattell 1946 and Eysenck 1947, for example) suggest that personality is a relatively fixed feature, and therefore it can be measured and is generally stable. If this is the case then it is likely that we could predict how a person might behave within a job. The research is based on the statistical study of groups using objective questionnaires, as well as exploring genetic links. The findings indicate that there are common personality traits that all individuals possess to a greater or lesser extent, and these can be clustered into categories. Table 3.1 illustrates some of the negative and positive traits that a person classified as an 'extrovert' and a person classified as an 'introvert' might exhibit.

TABLE 3.1 Nomothetic trait cluster for extroverts and introverts

Extrovert		Introvert	
Positive	*Negative*	*Positive*	*Negative*
Sociable	Impulsive	Responsibility	Unsociability
Expressive	Risk-taking	Control	Inhibition
Active		Carefulness	Inactivity
Practical	Irresponsible	Reflectiveness	

Table 3.2 lists some of the negative and positive traits that a person classified as having 'emotional stability' might exhibit.

TABLE 3.2 Nomothetic trait cluster for a person classified as having emotional stability

Positive	Negative
Calm	Anxiety
Self-esteem	Low self-esteem
Sense of health	Hypochondria
Freedom	Guilt
Happiness	Unhappiness
Autonomy	Lack of autonomy
Casualness	Obsessiveness

KEY THEMES Personality and leadership

Nicholson (1998), Professor of Organizational Behaviour at the London Business School, has carried out extensive research into the trait theories of personality and their impact on leadership. In his article 'How hardwired is human behaviour?' he states that 'the point is, along with each person's fundamental brain circuitry, people also come with inborn personalities'. He argues that the implications for leadership are significant. While leadership skills can be taught, 'the truth is that leaders are born, not made. They are not clones, but all of them share one common personality trait – a passion to lead'.

Q   Debate the idea that you are born either to lead or to be a follower.

One of the outcomes of the work of the nomothetic personality school of thought has been the development of personality tests to measure the clusters of traits exhibited by individuals, in order to be able to predict typical behaviour at work. Extensive research in this field has resulted in a wealth of data to establish norms for different groups – for example, men and women, different age groups and different occupational personalities. Well-known tests include Cattell's 16 PF, in which an individual is measured against 16 personality factors, including extroversion/introversion, cool/warm, affected by feelings/emotionally stable, shy/bold. The Occupational Personality Questionnaire developed by Saville and Holdsworth Ltd in the 1980s measures 30 personality dimensions. The main three groupings centre on:

- caring (considerate to others, helps those in need, sympathetic, tolerant)
- emotional control (restrained in showing emotions, keeps feelings back, avoids outbursts)
- forward planning (prepares well in advance, enjoys target-setting, forecasts trends, plans projects).

Personality questionnaires attempt to identify individual behavioural preferences – how you prefer to work, how you might respond to problems, and your level of resilience in the face of pressure.

SHL, a talent measurement company, provides some informative examples of personality test use, demonstrating the way that individuals answer questions about their behavioural preferences and personality, and how these might be interpreted. Take a look at the website, where you can complete a sample personality questionnaire to give you a feel for the sorts of questions that might be asked (**www.shl.com**).

ACTIVITY

Personality questionnaire examples

You might be asked to complete something like the following when applying for a job – but how might your answers be interpreted?

Please rate the following statements as to whether they are Most Like Me (M) or Least Like Me (L).

TABLE 3.3 Personality questionnaire example

	Most Like Me	Least Like Me
(1)		
(A) I have a wide circle of friends		
(B) I enjoy organizing people	X	
(C) I can relax easily		
(D) I seek variety		X
(2)		
(A) I like to help people with their problems		X
(B) I like to develop new approaches		
(C) I have lots of energy		
(D) I enjoy social activities	X	

The candidate is required to select from a group of four statements the statement that is most like them and the statement that is least like them. The example above might be interpreted as follows:

Question 1 – suggests that the person likes organizing, but is not keen on variety. This could be explored further in the interview process. If the job involves constant change, for example, and very varied responsibilities, this person may not be suited to the role.

Question 2 – suggests that the person enjoys social interaction, but would not enjoy working in a job that involved helping others to solve problems.

Reflective question

Do you think personality should be assessed as part of the selection process for a job, and if so, what traits do you think an organization might look for, and why?

The Resourcing and Talent Planning Survey conducted by the CIPD (2011d) into methods used to select applicants shows that 35 per cent of organizations use personality tests. The report indicates that online testing is growing in popularity, particularly among graduate employers, who face dealing with high volumes of applicants. For example, Sainsbury's graduate applicants have to complete a personality questionnaire online to help the company get to know the graduates better and assess how they would fit into the organization (**http://sainsburys.jobs/graduates/application/process**).

Personality questionnaires assess the individual's behaviour preferences; these are often classified as behavioural 'competencies', and personality tests are one of the ways that employers capture and measure an individual's preferred way of working.

CASE STUDY Behavioural competencies at Deloitte

Deloitte is a global professional services firm (**www.deloitte.com**). Its behavioural competencies include:

- **Communication** – We are looking for individuals who are expressive, clear and concise and have the ability to quickly form relationships with others in a variety of situations.

- **Achievement of goals** – We look for individuals who can demonstrate examples of persistence and energy when required to meet or exceed objectives or well-defined goals and also who respond well to pressure.

- **Commercial awareness** – this is the ability to demonstrate an interest in business and knowledge of any current issues that may be impacting your chosen field.

- **Career motivation** – We look for an individual who demonstrates knowledge of what a career in a professional services firm involves.

- **Planning and organizational skills** – We are looking for individuals who take responsibility for the completion of tasks and ensure that detail is not overlooked when involved in a project. You will need to have good time management skills and be able to prioritize tasks effectively.

- **Adaptability** – this competency assesses an individual's ability to be positive in the face of change and resourceful in responding to major changes.

- **Problem solving** – we are looking for individuals who can analyse, distil, and solve practical problems, generate new ideas and make sound judgements in complex situations.

Most recently, organizations have been approaching the assessment of personality through the use of situational judgement tests. These are tests that outline hypothetical and challenging situations that you might face at work and give you an opportunity to demonstrate how you would respond.

One of the key issues in relation to the use of personality tests for recruitment and selection purposes is the extent to which the results can be used to predict future performance in a job. The predictive validity of personality assessment is ranked as only 0.4, with 1.0 being certain prediction, meaning there is only a 40 per cent chance that measuring personality will help to determine the suitability of the candidate for a job role (Pilbeam and Corbridge 2010).

> **CASE STUDY** Situational judgement test in action at Waitrose (IDS HR Studies 2011)
>
> Faced with increasing numbers of graduate applicants, Waitrose has introduced a situational judgement test to assist in sifting out candidates not suited to the roles on offer in the early stages of the recruitment and selection process.
>
> The test, called 'Graduate Dilemmas', contains 20 scenarios that a branch manager may typically face, with four possible courses of action. Using a five-point scale, each applicant has to rate their response and the answers are automatically scored; those with the best scores progress to the next stage.

A further criticism of the use of personality tests is their reliance on self-reporting, which can be open to distortion, as candidates may answer the questions in the way they believe will impress the recruiting organization, rather than reflecting how they actually behave in practice. This further reduces the reliability of personality tests.

In addition, there is little research evidence to connect certain personalities with success in specific job roles. In an ideal world, a company with a large number of individuals employed in the same job role could assess the high performers and identify any common personality traits linked with success in the job. These traits could then form part of the selection criteria and candidates could be measured via the use of a personality test to assess their suitability for the job. This rarely happens in practice.

However, companies such as the Airmiles travel company maintain that since introducing personality assessment as part of their selection process they have been 'much better placed to employ the right type of person for our team' (*Personnel Today* 2006).

3.5 The idiographic debate

KEY TERM

Idiographic: this approach views personality as growing and developing in response to environment and social upbringing. It is therefore changeable and difficult to measure, and everyone is seen as unique.

The nurture debate put forward by psychologists such as Jung (1921), Kelly (1963), Rogers (1959) and Erikson (1950) offers a contrasting explanation of personality, as they see it being created through interaction with the environment and the influence of social and cultural processes. Rather than being fixed, they consider it to be adaptable and open to change, and each individual is said to be unique, with a personality that cannot be classified or grouped into any typology. One of the key aspects central to this approach is the notion of 'self-concept', which introduces a further complexity to the personality debate, in that it refers to the way that the individual sees themselves and perceives how others view them. Perception is seen to play a significant role in the way that we regard our own personality and the way that we categorize others. We will explore the process of perception later in this chapter.

This nurture approach to personality does not lend itself to the measurement of personality, as each individual is regarded as unique. From an organizational perspective, therefore, it is less likely to form part of an assessment process. However, some organizations do utilize the notion of self-concept as part of their management and development training programmes, and it can form part of the performance management process, particularly if a 360-degree feedback approach is utilized. (For further information about 360-degree feedback, take a look at the CIPD (2011b) 'Feedback – 360 degree' factsheet.)

3.6 The 'big five' personality characteristics

The 'big five': psychologists have agreed that there appear to be five common personality dimensions that form the basis of everyone's personality.

Psychologists continue to debate the nomothetic/idiographic issues, but more recently have come to acknowledge that a pattern of traits appears to be evident, regardless of the impact of nature or nurture. A number of research studies demonstrate that the basis of personality is centred on five dimensions, known as the 'big five' (see Figure 3.1). These five dimensions are explained below. McCrae and Costa (1995) suggest that the 'big five' are also consistent across the more developed industrialized national cultures.

FIGURE 3.1 The 'big five' personality characteristics (adapted from Arnold and Randall *et al.* 2010)

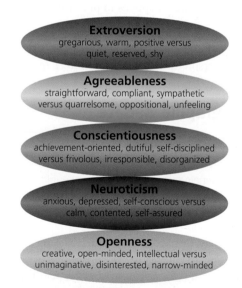

Research into the relationship of the 'big five' personality characteristics and job performance has highlighted some interesting relationships. Below is a brief insight into some of these results.

- Le Pine and Dyne (2001) suggest that conscientiousness, extroversion and agreeableness are all related to cooperative behaviour, but not to task performance.
- Barrick and Mount (1991) and Salgado (1997) found that conscientiousness was a valid predictor of job performance for all occupational groups in their studies.
- Furnham, Jackson and Miller (1999), in carrying out research into call-centre staff, found that extroverts were good in sales, but introverts were better suited to customer service.

● Judge, Martocchio and Thoreson (1997) found extroversion and conscientiousness to be predictors of absence. Extroverts tended to have higher levels of absenteeism, whereas conscientious people tended to be dutiful, rule-bound and reliable, and tended to take less time off work.

ACTIVITY

Choose a person you know very well (it could be yourself) and give some examples of their personality in action, using the 'big five' characteristics.

1 | What are the consistent and stable components of this person's personality?

2 | Now identify two or three possible situations in which this person might find themselves – for example, at a party, at work, on a date – and assess the impact that the situation might have on how the person behaves.

KEY THEMES Research into changing personality at work

A research study of 2,000 people conducted in 2006 found that employees were rather like chameleons, changing their identity and persona when at work in order to fit in, get ahead and be accepted:

● 59 per cent of respondents admitted to changing their personality and identity to some extent at work.

● 6 per cent admitted to changing everything about themselves.

● 63 per cent of women compared with 50 per cent of men admitted to changing their personality at work.

● 60 per cent of graduate trainees adopt new personality characteristics in order to get accepted.

● 56 per cent of employees believe that the higher you climb up the career ladder, the more personal compromises you make to your character and values.

KEY THEMES Are you in work mode?

To what extent do you agree or disagree with the following statement made by the Director of Resourcing at Vodafone, UK: 'We all make a switch at some point in the morning and say "I'm in work mode now"'. (Faragher 2006)

Personality is something that everyone has, and everyone also has a view about how it is formed. While the nature/nurture debate continues, with research into the 'big five' provoking further discussion, another dimension that has been recognized is the impact of emotions in the workplace.

3.7 Emotional intelligence

KEY TERM

Emotional intelligence: this refers to the concept of tapping into our emotional awareness and sensitivities to others, and using this to guide our interpersonal behaviour in a more powerful way.

Personality traits will clearly impact on our behaviour at work and determine to some extent how we behave and how we relate to others. More recent research into successful performance at work has identified that one of the key factors is linked to emotional intelligence. This term has been defined as 'the ability to sense, understand and effectively apply the power and acumen of emotions as a source of human energy, information, trust, creativity, connection and influence' (Cooper 1998, cited in Redman and Wilkinson 2009).

Another definition of emotional intelligence is provided by Mayer and Salovey (1990), who suggest that it comprises four elements:

- identifying emotions in oneself and others
- using emotions and feelings in communications
- understanding emotions
- managing emotions, which refers to the capacity to be able to regulate emotions in oneself and others in order to promote understanding and growth.

Goleman (1998) suggests that the more effective leaders work through emotions to achieve high levels of performance. He suggests that the rules for work are evolving: 'the new measure takes for granted having enough intellectual ability and technical know-how to do our jobs; it focuses instead on personal qualities, such as initiative and empathy, adaptability and persuasiveness'. Goleman claimed that 67 per cent of abilities considered essential for effective performance were emotional (i.e. soft) competencies. The CIPD (2010) argues that 'the skills of listening, empathy, self-management and relationship-building are critical, not optional.'

Some UK-based research by Higgs and Dulewicz (2002), working at Henley Management College, found that emotional intelligence comprised seven dimensions:

- **drivers** – motivation and decisiveness
- **enablers** – sensitivity, influence, self-awareness
- **constrainers** – conscientiousness and integrity, and emotional resilience.

During the course of their research into the emotional intelligence of successful managers attending courses at Henley Management Centre, Higgs and Dulewicz found that the 'enablers' had potential for development, but that the 'drivers' and 'constrainers' are more inherited characteristics that are therefore more difficult to develop.

CASE STUDY Emotional intelligence at work

When L'Oréal selected sales people for emotional intelligence, the company experienced 63 per cent less staff turnover and an increase in sales per head of over £60,000.

The US Air Force reduced annual staff turnover from 35 per cent to 5 per cent by selecting candidates with a high score in emotional intelligence.

Coca-Cola saw that those who had developed emotional intelligence competencies outperformed their targets by 15 per cent, whereas division leaders who did not develop emotional intelligence missed their targets by the same margin.

(Adapted from Talentsmart 2009)

Emotional intelligence has several limitations. Some argue that the definition of what emotional intelligence is has not been clearly agreed, and the nature of the concept makes it challenging to measure. We must also consider that any measure of the concept is typically based on an individual rating themselves, and the use of such self-report methodology is debatable. Woodruffe (2001) suggests that the qualities of emotional intelligence are not new. Landy (2005) claims that emotional intelligence does not allow us to predict outcomes – so if someone scores well on emotional intelligence, they may not have the necessary cognitive intelligence to be successful. A report by Kilduff and Menges at Cambridge's Judge Business School, and Chiaburu at the Mays Business School in Texas, argues that there may be a 'dark side to emotional intelligence', that it may be used in a competitive rather than a cooperative way, and may be used to 'manipulate, spin, intimidate and generally bend others to one's will' (Friday 2011).

3.8 Stress and personality

> **Stress:** experienced when pressure at work turns into a negative experience that an individual is unable to cope with.

According to the CIPD (2011a) absence management survey, stress has become the main reason for long-term absence from work, overtaking back pain as the major cause. This rise in stress-related absence has been put down to increased workloads, as other employees have lost their jobs and tougher economic conditions threaten job security. There has been a particular rise in stress-related absence in public sector organizations, as government cuts have impacted on jobs. If we consider some of the personality characteristics discussed above it might lead us to suggest that some personality types could be more susceptible to stress at work. Research evidence investigating the links between stress and personality characteristics, however, is mixed. Alarcon, Eschelman and Bowling (2009) found that only a weak relationship exists between neuroticism and extraversion and performance at work. They did find, however, that neuroticism can act as a predictor of feelings of 'distress', and those with a high score on the neuroticism characteristics were more likely to have difficulties finding appropriate coping behaviours.

Looking back at Type A and Type B personalities, there is some research evidence to suggest that there is a link between Type A behaviour and coronary heart disease, with males being more prone than females (Feldman 1996). Type A personalities are typically competitive, time-driven and impatient, whereas Type B personalities are less competitive, less concerned with time and demonstrate a more relaxed attitude in the workplace. Type A behaviour patterns are more likely to generate a more pressured pace of work, which, ultimately, can result in physiological changes, creating a higher propensity to heart disease. Bearing in mind the latest findings in relation to stress and long-term absence from work, it is important that organizations pay attention to this issue and that bodies such as the Health and Safety Executive promote the use of risk assessment strategies and the implementation of stress management training (**www.hse.gov.uk**).

Some interesting research conducted by Smith *et al.* (2010) investigated the notion of 'resilience', which is a dimension of emotional intelligence. They refer to resilience as 'the ability to bounce or spring back into shape, or position' – in other words, the 'ability to recover strengths, spirits, good humour etc. quickly' (Agnes 2005, cited in Smith *et al.* 2010). They also cite the definition of Bonanno (2004) as resilience being 'the ability to maintain a stable equilibrium in the face of stress.' Their research found that resilience was an important personal resource in the face of stress at work, and suggested that further research was needed to investigate more detailed outcomes.

Having discussed personality and the concept of emotional intelligence, we will now turn our attention to perception and attitudes, which also play a part in influencing how people behave and act at work.

3.9 Attitudes, perception and the psychological contract

CASE STUDY Clashes at engineering company

The authors interviewed a number of line managers within a large engineering company, as part of a research project looking at the 'Contribution of HRM to organizational success'. During the interviews it became clear that, without exception, the line managers had a negative perception of what the HR department did, and most suggested that they 'seem to act as a barrier to us achieving better levels of performance through our staff and in many cases have interfered with us being able to make suitable selection decisions.' The authors then interviewed some of the HR staff, who clearly perceived the line managers as being 'troublemakers' and 'resistant to any advice to help them to operate within the legislation'. The research also identified that the HR team had developed several very innovative and valuable HR policies and practices, such as flexible working initiatives, that some of the line managers were not aware of. These perceptual differences impacted in a negative way when trying to assess the contribution that HR had made – for example, where line managers had implemented flexible working opportunities within their department, they did not credit such initiatives to the HR staff. Perceptual differences can lead to misunderstandings and differences in attitudes and opinions.

Q   List some ideas as to how to change these negative perceptions held by line managers and HR staff within the organization.

Perception

KEY TERM

Perception: this refers to the process by which we make sense of different stimuli in the environment in order to make judgements and decisions that we then act on.

From the brief case study above, it is clear that the way that we perceive things at work is often based on fairly limited information, and perception can lead to negative behaviour and attitudes. This can result in power battles and conflict at work.

Perception is how we make sense of the world around us. We are bombarded with stimuli from the environment that we need to filter and interpret to be able to respond to. This filtering process is influenced by a number of factors, including:

- your mood
- your personality and concept of self
- your skills and experience
- your attitudes and what you value.

This filtering system, which is part of the perceptual process, allows us to operate in a very complex world, where there are millions of stimuli competing for our attention. Perception is influenced by the source of the stimuli and the context in which we experience it. In terms of organizational behaviour, one of the ways in which the process of perception, and how it can impact on our decision-making and behaviours, can readily be demonstrated during the use of interviews, which are typically an important part of any selection decision.

KEY THEMES The role of perception in interviews

There is much published research demonstrating how we form judgements and make decisions based on limited information. So what we perceive to be the case influences how we respond. This is particularly evident within the interview situation. Some of the possible perceptual errors that can occur include:

- **First impressions count** – this can be as simple as what someone is wearing or the strength of their handshake.

- **Halo/horns effect** – if a candidate is from the same city as us and supports our favourite football team, we are likely to see them in a positive light and put an image of a 'halo' above their head. From then on, they have little else to do to convince us that they are the person for the job. In contrast, 'horns' may be applied if early on

in the interview the candidate answers a question incorrectly and a negative image is then created that is hard to overturn.

- **Same image** – viewing candidates more favourably if they possess similar characteristics to ourselves – for example, age, social background, accent, educational level. Gilmore and Williams (2009) refer to this as 'Like Me' judgements.

- **Recency/primacy effect** – we allow our perceptions to be formed by the most recent encounter (recency effect) and the first encounter (primacy effect). Very simply, this suggests that candidates who go first or last in the interview line-up are more likely to be remembered, whereas those in the middle may be lost.

Perception is also a crucial element of how employees experience organizational culture, which is discussed in Chapter 9. In a summary produced by the CIPD (2011c) of the 'best thinking in HR', it is suggested that 'organization culture is a set of values, beliefs, norms and ways of behaving of the individuals that make up the organization', but that 'it should not come as a surprise to learn that the perceptions of our employees are as significant in shaping these desired behaviours as the formal mechanisms, or rules, that we set in place to encourage them'.

A key example of perception in action at work can also be provided by taking a look at the role of the psychological contract.

The psychological contract

KEY TERM

The psychological contract: an unwritten and undocumented set of expectations existing in the mind of both the employer and the employee about the offer of employment that has been made.

The psychological contract is unwritten and concerns the perceptions that employees and employers have in relation to their role at work. The contract is not written and therefore cannot be seen, but forms part of the 'deal' that is expected and revolves around mutual obligations. It can be inferred from how people behave in the workplace, and the organizational customs and practices that form part of the organizational culture (see Chapter 9).

The psychological contract is about 'fairness and trust', and both parties honouring the 'deal'. If an employee perceives that the deal is being broken, this can lead to negative behaviour, such as absenteeism or, ultimately, leaving the organization. If the employee perceives that their psychological contract is being met, high performance and commitment to the organization are likely to be the result. The CIPD (2011e) factsheet on 'The Psychological Contract' suggests that the establishment and maintenance of a positive psychological contract with employees is critical in order to produce sustainable business value.

TABLE 3.4 The psychological contract

Employer expects	Employee expects
• Work hard	• Pay commensurate with performance
• Uphold company reputation	• Opportunities for training and development
• Maintain high levels of attendance and punctuality	• Opportunities for promotion
• Show loyalty to the organization	• Recognition for innovation or new ideas
• Work extra hours when required	• Feedback on performance
• Develop new skills and update old ones	• Interesting tasks
• Be flexible – for example, by taking on a colleague's work	• An attractive benefits package
• Be courteous to clients and colleagues	• Respectful treatment
• Be honest	• Reasonable job security
• Come up with new ideas	• A pleasant and safe working environment

CIPD 2011e

ACTIVITY

Think about what your expectations might be in your first graduate job and what you think your employer will expect. To what extent do they match the lists in Table 3.4?

Attitudes

KEY TERM

Attitudes: beliefs that we hold which influence our approach to the way we work and how we treat others.

Employee attitudes are a key contributor to performance. They can be measured, and results can provide valuable indicators of the success or failure of management efforts (CIPD 2004).

Many employers today pay a lot of attention to the attitudes of their employees, through the use of such things as attitude surveys, which are used to measure and review how employees are thinking and feeling with regard to the workplace. The shared attitudes of employees within an organization can be very powerful and resistant to change, as explored in Chapter 9 on organizational culture and change. Sometimes such entrenched attitudes can lead to possible discriminatory behaviour or individuals feeling left out if they do not assimilate the prevailing attitudes and beliefs.

What do we know about attitudes?

- We have lots of them.
- They are difficult to change.
- We learn them over time.
- They shape our behaviour.
- They are invisible.
- They are usually positive or negative.

Attitudes are said to contain three interconnected elements: an emotional or affective element, a behavioural element and a cognitive element. In practice, this means that an attitude will provide an individual with signals as to how to feel, act and think about something or someone else – for example, about the particular equipment that is being used at work or the group of people that the individual has to work with. An attitude is not the same as personality, though; an attitude is formulated in relation to something else, whereas personality is something within the individual themselves.

Katz (cited in Mullins 2010) suggests that attitudes can have four roles:

1 They provide the basis on which we categorize and sort information.
2 They demonstrate to others who we are.
3 We use attitudes to help us to know how to react to others, based on positive or negative experiences.
4 Attitudes may be used to protect the individual from reality.

Companies often measure attitudes at work through the use of attitude surveys; the results can provide valuable information about a range of key areas that each organization can work on in order to maintain and develop competitive edge.

Such surveys generally ask questions about the following aspects at work:

- leadership and management
- the work itself – that is, job role, responsibilities and workloads
- motivation and engagement
- fairness and equal treatment at work
- loyalty and commitment
- training and development
- work–life balance
- communications.

The *Sunday Times* Best Companies to Work For survey uses a rigorous methodology, exploring employee attitudes to identify workplace performance and best practice, according to eight key factors:

TABLE 3.5 Key factors used by the *Sunday Times* Best Companies to Work For survey

Leadership	How employees feel about the head of the organization, senior managers, and the organization's values and principles
My manager	How employees feel about and communicate with their direct manager
Personal growth	What employees feel about training and their future prospects
Well-being	How employees feel about stress, pressure at work, and work–life balance
My team	Employees' feelings towards their immediate colleagues and how well they work together
Giving something back	The extent to which employees feel their organization has a positive impact on society
My company	The level of engagement employees have for their job and organization
Fair deal	How happy employees are with their pay and benefits

Sunday Times 2011

Table 3.6 shows two examples of the types of question that might appear in an attitude survey.

TABLE 3.6 The types of question that might appear in an attitude survey

Communication	Strongly disagree 1	2	No opinion 3	4	Strongly agree 5
1. I generally feel informed about changes that affect me within [*Company*].	☐	☐	☐	☐	☐
2. I usually know in plenty of time when important things happen.	☐	☐	☐	☐	☐
3. I can see the link between my work and [*Company*] objectives.	☐	☐	☐	☐	☐
4. Managers communicate clear objectives for the company to achieve.	☐	☐	☐	☐	☐

Teamwork	Strongly disagree 1	2	No opinion 3	4	Strongly agree 5
37. I believe that all the divisions in the company work together to achieve a common goal.	☐	☐	☐	☐	☐
38. The people I work with cooperate to get the work done.	☐	☐	☐	☐	☐
39. There is a spirit of we're all in this together within [Company].	☐	☐	☐	☐	☐
40. There is co-operation among team members.	☐	☐	☐	☐	☐

www.hr-survey.com/sdeoaq.htm

Attitude surveys provide a snapshot in time and, as a result, tend to be repeated on an annual basis. Attitudes can be very resistant to change, and education and communication are important approaches to use in the change process, as discussed in Chapter 9. If we think back to the section on behavioural competencies at Deloitte, what is beginning to emerge is an interest in recruiting employees in the first place who share the company values and attitudes, so will fit in with the organizational culture. Given the speed at which job roles change, an increasing emphasis is being placed on seeking out candidates whose attitudes match the company ethos. ASDA is a company with a strong emphasis on employing people who share its ethos. 'We recruit for attitude and train for skill. The company has a strong brand identity with a clear set of values, so it is key that our employees share those values' (*Personnel Today* 2006).

3.10 Summary

From our exploration into personality, attitudes and perception, it can be seen that individuals are both unique and complex. From an organizational perspective, having an understanding of individual characteristics can help to identify why certain situations arise in the workplace and enable those who manage people to be more sensitive to differences. Personality assessment, for example, can provide rich material to enhance an interview, by helping to provide a fuller picture of an individual and how they might behave in different situations. It can also help the organization to consider career development opportunities and redeployment arrangements. However, it is also important to remember that there is little established research evidence to suggest that there are strong links between success in a job and personality characteristics. The emergence of the 'big five' personality characteristics and subsequent research into their links to job performance is starting to provide a source of such evidence.

An awareness of the process of perception and assessing the strength of attitudes at work is increasingly recognized as providing a useful barometer for workplace commitment. The way that individuals perceive things at work can lead to distorted views of reality. This emphasizes the need for effective communication and rigorous and systematic approaches to the selection of new employees, for example.

Many organizations measure attitudes on a regular basis, to 'take the pulse' of the organization and identify where attention needs to be paid. Attitudes can be very difficult to change as they are often developed over time, but taking a snapshot of employee attitudes can help to identify action points for attention.

Key ideas

- The big debate about personality relates to whether we are born with our personality or whether it develops as we grow up and emerge into adulthood.
- Some early personality theorists suggested that our personality is linked to our physiology or body shape.
- Type theorists, from the simple Type A and Type B personality theorists to later, more complex trait approaches to personality, argue that we can all be classified into type/trait clusters.
- Personality testing is often used as part of the recruitment and selection process within organizations, but such use is not without its critics.
- More recent research into personality has led to the basic agreement that there are common characteristics against which we all can be measured, these being the 'big five' personality characteristics.
- Contemporary research suggests that it is emotional intelligence that generates success at work.
- The process of perception leads individuals to form quick interpretations of others, based on limited stimuli.
- The psychological contract, although invisible, is a powerful determinant of our level of satisfaction at work.
- The measurement of attitudes is increasingly being used by organizations to gather and evaluate employee views.

Review questions

1. How would you define personality and why are organizations interested in the concept?
2. What are the key characteristics of Type A and Type B personalities, and how will their behaviours be different in the workplace?
3. Differentiate between the nomothetic and the idiographic approaches to personality.
4. Researchers have agreed that personality comprises five major dimensions. Consider why these might be a useful foundation for further research into the link between personality and performance at work.
5. How would you define emotional intelligence, and why might it be of particular relevance for leadership?
6. How far do you think the psychological contract provides a useful indication of what an employee might expect in the workplace?
7. Explain why attitudes might be resistant to change.

Recommended reading

CIPD (2011) 'The psychological contract'. Factsheet, July. London: Chartered Institute of Personnel and Development. (Available at www.cipd.co.uk)

Woodruffe, C. (2001) 'Promotional intelligence'. *People Management*, 11th January, pp. 26–9.

Useful websites

www.talentsmart.com – provides interesting short articles related to emotional intelligence

www.shl.com – allows you to explore and complete sample personality tests, as well as offering access to an archive of published journal articles relating to the use of psychometric tests in the workplace

References

Alarcon, G., Eschleman, K. and Bowling, N.A. (2009) 'Relationships between personality variables and burnout: a meta-analysis'. *Work and Stress*, 23(3), July–September, pp. 244–63.

Arnold, J. and Randall, R. *et al.* (2010) *Work Psychology: Understanding Human Behaviour in the Workplace* (5th edn). Harlow: Pearson Education.

Barrick, M. and Mount, M. (1991) 'The big five personality dimensions and job performance: a meta-analysis'. *Personnel Psychology*, 44(1), pp. 1–26.

Butler, M. and Rose, E. (2011) *Introduction to Organizational Behaviour*. London: Chartered Institute of Personnel and Development.

Cattell, R.B. (1946) *Description and Measurement of Personality*. Oxford: World Book Company.

CIPD (2004) 'Managing the psychological contract: taking the temperature'. Survey Report. London: Chartered Institute of Personnel and Development. (Available at www.cipd.co.uk)

CIPD (2010) 'Using the head and heart at work: a business case for soft skills'. Research Survey, 10th November. London: Chartered Institute of Personnel and Development. (Available at www.cipd.co.uk)

CIPD (2011a) 'Absence management'. Survey Report. London: Chartered Institute of Personnel and Development. (Available at www.cipd.co.uk)

CIPD (2011b) 'Feedback – 360 degree'. Factsheet, May. London: Chartered Institute of Personnel and Development. (Available at www.cipd.co.uk)

CIPD (2011c) 'In a nutshell: our pick of the best thinking in HR'. Issue 6, October. London: Chartered Institute of Personnel and Development. (Available at www.cipd.co.uk)

CIPD (2011d) 'Resourcing and talent planning'. Survey Report. London: Chartered Institute of Personnel and Development. (Available at www.cipd.co.uk)

CIPD (2011e) 'The psychological contract'. Factsheet, July. London: Chartered Institute of Personnel and Development. (Available at www.cipd.co.uk)

Erikson, E.H. (1950) *Childhood and Society*. New York: Norton.

Eysenck, H.J. (1947) *Dimensions of Personality*. New York: Kegan Paul.

Faragher, J. (2006) 'UK workers changing their personalities to get ahead'. *Personnel Today*, 4th July.

Feldman, R.S. (1996) *Understanding Psychology* (4th edn). London: McGraw-Hill.

Freud, S. (1938) *The Basic Writings of Sigmund Freud*. New York: Modern Library.

Friday, R.A. (2011) 'The dark side of emotional intelligence'. *Management Today*, 1st April.

Friedman, M. (1996) *Type A Behaviour: Its Diagnosis and Treatment*. New York: Plenum Press.

Friedman, R.A. and Rosenman, R.E. (1974) *Type A Behaviour and Your Heart*. New York: Knopf.

Furnham, A., Jackson, C. and Miller, T. (1999) 'Personality, learning style and work performance'. *Personality and Individual Differences*, 27, pp. 1113–22. Oxford: Pergamon.

Gilmore, S. and Williams, S. (2009) *Human Resource Management*. New York: Oxford University Press.

Goleman, D. (1998) *Working with Emotional Intelligence*. London: Bloomsbury.

Higgs, M. and Dulewicz, V. (2002) *Making Sense of Emotional Intelligence*. Slough: National Foundation for Educational Research in England and Wales.

IDS HR Studies (2011) 'Recruitment'. Issue 941, May.

Judge, T.A., Martocchio, J.J. and Thoreson, C.J. (1997) 'Five-factor model of personality and employee absence'. *Journal of Applied Psychology*, 82, pp. 745–55.

Jung, C.G. (1921) *Psychological Types: Collected Works*. New Jersey: Princeton University Press.

Kelly, G.A. (1963) *A Theory of Personality*. New York: Norton.

Landy, F.J. (2005) 'Some historical and scientific issues related to research on emotional intelligence'. *Journal of Organizational Behaviour*, 26, pp. 411–24.

Le Pine, J.A. and Dyne, L.V. (2001) 'Voice and cooperative behaviour as contrasting forms of contextual performance: evidence of the differential relationships with big five personality characteristics and cognitive ability'. *Journal of Applied Psychology*, 86, pp. 326–36.

Mayer, J.D. and Salovey, P. (1990) 'Emotional intelligence'. *Imagination, Cognition and Personality*, 9, pp. 185–211.

McCrae, R.R. and Costa, P.T. Jr (1995) 'Trait explanations in personality psychology'. *European Journal of Personality*, 9, pp. 231–52.

Mullins, L.J. (2010) *Management and Organizational Behaviour* (9th edn). Harlow: Pearson Education.

Nicholson, N. (1998) 'How hardwired is human behaviour?' *Harvard Business Review*, July/August.

Personnel Today (2006) 'Nature or nurture?' 17th January.

Pilbeam, S. and Corbridge, M. (2010) *People Resourcing and Talent Planning: HRM in Practice* (4th edn). Harlow: Pearson Education.

Redman, T. and Wilkinson, A. (2009) *Contemporary Human Resource Management*. Harlow: FT Prentice Hall.

Rogers, C. (1959) 'A theory of therapy, personality and interpersonal relationships as developed in the client-centred framework'. In Koch, S. (ed.) *Psychology: A Study of Science. Vol. III: Formulations of the Person and Social Context*. New York: McGraw-Hill.

Salgado, J.F. (1997) 'The five-factor model of personality and job performance in the European Community'. *Journal of Applied Psychology*, 82(1), February, pp. 30–43.

Sheldon, W.H. (1954) *Atlas of Men: A Guide for Somatotyping the Adult Male at all Ages*. New York: Harper and Row.

Smith, B.W., Tooley, E.M., Christopher, P.J. and Kay, V.S. (2010) 'Resilience as the ability to bounce back from stress: a neglected personal resource'. *Journal of Positive Psychology*, 5(3), 3rd May, pp. 166–76.

Sunday Times Best Companies to Work For (2011) (Available at www.thetimes100.co.uk)

Talentsmart (2009) *The Business Case for Emotional Intelligence*. (Available at www.talentsmart.com)

Woodruffe, C. (2001) 'Promotional intelligence'. *People Management*, 11th January, pp. 26–9.

4 Motivation and engagement

*If a worker sees high **productivity** as a path leading to the attainment of one or more of his (or her) **personal goals**, he (or she) will tend to be a high producer.* (VICTOR VROOM)

*Real commitment is rare in today's organizations. It is our experience that 90 per cent of the time what passes for **commitment** is compliance.* (PETER SENGE)

CHAPTER OUTLINE

1 Introduction

2 What is motivation?

3 Content theories of motivation

4 Process theories of motivation

5 Employee engagement

6 Motivating and engaging different generations of employees

7 Summary

CHAPTER OBJECTIVES

By the end of this chapter you will understand:

- the term 'motivation' and differentiate between intrinsic and extrinsic factors

- content theories and process theories and how they differ

- some limitations of the main theories of motivation

- different motivational techniques used by organizations to motivate employees

- the concept of employee engagement and the impact that engaged employees might have on an organization

- research into attitudes and values of current and future entrants to the labour market and identify what this might mean for organizations.

4.1 Introduction

> **Motivation:** the force that drives individuals to take action.

Motivation is one of the most popular topics within OB; it is studied on undergraduate business degree programmes and is often included as a feature of management training and development. There has been a wealth of research into motivation, both from a general human point of view and with regard to the workplace, which has resulted in several published academic models and concepts. This research has led to much debate around the topic and created a great deal of interest concerning what organizations can do to encourage employees to work hard and drive them to a higher level of performance. Motivation theories, in fact, explain the term from a range of different perspectives and this has led to there being no universal agreement on how to motivate employees in practice. This chapter will focus on motivation at work, unravelling the complexity surrounding the term, and will examine how it can be tackled in practice.

 ## 4.2 What is motivation?

Motivation is often viewed as the force within us that propels us to do something. This can be as simple as going to the coffee machine at work to get a drink to satisfy thirst (a human need), or a more complex process, such as deciding whether to put in extra performance at work in the belief that this will result in promotion and more money, thus enabling the individual to go skiing (a human want and expectation). So at the root of the issue of motivation are several key terms – needs, wants, goals and fulfilment. Let us look at these in more detail.

The basic idea is that individuals have needs or wants that spur them into action to achieve a desired result.

Consider your response to the following question: what motivates you to work hard in a job? Below is a list of responses compiled from interviews with the following employees:

- 27-year-old female texture artist in the film industry
- 31-year-old male chartered surveyor in the commercial property sector
- 59-year-old male self-employed engineer in the petrochemical industry
- 42-year-old female planning manager in the residential property sector
- 25-year-old female HR manager in the charity sector
- 20-year-old male checkout operator for a large supermarket
- 29-year-old male newly qualified teacher.

The motivating factors cited by the interviewees were:

- money
- potential bonus

- impressing my boss
- working with friendly people
- being able to have a laugh at work
- having the opportunity to be creative
- having the freedom to make decisions
- a nice working environment
- being able to use the latest technology
- being able to work from home occasionally
- the feeling of contributing to society
- the chance of promotion
- working on challenging projects
- the chance to go on training courses and to learn new things
- doing the work in the order and the way that you want – having autonomy
- a good boss.

This list contains motivational factors that the organization can offer and also shows clearly that motivation comes from within the individual. For example, pay is determined by the organization, while the feeling of being liked and accepted by colleagues is more internal to the individual. To put this into academic terminology, the list can be divided into what are called **intrinsic** factors of motivation and extrinsic factors. Intrinsic factors come from within the individual and are to do with how people feel about things – for example, feeling valued, loved, accepted, making a contribution, making things better. Extrinsic factors relate to things that the organization can offer the individual and are external – for example, pay, promotion, the work itself, training, the working environment and technology.

Both intrinsic and extrinsic factors are a feature of most established motivation theories.

 ## 4.3 Content theories of motivation

Content theories: a body of research that suggests that motivation is driven by wants and needs.

Early motivation theories focused on the satisfaction of needs and these are classified as **content** theories. The basic premise is that individuals will be driven by their desire to satisfy their wants and needs. One of the most famous content theories of motivation was put forward by Abraham Maslow in 1943. He proposed a **hierarchy of needs** (see Figure 4.1), which individuals will strive to fulfil. In summary, the hierarchy suggests that we all have five levels of needs, and the lower-level needs (physiological and safety) should be mostly satisfied before embarking on the fulfilment of any of the higher-level needs, with the ultimate need being the fulfilment of what Maslow called 'self-actualization'.

FIGURE 4.1 Maslow's hierarchy of needs (Maslow 1998, originally published 1943)

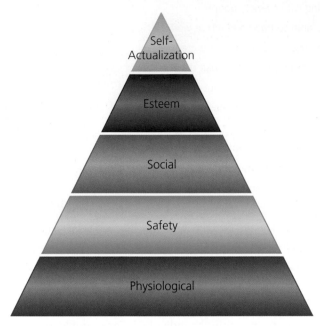

Maslow's work was put forward as a universal theory about what drives human beings. He suggested that we all have a set of needs that we must satisfy. His research was not focused directly on the workplace, although much of it has been used to explore how to ensure that employees are able to satisfy their needs at work. Table 4.1 summarizes the hierarchy of needs, illustrating the application of these in practice.

TABLE 4.1 Summary of Maslow's hierarchy of needs

Need	What does this mean in the work setting?	How can organizations fulfil this need?
Physiological	Hunger Warmth Thirst Shelter	Drinks machines Kitchen or restaurant facilities Heating and air conditioning Comfortable working environment Salary
Safety	Security Safety Feeling protected Stability	Health and safety at work Security guards Contracts of employment Communicating on business performance and planned changes
Social	Involvement with others Team-working Social atmosphere	Creating structures based on teams Staff associations and social clubs Open-plan offices Company sports teams

Need	What does this mean in the work setting?	How can organizations fulfil this need?
Esteem	Feeling wanted and valued Self-respect and the respect of others Status	Recognition schemes Regular feedback Job roles and titles Promotion Salary
Self-actualization	Growth and development Achieving potential Freedom to create and innovate at work Autonomy	Job roles that allow opportunities for challenge, creativity and continuous learning Having a say in decisions, freedom and control over your daily activities

In considering Table 4.1, it is interesting to reflect on intrinsic and extrinsic motivating factors. It can be seen that the lower levels of Maslow's hierarchy tend to be able to be satisfied by extrinsic factors with the higher-level needs being more intrinsically satisfied. In reality, it is sometimes hard to differentiate between intrinsic and extrinsic factors, as they can feed into each other. For example, a high salary not only satisfies physiological and security needs (many of which are extrinsic), but can also create a feeling of worth and bolster self-esteem, which would be considered intrinsic motivators.

Company practice

The winner of the Best Workplace in the UK (Great Place to Work with CMI 2011) was Baringa Partners, a small to medium-sized enterprise (SME) with 170 staff, specializing in the energy, utilities and financial services sectors. It satisfies **esteem** and **self-actualization** through an explicit policy of promotion based on ability rather than length of time in the organization. In 2010, 28 internal promotions were the result of this. Quarterly awards are given to employees nominated by colleagues, based on their contribution to the company's core values.

Siemens also provides opportunities for employees to satisfy the higher-level needs on Maslow's hierarchy. For example, **self-actualization** is satisfied by allowing employees to fulfil their potential in that they can get involved and take responsibility for their own jobs. They have autonomy to make improvements and changes. They work in a challenging environment, which requires innovation and creativity to solve problems. Training and development opportunities help to satisfy **esteem** needs, as engineers learn new skills that can lead to progression up the career ladder (*The Times* 100 Business Case Studies 2010).

Tesco motivates its employees in relation to Maslow's hierarchy.

TABLE 4.2 How Tesco motivates its employees

Need	What Tesco provides
Self-actualization	Tesco offers personal development plans, recognition of skills, abilities and talents, and opportunities for career progression. It has a fast-track management programme, which provides a clear pathway for talented staff.
Self-esteem	Tesco values highlight respect for others and praise for those who work hard. The appraisal system is designed to recognize the contribution of individuals, and achievements are celebrated.

Need	What Tesco provides
Social needs	Tesco puts a strong emphasis on team-working and creating a 'home-from-home' atmosphere.
Security needs	Tesco offers formal contracts of employment and benefits such as pensions and sickness schemes. Health and safety at work are a priority. Staff can join a union for further support.
Physiological needs	The company provides regular monthly pay, restaurants and lockers for staff.

Adapted from *The Times* 100 Business Case Studies 2010

Limitations

While Maslow's hierarchy of needs has generated much debate and provides an interesting perspective on human motivation, it raises several questions relating to the satisfaction of individual needs.

- The order in which the needs have to be satisfied is not clear. In his early work, Maslow suggested that the needs would be satisfied in order, with lower-level needs requiring fulfilment before progression to the higher-level needs. Later work suggests that the needs may require only partial satisfaction before moving on to the next level of need, or that the needs may be met in a variety of orders, according to what each individual places a value on.

- External pressures are not taken into account in the design of the model – for example, in the recent world recession, a person operating in a senior role, with their esteem and self-actualization needs satisfied, may suddenly face the threat of redundancy and the driving need becomes security.

- There is no one solution, as everyone is different and the depth of need will vary from person to person.

- Needs may change according to the stage the individual is at in his or her life (see the discussion on Generation Y later in the chapter).

- In applying the hierarchy to the workplace there are limitations, as some needs may be met outside of work – for example, by being captain of a successful football team in the local league, the person may satisfy his or her need for esteem outside of work.

- The set of needs is presented as a fixed model, whereas the context of work constantly changes – for example, in a global environment, can one set of needs be applied universally?

- In a later publication, Maslow (1998) indicated that self-actualization is actually achieved only by a very small minority (less than 1 per cent of adults), so should organizations bother with this level of the hierarchy?

- Some needs could be satisfied by the same factor. Money, for example, can help satisfy physiological needs, in terms of providing the cash to purchase food at work or pay rent outside of work; yet it also helps to fulfil esteem needs, in that money gained through a promotion can be used to buy a holiday in the Caribbean, which can demonstrate wealth and achievement to colleagues at work and friends outside of work.

These criticisms or observations of Maslow's work were partly addressed by Alderfer (1972), who adapted Maslow's five-tier hierarchy and reduced this to three main motivational needs: existence, relatedness and growth, known as 'ERG' theory. His explanation of motivational needs is helpful when reviewing motivation at work, as he proposed that needs could be met flexibly rather than in a strict order. The fluidity proposed by Alderfer is an interesting dimension to consider, as it suggests that needs will change and develop for individuals. In the workplace, for example, if there is not an opportunity for the satisfaction of growth needs, an individual may place more emphasis on one or both of the other needs to compensate. Alderfer referred to this as the 'frustration-regression effect'. While he did not present a hierarchy, he proposed that the three needs could be classified in order of importance, with growth needs being the most essential:

1 | Existence needs – similar to the physiological and safety needs of Maslow's hierarchy.
2 | Relatedness needs – overlaps with the social and esteem needs of Maslow's hierarchy.
3 | Growth needs – relates to the esteem and self-actualization levels on Maslow's hierarchy.

In contrast, a further content theory proposed by Frederick Herzberg (1959) was based specifically on research conducted within the workplace. He interviewed 203 accountants and engineers from different industries, but from the same geographical area of the USA. Interviewees were asked to identify times when they felt positive and times when they felt negative about their current or any previous jobs, and to explain why. The findings from the research led to the development of Herzberg's **two-factor theory of motivation**, in which he highlighted that there were two different sets of factors impacting on motivation and job satisfaction at work: the **hygiene** factors and the **motivators**. If we think back to the earlier part of the chapter when we discussed what motivation is, the terms intrinsic and extrinsic were introduced. We can relate these terms to the work of Herzberg. The hygiene factors are sometimes classified as extrinsic factors, which are issues external to the individual. On the other hand, the motivators can be viewed as intrinsic factors, which are related to feelings and perceptions within the individual.

TABLE 4.3 Herzberg's two-factor theory of motivation

Hygiene factors	Motivators
Reward and pay, working conditions and environment, company policy and procedures, job security, effectiveness of supervision, and interpersonal relations with colleagues	Growth and advancement, achievement opportunities, recognition, responsibility, and job role, design and content
Herzberg's research found that these factors were linked to dissatisfaction at work, but were not listed as motivational factors.	These factors were found to be the factors that actually motivate people and result in higher levels of productivity.

In summary, Herzberg argued that both hygiene factors (extrinsic factors) and motivators (intrinsic factors) need to be in place in an organization in order for work performance to be enhanced. By satisfying the hygiene factors, an organization is setting the context to enable employees to contribute in the workplace, through creating a fair and pleasant working environment and removing dissatisfaction. However, in order to create a motivated workforce, attention also needs to be paid to the motivating factors identified through his research. It is not that one set of factors has a higher priority than another, but that both play a part in generating motivation at work.

ACTIVITY

In small groups, identify what organizations can do in practice to satisfy both hygiene and motivator factors in the workplace. If no attention is paid to the motivators, how might employees respond, and what impact might this have on the organization?

Limitations

A key criticism of Herzberg's work was the nature and size of the sample on which it was based. Think of the workplace today: if you were to conduct research based solely on males working in a professional capacity, would the results be applicable to all employees? Interestingly, however, when Herzberg replicated his research using wider samples, the research did produce similar results. Butler and Rose (2011) point out that although the theory is relatively simplistic, it does provide a framework for managers to consider. Butler and Rose also raise a key dimension of Herzberg's research, which assumed a link between being satisfied in your job and being productive. This assumption has been widely criticized. For example, some people do not enjoy their jobs, but work hard and are productive. Others who love their job role may not sustain a high level of performance.

CASE STUDY   Insight into practice – W.L. Gore

W.L. Gore Associates has consistently been ranked by the *Sunday Times* as one of the 100 best companies to work for. Founded in 1958 in Delaware in the USA, the UK's sites are based in Scotland. The company makes advanced technology products as diverse as walking boots, jackets, electronic equipment and window screens. Some of the benefits it offers include childcare vouchers, dental insurance, a wellness programme, flexible working (homeworking, teleworking and annualized hours), a final pension scheme to which Gore contributes 15 per cent of pay, generous maternity and paternity leave, profit-related pay, free private healthcare, a share option scheme, and opportunities to learn and grow. In 2010, the company spent £300 per employee on 'fun activities'; it donates dividends from shares to charities and encourages staff to support good causes.

Interestingly, there are no managers and no formal chains of command. The organization is team-based and fosters personal initiative. Workers communicate directly with each other and are accountable to fellow members of their multidisciplinary team, with those closest to the project being involved in the decision-making.

In the *Sunday Times* 2011 survey, some of the results indicated:

- 85 per cent love their job so much they would not leave tomorrow
- 85 per cent would stay even if offered another job
- 87 per cent are proud to work for W.L. Gore
- 83 per cent feel they can make a difference to the organization
- 84 per cent believe they can make a valuable contribution to organizational success
- 80 per cent say work is stimulating
- 83 per cent say work is good for personal growth
- 70 per cent say there are opportunities to learn and grow.

(*Sunday Times* Best Companies to Work For 2011)

Q   1 Taking account of the motivation theories outlined above, which of Maslow's hierarchy of needs are being met by W.L. Gore Associates, and how?

2 What evidence is there to suggest that the hygiene factors and motivators identified by Herzberg may play a part in encouraging employees at W.L. Gore Associates to want to work hard?

3 From the above data, are there any questions you would like to ask W.L. Gore Associates in order to further explore its practices?

Content theories in summary

Content theories are well established and provide an interesting perspective on how to improve performance at work. It is clear that many organizations apply the theories in practice. They concentrate on human needs that we all can relate to. The simplistic nature of the various theories makes motivating people at work seem easy. In reality, this is not the case, and the process theories, which emerged later, address more complex human behaviour, which also needs to be considered when reviewing how to encourage people to achieve high levels of performance.

4.4 Process theories of motivation

Process theories: the notion that individuals weigh up the value of what they give in return for what they expect to get, so motivation also comprises a rational decision-making process.

Process theories focus more on the individual weighing up the consequences of working hard and the likely outcomes or rewards for doing this. The reference to process can be explained by thinking of yourself and the mental calculations you take to decide to do something, based on whether you value what you will get in return. A significant process theory is that of **expectancy**.

Expectancy theory

Expectancy theory, developed by Victor Vroom (1964), illustrates the process whereby an individual alters his or her behaviour according to what he or she expects to achieve, and the value he or she places on the reward on offer. For example, based on our experience of teaching in universities, many undergraduate students change their study habits and behaviours in their final year. They have an expectation that devoting more time to study in the final year will result in a higher level of performance and therefore the attainment of the degree classification that they want.

Vroom's theory can be presented in the form of a simple diagram, as in Figure 4.2.

FIGURE 4.2 Vroom's expectancy theory

In summary, Vroom proposed that a high level of performance would be achieved when employees could see a clear link between putting effort into their work and getting a desired outcome.

> ### Reflective questions
>
> Think of an occasion when you wanted to achieve something. Reflect on the effort you put in, how you behaved and what actions you took in order to achieve the reward that you wanted.
>
> Now think of an occasion when you put effort into something, but the reward was not met in the way that you valued. How did this make you feel?

If we think of the model in relation to work, the sorts of rewards that employees might value are opportunities to undertake some charity work, a thank you from their manager, promotion, increased salary, becoming more integrated within a team, being able to leave work an hour early and so on.

The basis of expectancy theory is that individuals must place a value on a reward and perceive that the reward will be given if effort is made. Of course, effort will be affected by one's skills and abilities and the resources available.

Goal-setting theory

Locke (1968) and Locke and Latham (2002) suggested that the setting of goals is critical to motivating people to perform. In the workplace, it is the idea that setting goals will help employees to be clear about expectations, give them a focus and drive them to achieve results. Mullins (2010) proposes that people with specific goals will be more productive than those with 'vague goals such as "do the best you can"', as these are unclear and the individual does not know what they are working towards.

Think about joining a gym. A goal of 'wanting to get fitter' is rather vague and will not allow you to know when you have achieved your goal. On the other hand, a goal such as 'I want to be able to take part in the 5 km run Race for Life on 29th March 2012 and achieve a time of 30 minutes' gives you a clear focus and is measurable.

At work, the organization may use appraisals as part of a performance management system. These are often used as the vehicle for managers to discuss and agree goals with employees. Research suggests that the most effective goals:

- push people
- are SMART in focus – that is, specific, measurable, achievable, realistic and timed
- are agreed and not imposed
- have a mechanism for continuous review and feedback
- are linked to the organizational strategy and targets.

Research by the CIPD (2010) suggests that while setting goals is important, it is not just the results that matter, but the way in which they are achieved. Many organizations now specify the set of behaviours or competencies that they want employees to demonstrate in achieving their goals. So organizational culture and values also play a part. These concepts are discussed in Chapter 9.

Equity theory

Another important variable when looking at motivation is an individual's **perception** of his or her situation. Equity theory argues that individuals will look for fairness at work. In terms of motivation, this means that they seek a balance between the effort they put in and the reward they receive. Adams' (1965) theory suggests that individuals assess their contribution against what they expect to get in return. This is often shown visually in the form of weighing scales. On one side of the scales are the 'inputs' (energy, effort, time, skills, knowledge, attitudes and so on) and on the other side of the scales are the 'outcomes' (pay, holidays, promotion, responsibility, job title and so on). If the scales are in balance, an individual is considered to be satisfied and will feel that he or she is getting a fair exchange and will be motivated. If the scales are unbalanced, the employee will perceive unfairness of treatment, which may alter his or her behaviour.

Organizations typically work hard to create fairness at work. This is achieved in lots of ways, including carrying out a market analysis of pay rates, equal opportunities and diversity policies, as well as job evaluation schemes that rank jobs and classify appropriate rewards and benefits.

But what if an employee perceives an imbalance? Adams suggests that several possible actions may follow:

TABLE 4.4 Adams' equity theory: actions and behaviour

Action	Behaviour
Change input	Negative actions: work more slowly; leave early; more days off 'sick'; spend more time moaning than working Positive actions: work longer hours; increased rate of productivity
Alter outcomes	Negotiate a higher level of pay or benefits; seek promotion; ask for additional training and development
Leave the organization	Move to another employer to achieve a more favourable balance or ask for an internal transfer
Comparisons	Use other groups of employees to compare yourself with so that the balance is restored
Rethink the balance	Sometimes distortion comes into play – for example, you may think you are working harder than you are and you can revisit and reflect on your perception of your input to achieve equity

CASE STUDY Insight into practice – Beaverbrooks

Featuring in the *Sunday Times* as one of the 100 best companies to work for (*Sunday Times* Best Companies to Work For 2011), the jewellery retailer Beaverbrooks motivates staff in numerous ways.

Benefits on offer at Beaverbrooks include performance-related pay, childcare vouchers, a pension scheme, target-based rewards, bonus schemes, coverage in the company magazine and a loyalty bonus. Money raised by staff is matched by the organization for local charities and 20 per cent of its pre-tax profits go to good causes; office equipment is donated to schools and charities as part of its recycling policy. Communication is key, with regular visits to the 60 stores from the senior management team, as well as conferences and focus groups. Forty-five per cent of employees who earn £15,000 or less feel they are fairly paid for the work they do compared with people in similar positions in other organizations and within Beaverbrooks. Staff are reported to be proud to work for the company and love their jobs. The firm is ranked second for 'Giving Something Back' and eleventh for a 'Fair Deal'. Scores of 72 per cent were achieved for fair treatment, 83 per cent for having fun with colleagues; 77 per cent of employees feel the organization puts a lot back into the community and works to protect the environment.

> **Q**   **Analyse which of Beaverbrooks' practices you would classify as potentially satisfying either intrinsic or extrinsic motivation, and why. Fit some of the benefits to expectancy theory, goal theory and equity theory, and explain how you think they fit and why.**

What do the process theories tell us about motivation and job satisfaction?

In summary, process theories take our understanding of motivation further. They emphasize the fact that individuals will internally process the rewards on offer and calculate how much effort they need to expend if they value the reward. They highlight that motivation, while different for all individuals, does not occur in a vacuum, in that employees will make comparisons with others and behave according to their internal assessment of fairness or value. One of the main assumptions of process theories is that individuals are rational and will think before they act. Do you always think before you act?

 ## 4.5 Employee engagement

KEY TERM

> **Employee engagement:** this relatively new concept explores the degree to which an individual forms an attachment to an organization.

Clearly, many of the content and process theories were published some years ago, and a question that is often asked is whether there are any more recent theories of motivation, given the changing nature of work and the changing context of organizations. The most recent development in this area is the notion of 'employee engagement', which goes beyond motivation and job satisfaction. Employee engagement examines the clarity of employees' perceptions of what is expected of them, their relationships with co-workers and managers, and how these contribute to their experience of and involvement in their work. Unlike motivation theories, which focus on job satisfaction and the fulfilment of needs, 'employee engagement' emphasizes that motivated employees who perform well in their jobs feel valued and involved in their work, in terms of three particular dimensions:

- **emotional** – they enjoy coming to work; they gain satisfaction and pleasure from the work that they do; and they feel connected to the people they work with
- **cognitive** – they feel that their job uses their skills and abilities appropriately
- **behavioural** – they are willing to put in more effort and increase performance as required (CIPD 2010).

Rankin (2008) considers that engagement goes beyond the more static notion of job satisfaction and motivation, and highlights the importance of the psychological relationship between the individual and the organization. MacLeod and Clarke (2009) argue that the organization has to develop and nurture engagement, and work towards building a two-way relationship between the employer and the employee. The CIPD (2010) stresses that engagement is something that the employee has to offer, and employees have to be motivated to want to connect with their work and really care about doing a good job. Much is said today about the importance of people at work and how they can provide an organization with a competitive edge in these difficult economic times. Eccleston (2011) reports that Ashley Ward, director of the people development company European Leaders, suggests that 'it's widely accepted that people performance is the biggest influence in business performance … if you look at the UK's best companies to work for, their focus on company values and employee engagement is right at the top of their agenda.'

So why has engagement generated so much interest?

There is interesting research evidence emerging that provides some indicators of the impact that an engaged workforce can have on a business. This is raising the awareness of many organizations about the importance of this concept. De Mello, Wildermuth and Pauken (2008) highlight the positive correlations between employee engagement and improvements in customer satisfaction, productivity, profits, turnover and safety records. MacLeod and Clarke (2009) report many instances of positive outcomes of having engaged employees – for example, they are 18 per cent more productive and create a 12 per cent increase in profitability (based on a Gallup survey conducted in 2006).

An analysis by Kanter and MacKenzie (from Hewitt 2010) of 900 global organizations between 2008 and 2010 showed a link between employee engagement levels and financial performance. Organizations with high levels of engagement (65 per cent or more of employees were engaged) outperformed the total stock market index. In 2009, total shareholder return was 19 per cent higher than the average. Companies with low engagement (where fewer than 40 per cent of employees were engaged) had a total shareholder return that was 40 per cent lower than the average.

CASE STUDY Insight into practice – Enterprise Rent-A-Car

Enterprise Rent-A-Car has taken the concept of engagement seriously. The company has highlighted the differences between 'engaged' employees and those 'actively disengaged'.

TABLE 4.5 Enterprise Rent-A-Car and the concept of engagement

Engaged	Not engaged	Actively disengaged
Work with passion	Sleepwalk through the day	Are unhappy
Have a strong bond with their business	Show only minimum engagement with their work	Undermine what their colleagues accomplish
Introduce new ideas and move the company forward	Put in their time without energy or passion	Add costs to business activity

The Times 100 Business Case Studies 2010

So what does engagement look like in practice?

- Answering the phone before the working day starts
- Working together as a team
- Regularly attending social work functions together
- Arriving early every day
- Organizing and preparing the office at the end of the day.

What are organizations doing to effectively develop engaged employees with high levels of motivation?

The CIPD (2010) suggests that a key driver of engagement is providing employees with an opportunity to feed their ideas upwards, as well as keeping employees informed about the business. Recent research from the CBI/IPA (2011) argues that:

> Employees must be informed and given voice. Having the opportunity to feed views upwards and feeling they are listened to affects the extent to which employees feel valued, committed and engaged.

CASE STUDY How some organizations keep their employees informed

- The Co-operative Group holds informal meetings where all team members are encouraged to contribute over coffee and cake.
- John Lewis partners are informed about strategic business decisions through a wide range of channels, including a suggestion scheme, management consultations and a culture of knowledge sharing. (MacLeod and Clarke 2009)
- PlasticCo set up cross-functional problem-solving groups to meet and discuss ideas for improving work processes. (Alfes *et al.* 2010)

The CIPD (2009a) suggests that a poor work–life balance and a lack of flexibility are barriers to achieving engagement.

CASE STUDY KPMG

As part of its engagement strategy, KPMG has introduced:

- a shorter working week
- home working
- job sharing
- unpaid leave
- annualized hours
- career breaks
- additional holiday purchases
- 'glide time', when the start and finish times of the working day can be adjusted.

The CIPD (2009b) argues that the key to engaging employees is effective line management – the proposition is that individuals do not leave their jobs; they leave individual managers.

CASE STUDY B&Q

B&Q has made managers accountable for engagement within their teams. Management training, along with action planning and performance review materials, have been provided to help them with creating an engaged staff. (Employers Forum on Age 2007)

So what if employees are disengaged?

While the evidence suggests that there are many favourable outcomes of having an engaged workforce, there are, of course, going to be employees who are disengaged.

ACTIVITY

Imagine you are the newly appointed HR manager for a large retail organization. The results of the company's annual attitude survey have revealed that employee engagement levels in the warehouse division are lower than those at head office. You have been tasked with investigating this.

1 | What action would you take?
2 | Identify what you think will be the impact on the business of a large group of disengaged employees.

4.6 Motivating and engaging different generations of employees

Contemporary research into generational groups highlights the complexity of trying to tap into people's wants and needs, as these are often quite different across the generations. For example, there is research that identifies that Generation Y (those born between 1977 and 1991) may be motivated by different factors than their parents. Some of the research highlights the following:

- Generation Y has different priorities – they care less about salaries and more about flexible working, having time to travel and better work–life balance opportunities (Asthana 2008).

- Tulgan (2005) argues that Generation Y is much less likely to respond to traditional 'command and control' styles of management. Martin (2005: 40) points out that members of Generation Y 'are independent, entrepreneurial thinkers who relish responsibility, demand immediate feedback, and expect a sense of accomplishment hourly. They thrive on challenging work and creative expression, love freedom and flexibility, and hate micromanagement.'

- Iyer and Reisenwitz (2009) found that Generation Y expects promotion in two years, rewrites the rules rather than accepts them, multitasks and expects regular feedback, does not expect to stay with one organization, assumes technology and celebrates diversity. They further highlight that Generation Y prefers to be given the chance to contribute to the community and prefers a boss who can be trusted and respected.

Of course, there is a new generation about to enter the labour market, called Generation C. 'The "C" stands for "connected, communicating, content-centric, computerized, community-oriented, *always* clicking". It is the generation born after 1990, whose whole reality has been shaped by the internet, mobile phones and social networking' (Friedrich, Peterson and Koster 2011).

What does this mean for motivating employees in the future?

It means that attention should be given to the changing needs and expectations of future generations, as motivation for these generations will have new dimensions. Some changes in practice are already emerging – for example:

- Procter and Gamble has adapted its recruitment efforts to place more emphasis on the intangible rewards – for example, flexible hours, chance to work from home, promise of regular three-month sabbaticals (Asthana 2008).

- Deloitte (2009) has identified the things employers need to think about in relation to Generation Y in its report. In response to the question 'Which of the following action items should your employer do to retain you?', members of Generation Y suggested some of the following: increase salary and/or bonus; provide opportunities for advancement; provide appropriate recognition for contributions; promote coaching and mentoring; offer flexible work hours; offer a variety of career paths.

4.7 Summary

In summary, motivation is a very complex issue, which many theorists have explored, producing some interesting findings that generate debate. Organizations implement a range of techniques to encourage high levels of performance and productivity, as it is recognized that people make a difference to the bottom line. However, human beings are complex and unique, and therefore there is no single solution to creating a highly motivated employee. Individuals all have different wants and needs, and, as highlighted, these can change across generations and as the individual gains knowledge and experience. What is clear is that motivation is more than just money, and intrinsic factors, such as emotions, feelings and perceptions, need to be taken into account.

Key ideas

- Motivation is seen as the driving force behind our actions.
- Content theories of motivation discuss the satisfaction of needs and how individuals seek to satisfy these.
- Process theories propose that motivation is a more rational consideration, where an individual weighs up whether to do something based on how much they value what they are likely to get in return.
- Goal-setting theory focuses on the importance of goals in driving behaviour.
- Equity introduces the variable of individual perception to the motivation debate, in that it is argued that individuals consider fairness of treatment.
- Motivation models and theories present an insight into how individuals may be motivated at work, but there is much debate centred on the limitations.
- Employee engagement is one of the latest ideas relating to motivation at work; it considers how connected employees feel towards the organization.
- Contemporary research highlights that people's wants and needs will differ across generations, resulting in a need to rethink how to motivate people at work.

Review questions

1. How would you define the term 'motivation'?

2. Some writers argue that theories such as Maslow's hierarchy of needs and Herzberg's two-factor theory focus more on the satisfaction of needs than on actual motivation. What do you think of this view?

3. A criticism of Maslow's work is that needs may change as we progress through life. To what extent do you agree with this point, and why?

4. Process theories suggest that our behaviour is based on rational decision-making, which will drive our motivation. Consider the limitations of this view.

5. Explain how the notion of employee engagement differs from traditional motivation theories.

6. What is the value to organizations of identifying the needs and expectations of different generational groups?

Recommended reading

Alfes, K., Truss, C., Soane, E., Rees, C. and Getenby, M. (2010) 'Creating an engaged workforce'. Findings from the Kingston Employee Engagement Consortium Project. London: Chartered Institute of Personnel and Development. (Available at www.cipd.co.uk/NR/rdonlyres/DD66E557-DB90-4F07-8198-87C3876F3371/0/Creatingengagedworkforce.pdf)

Asthana, M. (2008) 'Generation Y: they don't live for work … they work to live'. *The Observer*, Sunday 25th May.

Useful websites

www.bestcompanies.co.uk – the workplace engagement specialist, which identifies workplace performance and best practice

www.cipd.co.uk – access to a range of factsheets, surveys, reports and podcasts by the Chartered Institute of Personnel and Development; free to register as a guest.

References

Adams, J.S. (1965) 'Inequity in social exchange'. In Berkowitz, L. (ed.) *Advances in Experimental Social Psychology*. New York: Academic Press.

Alderfer, C.P. (1972) *Existence, Relatedness and Growth*. London: Collier Macmillan.

Alfes, K., Truss, C., Soane, E., Rees, C. and Getenby, M. (2010) 'Creating an engaged workforce'. Findings from the Kingston Employee Engagement Consortium Project. London: Chartered Institute of Personnel and Development. (Available at www.cipd.co.uk/NR/rdonlyres/DD66E557-DB90-4F07-8198-87C3876F3371/0/Creatingengagedworkforce.pdf)

Asthana, M. (2008) 'Generation Y: they don't live for work … they work to live'. *The Observer*, Sunday 25th May.

Buchanan, D. and Huczynski, A. (2010) *Organizational Behaviour* (7th edn). Harlow: Pearson.

Butler, M. and Rose, E. (2011) *Introduction to Organizational Behaviour*. London: Chartered Institute of Personnel and Development.

CBI/IPA (2011) *Transformation Through Employee Engagement: Meeting the Public Services Challenge*. London: Confederation of British Industry.

CIPD (2009a) 'An HR director's guide to employee engagement'. London: Chartered Institute of Personnel and Development. (Available at www.cipd.co.uk/hr-resources/research/employee-engagement-hr-directors-guide.aspx)

CIPD (2009b) 'Employee engagement in context'. London: Chartered Institute of Personnel and Development. (Available at www.cipd.co.uk/hr-resources/research/employee-engagement-context.aspx)

CIPD (2010) 'Employee engagement'. Factsheet. London: Chartered Institute of Personnel and Development. (Available at www.cipd.co.uk/hr-resources/factsheets/employee-engagement.aspx)

Deloitte (2009) 'Generation Y: power house of the global economy'. (Available at www.deloitte.com)

De Mello, C., Wildermuth, S. and Pauken, P. (2008) 'A perfect match: decoding employee engagement. Part 1: engaging cultures and leaders'. *Industrial and Commercial Training*, 40(3), pp. 122–8.

Dernovsek, D. (2008) 'Creating highly engaged and committed employees starts at the top and ends at the bottom line'. (Available at www.insala.com/employee-engagement/engaged-employees.pdf) Washington, DC: Credit Union National Association Inc.

Eccleston, J. (2011) 'Manager's poor communication blamed for low staff motivation'. *Personnel Today*, 8th June.

Employers Forum on Age (2007) 'Employee engagement, case study B&Q', EFA overview. (Available at www.mtropy.com/efa/policy/case_bq.asp) London: EFA.

Friedrich, R., Peterson, M. and Koster, A. (2011) 'The rise of Generation C'. *Strategy and Business*, spring.

Great Place to Work with CMI (2011) *UK's Best Workplaces: Great Place to Work® Special Report 2011*. (Available at www.greatplacetowork.co.uk)

Iyer, R. and Reisenwitz, T. (2009) 'Differences in Generation X and Generation Y: implications for the organization and marketers'. *Marketing Management Journal*, 19(2), pp. 91–103.

Kanter, M. and MacKenzie, L. (2010) 'Hewitt analysis shows steady decline in global employee engagement levels'. (Available at http://talentmgt.com/articles/view/hewitt_analysis_shows_steady_decline_in_global_employee_engagement_levels)

Linstead, S., Fulop, L. and Lilley, S. (2009) *Management and Organization: A Critical Text* (2nd edn). Basingstoke: Palgrave.

Locke, E. (1968) 'Towards a theory of task motivation and incentives'. *Organizational Behaviour and Human Performance*, 3, pp. 157–89.

Locke, E.A. and Latham, G.P. (2002) 'Building a practically useful theory of goal setting and task motivation: a 35-year odyssey'. *American Psychologist*, 57(9), pp. 705–17.

MacLeod, D. and Clarke, N. (2009) 'Engaging for success: enhancing performance through employee engagement'. (Available at www.bis.gov.uk/policies/employment-matters/strategies/employee-engagement)

Martin, C.A. (2005) 'From high maintenance to high productivity: what managers need to know about Generation Y'. *Industrial and Commercial Training*, 37(1), pp. 39–44.

Maslow, A.H. (1998) *Toward a Psychology of Being.* New York: John Wiley.

Mullins, L.J. (2010) *Management and Organizational Behaviour* (9th edn). Harlow: FT Prentice Hall.

Rankin, N. (2008) 'The drivers of staff retention and employee engagement'. (Available at www.xpertHR.co.uk/article/86942/.aspx#top)

Sunday Times Best Companies to Work For (2011) (Available at www.thetimes100. co.uk)

The Times 100 Business Case Studies (2010) (Available at www.thetimes100.co.uk)

Tulgan, B. (2005) *Recruiting the Workforce of the Future.* Mumbai: Jaico Publishing House.

Tulgan, B. and Marting, C. (2001) 'Managing Generation Y – Part 3'. *Bloomberg Businessweek,* 12th October. (Available at www.businessweek.com/smallbiz/content/oct2001/sb20011012_001.htm)

Vroom, V.H. (1964) *Work and Motivation.* New York: Wiley.

Groups and teams $\quad$ 5

Groups are seen as having a **motivating***, inspiring influence on the individual, drawing out the best in him or her, enabling him or her to perform feats that would be beyond him or herself as a detached individual.* **Groups** *can have a healing effect on individuals,* **bolstering** *their self-esteem and filling their lives with meaning.*

If groups are capable of great **deeds***, they are also capable of great follies.*

(MARION HAMPTON, cited in BUCHANAN and HUCZYNSKI 2010: 298 and 357)

CHAPTER OBJECTIVES

By the end of this chapter you will understand:

- how to define a team and identify the key characteristics

- why teams are growing in importance

- different types of teams and the challenges faced by a virtual team

- the five stages of team development, as suggested by Tuckman

- the nine team roles proposed by Belbin and their contribution to team effectiveness

- the processes that contribute to an effective team and some of the barriers that can lead to team problems

- the key team-working skills and competencies that employers look for.

5.1 Introduction

Most of us have experienced working within a team, either at school, college, university or work. There has been a considerable amount of research into team-working and this has revealed some fascinating results, which we have tried to capture in this chapter.

 ## 5.2 Definitions of a team

The CIPD (2011) defines a team as a 'limited number of people who have shared objectives at work and who co-operate, on a permanent or temporary basis, to achieve those objectives in a way that allows each individual to make a distinctive contribution'. From this definition we can see that key aspects of team-working are:

- **shared objectives**, which assumes that everyone has had a say in and a chance to create agreed goals
- **cooperation**, which is necessary for effective team-working
- **making a distinctive contribution** – utilizing the diverse set of skills and experience of team members
- **a limited number of people** – the ideal number of people to make up an effective team has been the focus of much research.

Clegg, Kornberger and Pitsis (2005) also introduced the concept of **collective responsibility**, and suggest that a team differs from a group in that individuals are more 'psychologically' aware of each other and become interdependent. This is an important point, as the key aspect of being a member of a team is the emotional link and commitment to common goals. So while a group of people waiting in a queue to see the latest rock band all have a common purpose, they would be classified as a group of individuals and not a team. In contrast, a football team has a fixed number of players, everyone has a role and a contribution to make, and co-operation is critical to achieving the shared objective.

Other authors introduce additional perspectives of a 'team'. Kozlowski and Bell (2003), for example, refer to the **organizational context** in which the team operates, which will influence, constrain and impact on the way the team-members work together. Factors such as location, resources and technology will all play a part in how the team operates.

Team: a group of people who work together and have shared goals, cooperating and working towards achieving their goals.

KEY TERM

 ## 5.3 Why are teams important?

In Chapter 10 you will find a discussion of the context in which organizations operate today. In a global environment where organizations are reducing staff levels and controlling costs, the use of teams appears to be a desirable way of connecting and engaging people psychologically and emotionally with the workplace.

The *Workplace Employment Relations Survey* of 2004 (Kersley *et al.* 2006) found that 65 per cent of organizations in the UK used team-working, and one of the top competencies required of new recruits by organizations today is 'teamwork'. GlaxoSmithKline, for example, as part of its recruitment and selection process, requires teamwork competency, which it explains as follows: 'involves others and is able to build co-operative teams in which group members feel valued and empowered and have shared values' (**www.gsk.co.uk**).

Veolia Water, for example, suggests that it places great emphasis on teamwork: 'We pool our knowledge and experience, ensuring that every success is a shared success' (**www. veoliawater.co.uk/about-us/our-values**). If the company is able to recruit people who are willing to share expertise among team members, then working in teams makes strong business sense.

Toyota Manufacturing UK visualizes team behaviour as similar to 'rowing a boat. Each person has their own role, and they become skilled at operating within it, but if any member of the team is missing, or cannot cope, it upsets the balance of the boat, and its ability to achieve maximum success' (**www.toyotauk.com**). Toyota suggests that the essential components of teamwork are shared goals, shared commitment, creativity and resourcefulness, along with the freedom to share views and speak openly, while at the same time exchanging knowledge and learning from others.

The *Sunday Times* Best Companies to Work For (2010) highlights Addleshaw Goddard, a law firm that uses team-working and sees team contribution as key to the success of the business:

- 80 per cent of staff are proud to work for the firm.
- 74 per cent believe in the firm's values.
- 78 per cent of staff would not leave tomorrow if offered another post. More than half of the workforce has been with the firm for five or more years.
- 78 per cent say members of their team go out of their way to help each other.
- 81 per cent say their team is fun to work with.
- 83 per cent are confident in the abilities of their colleagues – a score bettered by only 14 other companies in the national survey.

So it is clear that companies see lots of benefits in setting up structures based around teams. The CIPD (2011) identifies organizational benefits as being an increase in productivity and quality; enhanced customer focus with the knowledge sharing that is achieved; and an improved ability to respond flexibly to change. Some of the benefits highlighted for employees are improved job satisfaction, motivation and learning.

CASE STUDY Generation Y and team-working

The authors surveyed a sample of Generation Y employees (those identified as being born between 1979 and 1991) to find out what their experiences were of working in a team. All those interviewed worked part-time in a variety of organizations.

Positive experiences included:

- shared responsibility and workload
- the opportunity to work with different views and ideas, and to learn from each other
- improved confidence in the individual when supported by other team members

- a feeling of closeness is created, rather like a family
- tasks take less time, the job gets done more quickly, 'two heads are better than one'
- stress is reduced with the knowledge that there are co-workers who can help – less pressure on individuals
- transferable skills, such as social skills, are gained by working with a diverse range of people.

Challenges highlighted:

- Communication problems – it is harder to be heard and difficult to get everyone on the same page.
- If pay is based on individual bonuses it can increase competition.
- Effort is not always equal among team members, but everyone gets the same pay.

- Goals are not the same – there are multiple goals within the team, and some people want to be the boss.
- Arguments about how things should be done can make things take longer.
- Individuals are unable to work using their own initiative – they have to consult all the time.
- There is no individual recognition of work completed.
- It can be difficult to trust other employees.

Listen to the interview on YouTube conducted in 2008 with Thomas Mallone from the Massachusetts Institute of Technology, who presents the notion of 'collective intelligence' – that is, teams have the benefit of many minds (**www.youtube.com/ watch?v=ITQ7XYG8Tk4**).

Q **Think about the teams that you have been part of and reflect on the benefits and drawbacks that you have experienced and whether they match the lists in the case study. What would you add or take away from the list, and why?**

 ## 5.4 Types of teams

There are many different types of teams – for example, project teams, sales teams, departmental teams, production teams and cross-functional teams. Self-managed teams are used frequently in organizations; these allow the team a degree of autonomy and have devolved decision-making. In a restructuring exercise, DARA introduced 'self-directed teams', defining them as 'an empowered group of individuals working to a common goal using the resources made available to the group to achieve agreed outputs' (IDS HR Studies 2003). Research sponsored by the CIPD in 2011 found that working in self-managed teams has very positive benefits for the organization, including higher productivity, reduced labour turnover, reduced dismissals and more engaged employees.

Virtual teams, which involve people working in a team remotely, connected by technology, are growing in importance. Team members may be based in the same country or in different locations worldwide. Horn (2009) defines a virtual team as one 'where members are separated by distance and … meet virtually facilitated by technology'.

CASE STUDY   Virtual teams

At Cisco, virtual teams are a key feature in the organization, as they utilize cross-departmental global team-working to achieve results. Employees spend 50 per cent of their time working from home, and over 40 per cent are located in a different city to their manager. One of the key challenges was to make the virtual teams effective and encourage collaboration, without losing the 'personal touch'. How did they do this?

Video conferencing is a daily activity for most Cisco employees. Many offices are equipped with lifesize screens, to allow collaborative meetings to take place. 'Now we'll get together instantly and virtually, share the problem and come to a collective decision.' The company enhances communications through the use of instant-messaging facilities, blogs and 'top of the mind' videos, to constantly connect team members through technology (Smedley 2011).

Q   **Imagine that you are a member of a virtual team comprising seven people working in different parts of the world. What might be the challenges for team-working and how could these be overcome?**

KEY TERM

Virtual team: where team members are based in different locations, perhaps around the world, but are connected through technology.

5.5 Stages of team development

A popular model to describe how a group of people assigned to work together form and develop into a team was put forward by Tuckman (1965, cited in Arnold and Randall *et al.* 2010). This research provides an insight into the stages that teams typically progress through as they evolve. Implicit within Tuckman's work is the acknowledgement that shared objectives and a common purpose are critical to team success. Consideration is also given to the infighting and vying for position that occur as teams come together. Given constant change within the workplace, teams are fluid and often change in terms of their composition and remit; in response to this, Tuckman added the final stage of 'adjourning or moving on' (see Table 5.1).

TABLE 5.1 Tuckman's model in summary

Forming	This is when group members first come together and almost test each other, to establish experience, skills, personality and so on. The group members are often polite, formal and careful about what they say. People may be guarded.
Storming	This stage can involve a lot of infighting, as people establish roles, vie for positions and confront each other's strengths and weaknesses; it can result in some members being sidelined.

Norming	This is the 'doing' stage. Work is started and the team is getting organized and establishing how it will work; the focus is on the task. Issues are confronted using the established communication channels.
Performing	The group now becomes a team, with a full 'identity', and provides each member with support and a sense of cohesion and closeness. It is a mature phase, with everyone working effectively towards the goals.
Moving on – this has been described as 'mourning' (CIPD 2011) or 'disbanding' (Arnold and Randall et al. 2010)	This is when the task is complete and the team moves on. With a very cohesive team, a sense of sadness and concern for the future can be felt. Some will reflect on the experience and learn from it.

This research indicates that teams progress through clear stages, as team members get to know each other and establish ways of working and clarify objectives. These stages can occur at the outset of team-working, when all members are new, but also as new members join the team and strengths and weaknesses are established. As the team settles down again to working, it will become clear what role each member plays, often related to an individual's strengths, but also related to the balance of roles played by team members and any gaps that need to be filled.

Reflective questions

Think of two teams that you have been part of, one successful and one that was less effective. Reflect on Tuckman's stages of team development in relation to both teams.

1 | Can you think of examples based on your experience within the two teams to illustrate each stage?
2 | Was the ease of progression through each stage a factor that contributed to team success or not?
3 | What conclusions can you draw about Tuckman's research?

 ## 5.6 Does team size matter?

The stages of team development, while important, are not the only contributing factor for effective team-working. There has been much research and debate into roles that people play within teams and the ideal number of individuals to make up a 'perfect' team.

Research by the authors was conducted into team-working within one of the *Sunday Times* top 100 companies to work for. The company scores highly on team-working and is structured on the basis of ten sales teams, with six employees in each, who each spend their time on the phone or connecting with their own set of clients, to market, sell and provide advice on a range of technology-based products. The teams all have a team leader, whose responsibility it is to communicate to the team any product changes, agree targets, monitor progress and support each team member to be successful. As the business expands, the teams have increased in size, but there remains a very close, cohesive feel to the organization, as team members have a 'voice' in decision-making and there is an element of competition between teams. One team member said, 'the team is like a family in a way, as although the company is growing rapidly it still feels personal and you still feel connected to people as you are in a team. Somehow it makes you feel valued.'

This company has so far operated with small teams of six, and it is interesting to note that research into the optimum size of team suggests between six and nine team members. In addition, the experience of the team member clearly indicates the psychological connection that she felt in working for the organization.

In the case study above, the organization had made a clear decision to structure employees on the basis of sales teams. Although team members had individual targets, they were clearly connected to a team with a team leader, chose their own team name and were also set some team targets, to encourage a degree of competition between teams. Other organizations may utilize team terminology in a much looser way, with employees assigned to a large production team or departmental team, with the emphasis placed more firmly on individual contribution.

5.7 Team roles

The most well-established investigation carried out into team roles is the work by Belbin (1993) and his team of researchers at Cambridge University. They investigated team roles over a period of time and identified some common roles that appeared crucial to effective team-working. In each team, individuals tend to adopt a preferred role or set of roles. The research is based on individuals completing a self-perception inventory, the results of which highlight the dominant team role and the secondary team roles that the individual will typically play. The research is ongoing, and while initially eight roles were identified, this was later extended to nine. In Table 5.2, Belbin's nine team roles are described, along with a brief interpretation of each one. To find out what your preferred team role is, you can visit **www.belbin.com**

TABLE 5.2 Belbin's team roles

Role	What this means in practice	The downside
Plant	Creative, imaginative, unorthodox. Solves difficult problems.	Ignores details. Too preoccupied to communicate effectively.
In summary: the Plant has lots of ideas and will think outside the box and be good at problem-solving, but may not get involved in the team dynamics, or pay attention to the detail.		

Role	What this means in practice	The downside
Resource Investigator	Extrovert, enthusiastic, communicative. Explores opportunities. Develops contacts.	Over-optimistic. Loses interest once initial enthusiasm has passed.

In summary: the Resource Investigator likes to make contacts outside the team to gather data and information and will build links for the team. Their enthusiasm may not last and they may promise to deliver what is not possible.

Role	What this means in practice	The downside
Coordinator	Mature, confident, a good chairperson. Clarifies goals, promotes decision-making. Delegates well.	Can be seen as manipulative. Offloads personal work.

In summary: the Coordinator is like a chairperson, pulling the team together to keep focused on the task in hand, getting the best out of people and ensuring that everyone knows what is required. By delegating, they can be seen by others as not getting involved in the work themselves.

Role	What this means in practice	The downside
Shaper	Challenging, dynamic, thrives on pressure. Has the drive and courage to overcome obstacles.	Can provoke others. Hurts people's feelings.

In summary: a Shaper has strong opinions and expresses these to get things moving. Others can find this irritating and some may be upset by their 'pushiness'.

Role	What this means in practice	The downside
Monitor-Evaluator	Sober, strategic and discerning. Sees all options. Judges accurately.	Lacks drive and ability to inspire others.

In summary: a Monitor-Evaluator likes to check things for accuracy. They are ordered and logical in their approach, and have an analytical style rather than motivating and driving the team forward.

Role	What this means in practice	The downside
Team Worker	Cooperative, mild, perceptive and diplomatic. Listens, builds, avoids friction.	Indecisive in crunch situations.

In summary: a Team Worker is a solid team player who likes to involve everyone and create cohesion. May spend too long working on team bonding, which can result in slow decision-making.

Role	What this means in practice	The downside
Implementer	Disciplined, reliable, conservative and efficient. Turns ideas into practical actions.	Somewhat inflexible. Slow to respond to new possibilities.

In summary: an Implementer gets things done by translating ideas into specific actions. Once started, they are keen to see things through, so may resist any changes to the agreed actions.

Role	What this means in practice	The downside
Completer	Painstaking, conscientious, anxious. Searches out errors and omissions. Delivers on time.	Inclined to worry unduly. Reluctant to delegate.

In summary: a Completer gets detail right and pays attention to ensure that the task is completed accurately and on time. Likes to control, so may not trust people to get things done.

Role	What this means in practice	The downside
Specialist	Single-minded, self-sharing, dedicated. Provides knowledge and skills in rare supply.	Contributes only on a narrow front. Dwells on technicalities.

In summary: a Specialist provides a source of expertise. Their knowledge and skills may be too specialist and they may not be able to see the bigger picture.

It is acknowledged by Belbin Associates that the ideal team has a balance of roles within it and, typically, individuals may play more than one role, depending on the make-up of the team and the task in hand. Belbin makes the point that 'no one's perfect, but a team can be' (Belbin 1993, cited in Mullins 2010: 343).

TABLE 5.3 Some questions for debate

Is it likely that men and women may interpret and answer the questions about their role in a team in a different way?	You may be interested to learn, for example, that Anderson and Sleap (2004) have suggested that women may score more highly on the role of Team Worker.
What are the pros and cons of completing a questionnaire based on your self-perception of how you behave in a team?	In fact, Belbin has developed an Observer Assessment Sheet to provide a more rounded assessment of the individual (Arnold and Randall et al. 2010).
Can you fit people into neat boxes or does their behaviour change according to the team dynamics and over time?	See Chapter 3 on the individual: personality, perception and attitudes. Some psychologists suggest that our personality develops over time and behaviour may therefore change as we gain different experiences. Others argue that personality is relatively fixed and stable, so categorizing people into boxes can be appropriate.
What impact might a gender mix within a team have on team dynamics?	Some recent research into teams by the Massachusetts Institute of Technology (2010) has found that teams with higher levels of 'social sensitivity' and those with a higher number of women tend to cooperate more effectively. Social sensitivity is described as 'the willingness of the group to let all its members take turns and apply their skills to a given challenge'. This research has implications for the current research being conducted by Cranfield University (Vinnicombe et al. 2010) into female representation on boards of directors. Evidence such as the work by MIT indicates that having more women as part of the 'top team' could improve its effectiveness.

KEY TERM

Team role: an individual's preference for a particular style of behaviour or way of contributing in a team situation. The role is usually based on the individual's past experience of team-working.

5.8 Effective team-working

What is it that makes an effective team, and what are the skills needed by an individual in order to become a great team player? These are questions that have formed the basis of much research over the years, and have resulted in useful insights into how to improve team-working, to the extent that the word 'team' has been defined as 'together everyone achieves more' – a little clichéd perhaps, but the evidence suggests that it might be true.

Successful team-working requires attention to the following issues:

- clear and shared goals
- open communication between team members
- agreed ways of working
- cooperation and support rather than point-scoring
- effective listening
- arrangements in place for monitoring progress and correcting things if need be
- awareness and achievement of deadlines
- enthusiasm and motivation
- reviewing outcomes and changing actions where necessary for future team efforts.

(Adapted from the University of Hertfordshire Academic Skills Unit guidance on team-working.)

Armstrong (2009) highlights these processes in a model that demonstrates how these feed into each other as a continuous cycle (see Figure 5.1).

FIGURE 5.1 Successful team-working (adapted from Armstrong 2009)

It is also interesting to consider some of the behaviours that interfere with effective team-working, such as:

- not preparing for the meeting or carrying out the task that you have agreed to complete
- talking too much in team meetings and focusing attention on yourself
- reacting emotionally when improvements are suggested
- not listening to what other team members are trying to say
- introducing a completely different point when the team is discussing something
- withdrawing from the group and making no attempt to join in
- being late for meetings and leaving early
- lack of personal clarity of the team brief, because you have not explored it fully and ensured complete understanding (adapted from Cameron 2009).

In an interview with Coutu (2009), J. Richard Hackman, Edgar Pierce Professor of Social and Organizational Psychology at Harvard University, and a leading expert on teams, talked about why teams do not work. Some of his research findings suggest that teams can underperform, so the benefit of collaborative working is not always achieved. This can be due to many factors, including the lack of agreement on team goals and problems with coordination and motivation, compounded as the team grows in size and boundaries may become unclear. Furthermore, Hackman sees competition between teams as a barrier to effectiveness, and highlights that teams can become too comfortable and familiar, and therefore fail to confront weaknesses. He suggests that a team should be made up of no more than six people, arguing that if a team is any bigger than this, it is harder to get the links to work in unison.

ACTIVITY

Imagine that you are a member of a small project team that is not working well together.

1 | One team member constantly takes over the running of team meetings, and does not allow others to have their say. What could you do to help to overcome this problem?

2 | Another team member often misses meetings or rushes in at the last minute unprepared. What action can the team take to fully engage this team member?

Do you have what it takes to be an effective team member?

Many organizations today are keen to recruit people who can provide evidence that they are as capable of working on their own as being able to make a strong contribution within a team.

For example, GlaxoSmithKline looks for 'team players', who can 'involve others' and who are able ' to build co-operative teams in which group members feel valued and empowered and have shared values' (**www.gsk.co.uk**).

This may not quite match up to your experience of working in a team, as you might have found that not everyone in the team pulled their weight, and that some members were not entirely sure what the team hoped to achieve, or they went off in different directions. The abilities of different team members often vary, and working on group projects at college, university or in the workplace can often result in frustration and fear that the final grade or outcome will be affected by lack of effort on the part of some members. You may also have found that to overcome some of the weaknesses of the team, you step in and take over someone else's work, just to make sure that the project is completed to the standard that you, as an individual, would expect. This can be frustrating and create resentment, so it is worth trying to face up to some of the possible problems at the early stages of team-working, to ensure that everyone is clear about what is expected and all members have the chance to contribute to the task, using their unique set of skills.

On the other hand, you may have had very positive experiences of working in teams. When all team members have a shared sense of what they want to achieve and are prepared to support each other, the results can be a highly satisfying experience that can stay in your memory for years to come.

Team-working can sound quite daunting if you add into the mix the issues of diversity, personality, skills, different cultures, gender, age, experience and so on, but often it is the very existence of such a mix of individuals that creates for an effective, innovative end result. Half the battle is to be aware of your own position and the contribution that you have made to teams and how you can develop yourself further. It is clear that teams feature strongly in the workplace, and being able to work in and contribute effectively to a team are qualities that are valued by employers of new recruits. Team-working is a key behavioural competence, as we will explore in the next section.

5.9 Team competencies

To help you to consider your potential contribution to team-working, we have compiled some examples of questions that graduate recruiters typically ask of job applicants.

> **ACTIVITY**
>
> Working in a small group, share the roles of interviewer, interviewee and observer. Select some questions from the list below and ask each other for a response. One of the group members can observe and make notes to give feedback, allowing the group to reflect on the experience. As a group, produce what you think is a very good response to each question.

- Give an example of a successful team you were part of. What was your role? Why was the team successful?
- Have you been a member of a team that struggled or failed to accomplish its goal? If so, what were the reasons for the failure and how did you respond?
- Have you ever had to work in a team with someone you did not like, or who was not doing their fair share? If so, what did you do to overcome this?
- What do you think are the key ingredients of a successful team?
- Describe the best team that you have been part of, and explain why it was so good.
- Thinking about your experience of working in a team, what would you say is your typical team role, and why?
- Reflect on a team that you have been part of and identify how you could develop your contribution.

CASE STUDY   Assessment centres in action

Within the selection process, graduate recruiters often assess team-working skills not only through interviews, but also as part of an assessment centre. Take a look at the following experiences, which were recently reported by two new graduates – one from the University of Hertfordshire and one from the University of Warwick.

" *We did a section in the assessment centre called 'Hot Air Balloon', where we debated as a team which celebrity we would throw out to keep the balloon afloat. We all had to choose to be a celebrity and give reasons why we should stay in the balloon. I found this challenging, as it was hard to get my points across, and some of the other candidates formed a subgroup and started another debate between themselves. You soon learn what the assessors are looking for in* relation to team contribution – *it is important that you get your points across, that you listen and demonstrate co-operation, while keeping focused on the task in hand within the time frame.*

" *On my assessment centre we were all given a charity that our manager wanted to support and had to attend a meeting on his behalf to put forward his views. The team had to come up with one charity to support. It seemed a fair way to allocate the roles, as everyone had some points of view to contribute. It was less about the content and all about how you influenced and persuaded others to listen. What was interesting to me was that some candidates were from Spain and Russia, and their view of charitable donations differed, so listening and understanding alternative viewpoints was critical.*

Q   To see an assessment centre in action, visit the PricewaterhouseCoopers YouTube clip at www.youtube.com/watch?v=v5SvzsFs-60&feature=related

KEY TERM

Team competence: an ability, skill or expertise related to working within a team. Many organizations today seek evidence of competence in team-working from applicants applying for a job.

 5.10 Summary

Team-working is a key facet of organizational life. There is much debate and research into what makes an effective team, and graduates are increasingly expected to provide evidence of their contribution and skills in team-working in order to succeed. The key debates concern team processes and the ideal size of a team, and the latest research suggests that team diversity and the gender mix are also important aspects to take into account. In order to get the best out of a team, there are a number of team-based skills and competencies that organizations can consider when putting a team together. The roles that people play within a team have been investigated, and there is research evidence that having a balanced set of roles helps team effectiveness.

Key ideas

- A team has a shared purpose, a common goal and works in collaboration to achieve the goal.
- Teams are a key feature of organizational life, with many positive benefits, but also challenges that need to be considered.

- There are many different types of teams, and technology now allows teams to work together on a virtual basis.
- Teams appear to progress through a series of stages as they develop.
- The size of the team can impact on its effectiveness.
- Research suggests that we have a preferred team role and that it is useful to ensure that every team has a balance of different roles within it.
- To be effective as a team, there are a number of considerations and behaviours that need to be present.
- Organizations are increasingly building into their recruitment and selection process the identification of team competencies.

Review questions

1. Explain why teams are used by organizations.
2. Why might team-working go wrong?
3. Teams are said to progress through a series of stages as they develop. Identify the stages and suggest why this categorization might be helpful.
4. Reflect on your own contribution in a team that you have been part of, and the role that you played. How does this fit with Belbin's research into team roles?
5. Identify the skills needed for effective team-working.
6. Now that organizations are carefully defining team-working competencies, how might this help them to select the best person for the job and to fit the team?

Recommended reading

CIPD (2011) 'Team working'. Factsheet. London: Chartered Institute of Personnel and Development. (Available at www.cipd.co.uk)
Coutu, D. (2009) 'Why teams don't work'. *Harvard Business Review*, 87(5), May, pp. 99–105.

Useful websites

www.belbin.com – the official website for Meredith Belbin's research work into teams, allowing you to experience some of the questions Belbin included in his team roles questionnaire

www.youtube.com/watch?v=ITQ7XYG8Tk4 – a short video clip offering an interesting insight into the development of collective intelligence within teams

www.youtube.com/watch?v=v5SvzsFs-60&feature=related – a short video clip of how a major employer seeks to identify team-working skills as part of the selection process

References

Anderson, N. and Sleap, S. (2004) 'An evaluation of gender differences on the Belbin team role self-perception inventory'. *Journal of Organizational and Occupational Psychology*, 77, pp. 429–37.

Armstrong, M. (2009) *Handbook of Human Resource Management Practice* (11th edn). London: Kogan Page.

Arnold, J. and Randall, R. *et al.* (2010) *Work Psychology: Understanding Human Behaviour in the Workplace* (5th edn). Harlow: Pearson Education.

Belbin, R.M. (1993) *Team Roles at Work* (2nd edn). Oxford: Butterworth-Heinemann.

Belbin, R.M. (2004) *Management Teams: Why They Succeed or Fail* (3rd edn). Oxford: Butterworth-Heinemann.

Buchanan, D.A. and Huczynski, A.A. (2010) *Organizational Behaviour* (7th edn). Harlow: Pearson Education.

Cameron, S. (2009) *The Business Student's Handbook* (5th edn). Basingstoke: FT Prentice Hall.

CIPD (2011) 'Team working'. Factsheet. London: Chartered Institute of Personnel and Development. (Available at www.cipd.co.uk)

Clegg, S., Kornberger, M. and Pitsis, T. (2005) *Managing and Organizations*. London: Sage.

Coutu, D. (2009) 'Why teams don't work'. *Harvard Business Review*, 87(5), May, pp. 99–105.

Horn, R. (2009) *The Business Skills Handbook*. London: Chartered Institute of Personnel and Development.

IDS HR Studies (2003) 'Teamworking'. Issue 763, December.

Kersley, B., Alpin, C., Forth, J., Bryson, A., Bewley, H., Dix, G. and Oxenbridge, S. (2006) *Inside the Workplace: Findings from the 2004 Workplace Employment Relations Survey*. London: Routledge. (Copies of the questionnaires used in 2004 are available at www.bis.gov.uk/policies/employment-matters/research/wers/wers2004)

Kozlowski, S.W.J. and Bell, B.S. (2003) 'Work groups and teams in organizations'. Cited in Borman, W.C., Ilgen, D.R. and Klimoski, R. (eds.) *Industrial/Organizational Psychology*, vol. XII. Chichester: John Wiley and Sons.

Mallone, T. (2008) 'Collective intelligence'. YouTube interview video clip with Thomas Mallone from MIT. (Available at www.youtube.com/watch?v=ITQ7XYG8Tk4)

Massachusetts Institute of Technology (2010) 'Are women better team players?' *People Management*, 11th October. (Available at www.peoplemanagement.co.uk)

Mullins, L.J. (2010) *Management and Organizational Behaviour* (9th edn). Harlow: Pearson Education.

Penna and CIPD (2008) 'GEN UP: how the four generations work'. Joint Survey Report. September. (Available at www.cipd.co.uk)

Smedley, T. (2011) 'Interview with Charlie Johnston: leadership and virtual communications'. *People Management*, April, p. 32.

Sunday Times Best Companies to Work For (2010) (Available at www.thetimes100.co.uk)

Vinnicombe, S., Sealy, R., Graham, J. and Doldor, E. (2010) *The Female FTSE Board Report 2010: Opening up the Appointment Process*. Cranfield University, School of Management: International Centre for Women Leaders.

6 Leadership

*The new **leader** is one who commits people to **action**, who converts followers into leaders, and who may convert leaders into **agents of change**.* (WARREN BENNIS)

CHAPTER OBJECTIVES

By the end of this chapter you will understand:

- what is meant by 'leadership'

- leadership in history

- the main theories of leadership and their application

- recent approaches to leadership and their application

- critical perspectives on leadership

- gender and leadership.

6.1 Introduction

What do you think of when you hear the term 'leadership'? For many of us, what will come to mind are certain individuals who are seen as great leaders and thus have come to epitomize the term – Churchill, Napoleon or Gandhi, for example. And these examples may occur in a variety of fields: politics, war, sport, business. Some will be seen in a positive light, others more negatively. Some may be viewed as having changed the course of world history, others to have had a more localized effect.

Leadership is seen as being crucial to organizational success, and in the challenging environment faced by today's organizations this is even more likely to be the case. Leaders who have spearheaded the growth of a successful business, such as Richard Branson with Virgin or Steve Jobs, the co-founder of Apple, are feted and praised, while those who are seen to have made errors of judgement are widely and publically criticized for their actions.

CASE STUDY A profile of Richard Branson

Sir Richard Branson started his business life as a hippy entrepreneur. He went into business at the age of 16, publishing the *Student* magazine. He initially started Virgin as a mail-order music business, before opening his first record store on Oxford Street. Virgin Atlantic Airways came next, and Branson's organization has also expanded into mobile phones, finance, retail, hotel and leisure, and rail travel. One of his latest ideas is to take tourists into space. In the mid-1980s the Branson company was floated on the Stock Exchange, but he later bought the company back from the shareholders, selling Virgin Records to Thorn-EMI in order to do so.

Branson is known as an ambitious showman, with a talent for self-publicity and a maverick streak. On more than one occasion he has had to be rescued following record-breaking attempts. He has been characterized as a 'transformational leader', one who stresses informality and ideas. In his autobiography he writes:

> *My interest in life comes from setting myself huge, apparently unachievable challenges and trying to rise above them ... from the perspective of wanting to live life to the full, I felt that I had to attempt it.*

What we mean by leadership and what makes for effective leadership is a topic over which there has been, and continues to be, much discussion. Crainer (1995) points out that there are over 400 different definitions of leadership and thus little agreement as to the meaning of the term. Ball (2007), however, suggests that an analysis of these definitions shows that three common elements can be discerned:

- goal-setting and achievement
- group activities
- influence on the behaviour of others.

Anita Roddick was the founder of The Body Shop, a company producing and selling cosmetics and beauty products. The company became known for its ethical stance – on prohibiting animal testing and promoting fair trade, for example. Roddick had a strong personal sense of social responsibility and environmental activism. By 2004 The Body Shop had nearly 2,000 stores, serving 77 million customers all over the world. In 2006 L'Oréal bought the company for £652 million. Although criticized for 'selling out', Roddick believed that by selling her business to such a large firm as L'Oréal she could influence its decisions. Roddick died in 2007.

Although it is difficult to generalize about leadership, Mullins' (2010) definition (see Key term: leadership) is useful.

KEY TERM

Leadership: 'a relationship through which one person influences the behaviour or actions of other people' (Mullins 2010: 373).

Mullins also suggests that the changing nature of work and work organizations has led to a move away from command-and-control leadership towards an increased emphasis on coaching, support and empowerment, with teamwork also highlighted.

6.2 Leadership and management

Another area for debate is the relationship between *leadership* and *management*, and the differences between the two. Leadership is normally seen more in terms of providing vision, inspiration and strategy, with management seen to be more about getting things done on a day-to-day basis and ensuring consistency. Bennis and Nanus (1985: 21) have summed this up with the saying that 'managers do things right, whilst leaders do the right thing'. In practice, it is often found that the two overlap. Arguably, one important aspect of the debate is the reminder that leadership is not necessarily dependent on job title or position in the hierarchy; it can be demonstrated by individuals throughout an organization, in different ways and at different levels.

This leads us to another potentially useful distinction: that between *leaders* and *leadership*. As we will see, the main focus historically has been on the former – that is, great leaders. In organization and management writings and in practice, however, there is now a shift to looking more closely at leader*ship* – that is, something that may be displayed in different situations at a variety of levels in an organization. Thus the chief executive of a large corporation may symbolically be 'the leader' of that organization and may be viewed as such by the outside world, yet 'leadership' will need to be shown by other managers at senior, middle and junior levels, as well as by employees in general – for example, in influencing others in a team-based situation.

ACTIVITY

Some commentators argue that leadership is one aspect of good management, but that leadership is not necessarily displayed by managers only.

1 | Give examples of leadership at work that may be shown by others – that is, not necessarily managers.

2 | In your experience of class activities at your university or college, describe examples where you have shown leadership yourself.

6.3 Leadership in history: implications for business

Historically, leadership was probably most frequently associated with the battlefield. From Spartacus in Ancient Greece, through Flavius Aetius the Roman general, and Boudicca (or Boadicea), who led an uprising against the Roman Empire, to Joan of Arc and Robert the Bruce, these early leaders were able to inspire others through their charisma and fighting prowess on the field of battle. Later military leaders, such as Field Marshal Montgomery, the US General Patton or the German Field Marshal Rommel in the Second World War, combined inspiration with strategic planning, coordination and tactical decision-making.

Consideration of leadership in the context of business organizations came after the initial military examples, although to begin with the portrayal of business leaders tended to mirror that of the military, directing and inspiring their employees to greater effort. However, although military leadership undoubtedly had a large element of command and control to it, it can still be seen to provide useful lessons for corporate leadership at times. Consider the following quote from Field Marshall William Slim (1891–1970) in his book *Defeat into Victory* (cited in Crainer and Dearlove 2001: 537):

Morale is a state of mind. It is that intangible force which will move a whole group of men to give their last ounce to achieve something, without counting the cost to themselves; that makes them feel they are part of something greater than themselves. If they are to feel that, their morale must, if it is to endure – and the essence of morale is that it should endure – have certain foundations. These foundations are spiritual, intellectual, and material, and that is the order of their importance. Spiritual first, because only spiritual foundations can stand real strain. Next intellectual, because men are swayed by reason as well as feeling. Material last – important, but last – because the highest kinds of morale are often met when material conditions are lowest.

Reflective question

What do you think are the implications of William Slim's ideas on military leadership for business leaders?

While the early examples of military leadership stressed the qualities of the individual leader (bravery, courage, strength, resolution), later approaches suggested that leadership was something that could be developed through experience. Thus Slim argued that the leadership lessons he had learned in the army could be applied to business, while the leadership writer John Adair, who also spent time in the army, based his approach to leadership on the notion that it could be learned, like any other skill. Adair identified a list of key leadership functions: planning, initiating, controlling, supporting, informing and evaluating.

 ## 6.4 Trait theories of leadership

As was suggested in Section 6.3, historically the earliest perspectives on leadership viewed it in terms of the personality traits of great leaders – that is, their personal qualities. This could be in the military, such as Napoleon, in politics, as with Churchill, or in sport. This view can also be applied to business leaders – Richard Branson, for example, has been described as innovative, charismatic, energetic and risk-taking. It has been suggested that these are some of the characteristics of a good leader. From the point of view of the trait approach, leaders are 'born not made', and therefore it would not be possible to train people in leadership.

> **Trait theories of leadership:** approaches based on the belief that leaders have certain personality traits and attributes that can be identified.

KEY TERM

There are limitations with this approach, however. First, it proved impossible to arrive at a generally agreed list of required characteristics that a leader should have; different people came up with different lists. Second, the characteristics tended to be rather generalized. For example, Ralph Stogdill (1974), in reviewing trait studies, came up with a list that included the following:

- strong drive for responsibility
- focus on completing a task
- vigour and persistence in pursuit of goals
- originality in problem-solving
- self-confidence
- willingness to accept consequences of decisions or actions
- ability to influence the behaviour of others.

While such qualities would undoubtedly be useful in a leader, they would also be important in many other situations, not just leadership ones. Many of the traits are also rather vague. A final shortcoming of the trait approach is that it takes no account of the specific situation, yet in reality what works well in one situation may not work in another.

To summarize, the attempts to produce definitive lists of leadership traits have not been successful. This is not to say, however, that there is no link between personality and leadership. Recent research on the 'big five' personality framework (see Chapter 3) has suggested that some general traits, such as extroversion, conscientiousness and openness to experience, are related generally to leadership. Similarly, recent interest in emotional intelligence has suggested that it may predict effective leadership (Robbins, Judge and Campbell 2010). But such characteristics are very general; it may well be that an extrovert is more likely to be a leader than an introvert, but this is a matter of degree, and the form that the extroversion takes in practice may also vary. Not only that, but later approaches to leadership have shown that while personality traits may play a part in leadership, it is only one part.

6.5 Style approaches

The limitations of the trait approach led to interest in leadership styles or behaviours. Two important studies in this area were the Ohio State Leadership Studies and the University of Michigan Studies (Robbins, Judge and Campbell 2010). Both had similar findings in identifying two dimensions of leadership behaviour, one focusing on the getting the job done (task- or production-centred) and the other focusing on employee needs and relationships (person- or employee-centred).

KEY TERM

> **Style theories of leadership:** characterize leadership behaviour patterns in order to identify effective leadership styles.

Drawing on such findings, Blake and Mouton (1964) developed a leadership grid (see Figure 6.1). This has two axes: one depicting concern for people and the other concern for production. A manager displaying 9,1 style would be heavily focused on the task, with little concern for employees; a 1,9 manager would focus on concern for employees, but to the neglect of the task. Not surprisingly, it was suggested that a 9,9 style of management, termed 'team management', was best.

FIGURE 6.1 Leadership grid (adapted from Blake and Mouton 1964)

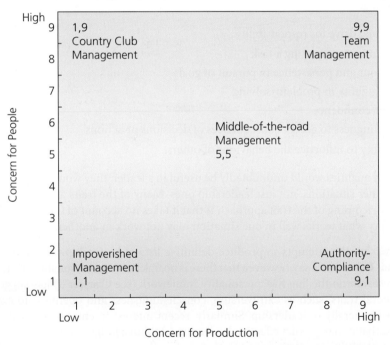

These results may appear both unsurprising and, from a modern viewpoint, rather obvious. Yet at the time the studies were undertaken they were important for at least two key reasons: first, they got managers to think beyond simplistic Taylorist scientific management notions (see Chapter 2), of focusing on the mechanics of getting a job done to the exclusion of concern for people; and second, they switched attention from selecting leaders purely on the basis of their personality traits, to identifying relevant leadership styles and training leaders in these.

These studies focused attention on the style of leadership towards employees and the focus of power of the leader. Three basic styles could be discerned:

- **The autocratic style**, in which the manager has the power and takes an authoritarian command-and-control approach, telling the employees what to do.
- **The democratic style**, where power is more shared among the team as a whole and the employees have a greater say in decision-making.
- **The laissez-faire style**, which is more a non-leadership approach, in that the manager leaves all decision-making and control to the group.

Not surprisingly, the democratic style was argued to be the best, in that it would be both effective in terms of getting things done, and also lead to high worker satisfaction; it therefore also tended to be the employees' preferred style.

Reflective question

Compare and contrast the trait and style approaches to leadership.

KEY THEMES The swinging sixties

We tend to see management and leadership writings and theories from a modern perspective, with the eyes of someone living in the second decade of the 21st century. Yet it is also important to try to put ideas into their historical context – that is, to understand the life and times that the authors were living in.

Thus, for example, F.W. Taylor (see Chapter 2) was writing his ideas on scientific management in the USA in the late 1890s and early 1900s. At that time, the factory system was a new phenomenon, and was recruiting workers whose only experience up to that point had been farmwork. There was also much emigration to the USA from other countries, including Europe, so recruits were coming from different cultures and speaking different languages.

It is not surprising, therefore, that Taylor developed a system of management that stressed close supervision of workers, as well as simplified and repetitive tasks, as the way to efficiency.

By the late 1950s and early 1960s, the context was very different. In what has become known as 'the swinging sixties', something of a social revolution was occurring, in which those in authority, whether political or organizational leaders, were increasingly questioned. The era stressed individual freedom and change. Again, therefore, it is not surprising that leadership and management writings of the time focused on participation and democratic approaches, in contrast to the more authoritarian command-and-control approaches that had gone before.

6.6 Contingency approaches

Approaches such as those of the Ohio and Michigan studies offered useful insights into leadership styles and behaviours, and allowed organizations to switch their focus from simply selecting leaders on their personality traits to the training and development of leadership. A major limitation of both trait and style approaches, however, was that they attempted to give 'one best way' solutions to the question of leadership. With the style approaches the suggestion was that leaders should show high concern for task and people, and democratic leadership styles were favoured. But any one leadership style is unlikely to suit all situations or circumstances. For a teacher facing a disruptive class, a sergeant major leading troops under fire or a manager faced with tight deadlines, the democratic approach is unlikely to be relevant. Such considerations led to situational or contingency approaches, in which it is suggested that the relevant approach to leadership will depend on the particular context.

Contingency theories of leadership: the most appropriate approach to leadership will depend on the particular situation.

In an extension to the style approaches, Tannenbaum and Schmidt (1958), in an article entitled 'Should a manager be democratic or autocratic – or something in between?', suggested a continuum from 'boss-centred leadership' at one end to 'subordinate-centred leadership' at the other (see Figure 6.2).

FIGURE 6.2 The Tannenbaum and Schmidt continuum of leadership behaviour (adapted from Tannenbaum and Schmidt 1958)

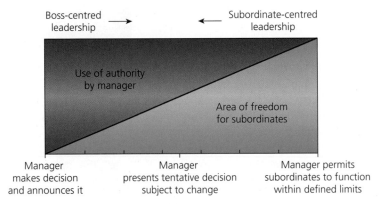

This gave managers a 'toolkit' of styles to choose from, depending on the situation they faced. How should managers choose the most relevant approach in any one particular situation? Tannenbaum and Schmidt argued that they need to consider three interrelated forces or influences:

- **characteristics of the manager** – personality, values, beliefs, confidence in subordinates
- **characteristics of subordinates** – need for independence, tolerance of ambiguity, level of knowledge
- **characteristics of the situation** – organizational customs and norms, size of group, nature of the problem.

A number of other studies concentrated on diagnosing the particular context in which a manager might operate; the contingency theory of Fiedler (1967) is one such example. As a starting point, Fiedler developed a measure of a leader's approach to managing people – that is, were they naturally more relationship-oriented and democratic, or task-oriented and autocratic? He did this by use of a questionnaire that asked leaders to think first of all of the most difficult person they had ever worked with, their 'least preferred co-worker' (LPC), and to rate that individual on a number of dimensions.

Your LPC score

Answer the following questions in order to determine your score.

1 | Think of someone whom you would find it the most difficult to work with (it could be someone you work with now or someone you have worked with in the past).

2 | Describe that person as he or she appears to you for each of the dimensions below, by placing a cross on the score that most closely matches them. Do this quickly, without thinking about it for too long. Mark every item, but only once.

3 | Once you have finished, compare your scores with those of your classmates.

Pleasant	8 7 6 5 4 3 2 1	Unpleasant
Friendly	8 7 6 5 4 3 2 1	Unfriendly
Rejecting	8 7 6 5 4 3 2 1	Accepting
Helpful	8 7 6 5 4 3 2 1	Unhelpful
Unenthusiastic	1 2 3 4 5 6 7 8	Enthusiastic
Tense	1 2 3 4 5 6 7 8	Relaxed
Distant	1 2 3 4 5 6 7 8	Close
Cold	1 2 3 4 5 6 7 8	Warm
Cooperative	8 7 6 5 4 3 2 1	Uncooperative
Supportive	8 7 6 5 4 3 2 1	Hostile
Boring	1 2 3 4 5 6 7 8	Interesting
Quarrelsome	1 2 3 4 5 6 7 8	Harmonious
Self-assured	8 7 6 5 4 3 2 1	Hesitant
Efficient	8 7 6 5 4 3 2 1	Inefficient
Gloomy	1 2 3 4 5 6 7 8	Cheerful
Open	8 7 6 5 4 3 2 1	Guarded

(Adapted from Mullins 2005: 322–3)

This gives you an insight into how LPC scores are measured. High scores (5–8) in the above questions equate with high LPC and low scores (1–4) with low LPC.

Leaders with high LPC scores tended to see their co-workers more positively and favoured more democratic styles of leadership than those with low LPC scores.

The LPC scores of leaders were just one consideration though. Fiedler argued that leadership effectiveness is influenced by three other factors:

1 | The degree of structure of the task.
2 | The leader's position power.
3 | The relationship between leader and followers.

This can be illustrated with an example:

● | The task is unstructured.
● | The leader's position power is low.
● | Relationships between subordinates and leader are moderately good.

It is argued that, in these conditions, leaders with high LPC scores (relationship-oriented) will get better results, because of the unstructured nature of the task combined with the need to maintain good relationships.

There are, however, a number of possible problems with Fiedler's approach:

1 | The idea of the 'least preferred co-worker' can be somewhat confusing and difficult to measure.
2 | It can also be difficult to assess the key variables of task structure, power and relationships.
3 | The needs of subordinates are not taken into account.
4 | The approach ignores the technical requirements of the leader.

However, Fiedler's theory has the advantage that it goes beyond the 'one best way' approaches and encourages leaders to think about the importance of contextual factors. Interestingly, Fiedler felt that most managers would have difficulty changing their preferred style and should therefore seek work and organizations that match their style. Other theories and approaches placed greater emphasis on leaders selecting an appropriate style. Hersey and Blanchard (1988), for example, put forward a model that has four basic leadership styles:

1 | **Telling:** focus on the task, telling subordinates what to do as well as how and when to do it.
2 | **Selling:** high amounts of both task and relationship behaviour.
3 | **Participating:** focus on relationship behaviour and support, less direction or task behaviour.
4 | **Delegating:** little in the way of task or relationship behaviour. Allows followers to take responsibility.

Hersey and Blanchard argued that the readiness of followers to perform a task was also a key factor. Thus a 'telling' style was more suitable for low follower readiness, a 'selling' style to a situation with low to moderate follower readiness, a 'participating' style for moderate to high follower readiness, and a 'delegating' style was seen as best where follower readiness was high. This view, in which insecure and reluctant subordinates need telling, while confident and able ones can be delegated to, is also supported by other theories.

CASE STUDY 'Herding cats'

A number of authors of books giving advice on the leadership of scientists and researchers have likened it to attempting to herd cats. Thus Cohen and Cohen (2005) point out that scientists are trained in scholarship and technical skills, but not often in how to relate to and deal with their peers, subordinates or supervisors. In relation to managing scientists, they suggest that 'the people you are managing are focused on technical and quantitative aspects of their jobs, at the expense of the interpersonal and social aspects'. This can potentially make managing such staff, and organizing work in teams, difficult.

In referring to academic and research institutions, Garrett and Davies (2010) suggest that they have one important characteristic in common when it comes to deciding how best they should be managed and led: both are staffed by people of high intellectual ability who like to think and act independently and be creative. There is usually no culture of uniformity or 'towing the line'. This can mean that such institutions need a somewhat different set of leadership skills than might be the case in other organizations.

Q   Taking a contingency approach to leadership, what advice would you give a prospective leader of researchers, scientists or academics as to what leadership style(s) to adopt?

In summary, the contingency theories of leadership provide food for thought for those in leadership positions. Most importantly, they suggest that different approaches to leadership will be needed, depending on the particular situation. Some of the more basic theories appear rather prescriptive, suggesting that in situation A, the manager should do B. This sort of 'contingent determinism' is likely to be too simplistic and does not allow for management choice. On the other hand, the challenge for more sophisticated contingency theories is which variables to focus on; in reality, any one particular situation is likely to be the product of a complex interaction of many variables, and thus it is difficult for managers to get clear guidance. Another limitation is that the contingency approach tends to concentrate on more conventional middle management or supervisory situations – that is, when a manager or supervisor is leading a group of subordinates. Arguably, it has less to say about leadership at a strategic level, or about leadership as a process among members of a group or team – that is, outside of the hierarchical system.

Reflective question

Sum up the strengths and weaknesses of the contingency approach to leadership.

CASE STUDY Leadership in sport

The following is based on an interview by the author with Steve Borthwick, a rugby union player who is the current captain of Saracens and former captain of the England team.

Leadership

What do you understand by the term 'leadership'? (What would your definition of 'leadership' be?)

Leadership is the ability to influence people to move in a direction to achieve one or more goals, influencing people to give all of their personal qualities and efforts towards an objective. Leading people means helping them maximize every aspect of their abilities and extending their beliefs of what they thought possible. It means adding value to those around you, and bringing out strengths in them that may not have appeared otherwise.

Do you consider leaders to be 'born' or 'made'? Is it possible to train people in leadership?

In many ways, we are a product of the experiences we have. It is these experiences that go some way to shaping our character, which helps mould what type of leader we can become. Hence, I believe that leaders can be made.

Leadership skills may be enhanced and it is important to set the example of constantly striving to improve. It is from being exposed to different ideas and experiences that learning can occur. This is a constant evolution and no leader is ever the finished article – we can all develop. The key, however, is the character that the individual brings to the organization. Each leader has a different blend of skills and has strengths in different areas, but it is the behaviours that are displayed in the most challenging of times that people will see. People then make their own assessment of whether to follow the individual or not. The behaviours shown illustrate the character and values of the person.

Understanding of tactics, situations, teammates, and opposition are important, but clear knowledge and understanding of yourself are vital – and it can take time to develop these. Knowing when to be positive and encouraging, but also recognizing when to be firm, being able to remain calm and collected in stressful times, understanding when to display fierce intensity, but also knowing when to relax — these are all aspects that can be developed and enhanced over time.

How would you describe the leadership of the rugby club as a whole?

The Director of Rugby has overall control of all aspects of the team. He will guide the group in the way he wants the team to play and he will set the ethos for the group as a whole. He will lead the recruitment that brings people into the team and it will be him who sets the values around which the team operates. Working with him is a team of coaches who all have different areas of speciality – specific areas of the game that they focus on. The coaches will then work closely with some key players in each specific area, so that those players will lead those areas. This ensures that the team will also have key on-field leadership, both in training and matches, when the coaches are not there. The players who lead each area will work closely with the coach to ensure a continual development. While the coach leads, the players will work to re-emphasize the messages and goals, while also giving feedback and opinion.

There is a Club Captain and it is important that he works closely with the Director of Rugby. This ensures that the messages and beliefs of the Director of Rugby are constantly emphasized within the team. The leadership of the players within the team must be constantly congruent with the leadership of the Director of Rugby. There will usually be at least one or two Vice Captains. Throughout the course of the season, while playing many games week after week, the Club Captain will not play every game. This means it is very important to have other members of the group who can also lead the team.

For a successful team, the Director of Rugby, coaches and all leaders within the organization must be empathetic with each other. Each person must feel that there is a way that their voice is heard and their opinion valued. This may be by speaking via the Club Captain or other senior player, or speaking directly to one of the coaching staff, but it may also be during team meetings, when open discussion is encouraged to ensure that every player is very clear about the plan.

What, in your opinion, makes for good leadership in rugby, both on and off the field?

People may lead in different ways within a sports team, but what is constant is the need for integrity of character. The leaders must be honest and trustworthy, selfless people who will put the needs of the team first, courageous people who will push themselves as far as they can possibly go. It is only with this integrity that a leader can earn respect, and

it is only with respect that leaders can help others go as far as they can – possibly further than they originally thought possible.

In a team sport, it is essential that the leaders within the group lead by example. This means that all aspects of their preparation are crucial, on the training field, in meetings, around the club, prior to a game, and also the other commitments that come with being a professional rugby player – the interaction with supporters and sponsors. This must continue on the field, where the leaders of a group must consistently play to a high standard. This is a major challenge, as the leader must concentrate on personal performance, while also being aware of the game as a whole and the team generally. It means putting the team first, but understanding the need to concentrate on personal performance. It is vital to have this greater understanding and awareness of the game, but it must not detract from the personal performance. This means that the team must have key leaders in decision-making roles, people who take responsibility and are aware of aspects of the game. Leadership of the team is a shared responsibility, and the Club Captain and other leaders within the group must have the discipline to constantly epitomize the values that the group as a whole aims for.

Rugby teams tend to be a very diverse group: from players who have just left school to those in their mid-thirties, players from all round the world who speak different languages, players who play at the top of world rugby and players who are just starting their careers. Hence it is very important to spend time getting to know the individuals. While rugby is a team sport, every player has an individual personality and will have different ways of motivation. That is why understanding each individual in this diverse group is so important – it is needed to help get the very best out of each individual, which then goes a long way towards team success.

Are there any lessons for leadership in business that can be learned from sport?

I believe that there are many similarities between leadership in business and sport, and there are also some key differences. Being a leader within a team sport ensures constant interaction with every member of the organization. It also means that the performance of the leader is constantly displayed. The standards that the leader displays, both in performance and also in values and behaviours, will be assessed by other members of the team. It is by constantly striving to be the best that they can be, by setting the example, that a leader in sport earns respect. This respect from your teammates and coaches, and others around the group, is vital to being a successful leader. It can take an incredible amount of hard work to earn this respect, and it takes dedication every day to maintain and enhance it.

Q   Consider the case study above. What potential similarities and differences do you perceive between leadership in sport and leadership in business?

6.7 Recent approaches to leadership

In their best-selling book *In Search of Excellence*, Peters and Waterman (1982), in analysing some of what they considered to be the most successful companies in the USA, emphasized the importance of the 'transforming leader'. This was someone who was able to clearly articulate a vision for the organization and, through their personal qualities and communication skills, inspire others to share that vision and thus transform the culture of the organization.

These ideas can be seen to form a 'new paradigm' on leadership (Alban-Metcalf and Alimo-Metcalf 2002). This is because the focus of previous theories of leadership was the leadership of organizations in times of relative stability, while the focus of 'modern' leadership was on managing change in turbulent and unpredictable environments.

The term 'transformational' was used to describe leaders' ability to transform followers, to perform beyond expectations. Transformational leaders are seen as being able to motivate others to:

- view their own work from new perspectives
- have an awareness of the mission and vision of the organization
- attain high levels of ability and potential
- look beyond their own interests to those of the group.

Transformational leadership was contrasted with transactional leadership, in which the leader rewards followers for specific task performance or behaviours. Transactional leadership can therefore be equated with management.

KEY TERM

Transformational leaders: leaders who have the ability to transform followers to perform beyond their expectations.

Leadership versus management revisited

The contrast between transformational and transactional leadership can be seen to mirror the differences between leadership, on the one hand, and management, on the other, with leadership being something visionary and inspirational, while management focuses more on getting the job done through others. It has been argued that both are important. The need for both and their complementary nature is illustrated in Table 6.1. Some authors have argued that leaders and managers are different kinds of people, with different personality types and orientations to work – leaders being the risk-takers who create excitement, while managers are more cautious and methodical (Alban-Metcalf and Alimo-Metcalf 2002).

Distributed leadership

As we have seen, certain approaches to leadership concentrate on the individual, often at a senior level in the organization. Thus the trait theories seek to identify the personality characteristics that will make for great leaders, and transformational leadership focuses on the vision and charismatic role of the leader in order to inspire followers.

A very different approach is that of distributed leadership, which takes the view that leadership can and will be found throughout the organization. Buchanan and Huczynski (2010: 619) suggest that distributed leadership involves a number of people acting together in formal and informal roles, which may be spontaneous and intuitive. Leadership functions may be shared and the leader role may shift from one person to another as circumstances change. It is argued that distributed leadership has become more important as organizational structures have become flatter and less centralized. Networked organizational forms, teamwork and knowledge work are other influencing factors. Self-managed teams, for example, may have no formal leader, or emphasis may be placed on the coaching and facilitator role of any leader that there is.

TABLE 6.1 Comparison of leadership and management

Activity	Leadership	Management
Agenda creation	*Establishing direction*: Developing future vision and articulating this to inspire.	*Planning/budgeting*: Developing detailed strategic plans. Allocating resources.
Human resource development for achievement	*Aligning people*: Enthusing and engaging others. Creating teams to achieve the vision.	*Organizing/staffing*: Developing planning and staffing structures, aims and objectives. Providing policies and procedures. Monitoring systems.
Execution	*Motivating/inspiring*: Energizing staff to overcome barriers to change by inspiring others.	*Controlling/problem-solving*: Detailed monitoring of results. Organizing corrections.
Outcomes	*Tends to produce*: Change, often dramatic. Potential for effective change.	*Tends to produce*: Order/predictability, efficiency. Results expected by shareholders.

Adapted from Kotter in Alban-Metcalf and Alimo-Metcalf 2002

KEY TERM

Distributed leadership: leadership that is found throughout the organization.

The increased importance of distributive leadership should not be taken to imply that it is unproblematic, or that it signifies a complete shift away from more individually focused views of leadership. Potential problems can include the difficulty of coordinating efforts, plus the wasted effort and personality clashes that may occur in groups without an appointed leader. Another potential problem with distributed informal leadership is that the qualities and contributions of those involved may be difficult to recognize and measure. It is also argued that a 'twin-track' approach is needed, with a leader or leaders providing inspiration and vision at a senior level, working with dispersed leadership that is not tied to the organizational hierarchy.

6.8 Critical perspectives on leadership

In Chapter 1, it was argued that there were different possible perspectives on organizational behaviour, and this also applies to the different topics that make up the study of OB. In this chapter on leadership, the theories outlined and the arguments presented are located predominantly in what Knights and Willmott (2007: 265) term 'the mainstream agenda'. This agenda focuses on how best to manage and lead in order to optimize performance. In general, it assumes a fair degree of agreement or consensus between different individuals and groups within the organization – management and employees, for example – as to values and goals, and this is also seen to apply to society more generally. This is the perspective predominantly taken by the authors of this book, with the rationale for this being that the book aims to provide an introduction to the subject for business and management students.

However, it is also the aim of the book to introduce the reader to other possible perspectives and to encourage critical thinking. Mainstream approaches focus on how managers can best meet existing goals, rather than questioning the nature of the goals themselves. They also assume the managers' 'right to manage'. Yet alternative or critical perspectives challenge these assumptions and question the goals and the legitimacy of management. From such alternative perspectives, management and leadership techniques may be viewed as manipulative and controlling.

What is the value of considering such alternative views? First, they remind us that the goals of organizations and how these organizations are managed are not a given; they are not written in tablets of stone. Rather, they are influenced by a variety of factors and societal attitudes, and they change and progress over time. Recent interest in corporate social responsibility (CSR) and ethical trading are examples of this. Second, they remind us that organizations, via their managers, can behave badly towards their employees and society more generally – with poor working conditions and 'sweatshop' labour supplying some of the big names in the clothing and fashion industry providing just one example, while recent revelations about phone hacking by journalists at the *News of the World* provide another. Lastly, on a more macro scale, the financial crash in 2009, and the actions of banks and other financial institutions that contributed to this, have led many to question our economic and monetary system. On a political level, recent populist uprisings in the Middle East, leading in some cases to changes in government, show that to always locate our view in mainstream perspectives can be very blinkered: things can and do change quite fundamentally and new paradigms emerge.

In terms of leadership specifically, critical perspectives question the assumed consensus in organizations, or argue that this consensus may be more apparent than real. Such perspectives highlight the power differences in organizations, and also issues of dependence. Employees may not follow a leader because of his or her inspirational qualities or vision, but merely because they do not have the power to do otherwise and wish to retain their jobs. Knights and Willmott (2007) introduce what they term a 'constitutional' approach, which questions not only the idea of universal leadership characteristics put forward by trait approaches to leadership, but also the notion that the context or environment of contingency approaches is a self-evident, objective reality. What do they mean by this? A full review of their ideas is beyond the scope of this book, but in essence their argument is that a key element of leadership is 'management of meaning', of educating their followers about what the 'real' situation is. Once followers accept this, they are also more likely to accept the legitimacy of the leader – that is, the person who has defined the situation they find themselves in. If a manager can mobilize appropriate resources – financial, informational, plus support – he or she is more likely to become a leader, and will then be in a more powerful position to remain such.

 ## 6.9 Gender and leadership

Historically, much of the research on leadership has been based on men's perceptions of the subject; indeed a common assumption has been that leaders would be men. Since the 1990s, however, there has been an increased interest in the subject of gender in leadership and management, particularly when attempting to explain the under-representation of women in management positions. In terms of leadership behaviours, few significant differences have been found between men and women (Powell 1993), though there was the suggestion that women were more likely to be participative and democratic in decision-making and more team-oriented. Interestingly, there is also some evidence to suggest that women are more likely to display transformational behaviours than men. It has also been suggested that, faced with flatter structures and thus the increased importance of communication, collaboration, consensus and team-working (qualities associated with women), we are seeing a 'feminization' of management.

KEY THEMES   Women in the boardroom

Figures show that although women make up nearly half the workforce and one-third of managers, very few make it to senior management positions. The Female FTSE Board Report from Cranfield University, School of Management (cited in Hofman and Hofman 2010) showed only four female chief executives of FTSE 100 companies in the UK, and that only 10 per cent of board directors are women. This situation is mirrored across Europe, apart from in Norway where, since 2008, Norwegian companies must by law make sure that at least 40 per cent of the board directors are women.

Apart from fairness/equity considerations, increasingly a persuasive business case is being made for greater equality in the boardroom, with the recent financial crisis making this even more of an imperative. Maitland (2009) points to substantial evidence that a better gender balance has a positive impact on company performance and profitability. This is most significant when there is a 'critical mass' of women of 30 per cent or more.

Helen Alexander, the first woman president of the CBI, the UK employers' organization, has warned against the danger of homogeneous leadership teams leading to 'groupthink' (Witenberg-Cox 2009). It is argued that there is a convincing business case for designing organizations that attract and retain women at the top and that more diverse leadership teams tend to make better decisions.

(Adapted from Smith 2011)

 ## 6.10 Summary

This chapter reviewed a key topic in organizational behaviour, that of leadership. The key debates concerning leadership have been outlined, including debates about the meaning of the term and the differences between leadership and management.

Leadership in history and the historical development of ideas on leadership were outlined, and trait, style and contingency approaches were reviewed and evaluated. Recent approaches to leadership include the concepts of transformational leadership and leadership that is distributed. The chapter concluded by looking at critical perspectives on leadership and gender and leadership.

Key ideas

Meanings and importance of leadership:

- Leadership is seen as crucial to organization success.
- There are many different definitions of leadership and thus little agreement as to the exact meaning of the term.
- It has been suggested, however, that there are three common elements to leadership: goal-setting and achievement; group activities; and influence on the behaviour of others.
- Differences between leadership and management have been much debated.
- While leadership is usually seen in terms of providing vision, inspiration and strategy, management is viewed more in terms of getting things done on a day-to-day basis.
- Historically, leadership was probably most closely associated with war and the battlefield.

Traditional approaches to leadership:

- Three main approaches to leadership can be discerned: trait, style and contingency.
- Trait theories rest on the assumption that leaders possess certain personality traits and attributes that can be identified and measured.
- Style or behaviour theories identify effective and ineffective leadership styles.
- Contingency approaches to leadership suggest that the most appropriate approach to leadership will depend on the particular situation.
- Contingency approaches seek to identify the key contingent variables that will influence leadership.

Recent approaches to leadership:

- A new paradigm of leadership has been suggested, suitable for managing change in turbulent and unpredictable environments.
- The term 'transformational leaders' refers to the ability to inspire others to perform beyond expectations.
- Distributed leadership is viewed as being found throughout the organization, at all levels.

Critical approaches:

- Mainstream approaches focus on how managers can best meet existing goals, rather than questioning the nature of the goals themselves.
- Critical approaches stress alternative perspectives.
- Historically, much of the writing and research on leadership have been from a male perspective. There is now interest in the role of gender and leadership.

Review questions

1. How would you define leadership? What are the common elements of leadership?
2. What are seen to be the main differences between leadership and management?
3. What are the main shortcomings of trait approaches to leadership?
4. Outline Tannenbaum and Schmidt's continuum of leadership behaviour.
5. Assess the strengths and weaknesses of contingency approaches to leadership.
6. What is meant by 'transformational leadership'?
7. Give a practical example of distributed leadership.

Useful websites

www.i-l-m.com – provides news and information on leadership from the Institute of Leadership and Management

www.leadershipnow.com – interesting quotes and an historical review of leadership

Recommended reading

Brown, M. and Treviño, L. (2006) 'Ethical leadership: a review and future directions'. *The Leadership Quarterly*, 17, pp. 595–616.

Northouse, P.G. (2009) *Leadership Theory and Practice*. Thousand Oaks, CA: Sage Publications.

Pugh, D.S. and Hickson, D.J. (2007) *Writers on Organizations*. London: Penguin Books.

References

Alban-Metcalf, R.J. and Alimo-Metcalf, B. (2002) 'Leadership'. In Warr, P. (ed.) *Psychology at Work*. London: Penguin Books.

Ball, S. (2007) 'Leadership of academics in research'. *Educational Management Administration & Leadership*, 35(4), pp. 449–77.

Bennis, W.G. and Nanus, B. (1985) *Leaders: The Strategies for Taking Charge*. New York: Harper and Row.

Blake, R.R. and Mouton, J.S. (1964) *The New Management Grid*. Houston, TX: Gulf.

Branson, R. (2009) *Losing My Virginity: The Autobiography*. London: Virgin Books.

Buchanan, D.A. and Huczynski, A.A. (2010) *Organizational Behaviour*. Harlow: Pearson Education.

Cohen, C.M. and Cohen, S.L. (2005) *Lab Dynamics: Management Skills for Scientists*. New York: Cold Spring Harbor Laboratory Press.

Crainer, S. (1995) 'Have the corporate superheroes had their day?' *Professional Manager*, March, pp. 8–12.

Crainer, S. and Dearlove, D. (eds.) (2001) *Financial Times Handbook of Management*. Harlow: Pearson Education.

Fiedler, F.E. (1967) *A Theory of Leadership Effectiveness.* New York: McGraw-Hill.

Garrett, G. and Davies, G. (2010) *Herding Cats: Being Advice to Aspiring Academic and Research Leaders.* Axminster: Triarchy Press.

Hersey, P. and Blanchard, K.H. (1988) *Management of Organizational Behavior: Utilizing Human Resources.* Englewood Cliffs, NJ: Prentice-Hall International.

Hofman, A. and Hofman, T. (2010) 'Why are senior managers so rare in finance?' *Financial Times*, 21st May.

Knights, D. and Willmott, H. (2007) *Introducing Organizational Behaviour and Management.* London: Thomson Learning.

Maitland, A. (2009) 'FT top 50 women in business'. *Financial Times*, 25th September.

Mullins, L.J. (2010) *Management and Organizational Behaviour.* Harlow: Pearson Education.

Peters, T.J. and Waterman, R.H. (1982) *In Search of Excellence: Lessons from America's Best-run Companies.* New York: Harper and Row.

Powell, G.N. (1993) 'One more time: do male and female managers differ?' *Academy of Management Executive*, 4, pp. 68–75.

Robbins, S.P., Judge, T.A. and Campbell, T.T. (2010) *Organizational Behaviour.* Harlow: Pearson Education.

Smith, P.E. (2011) 'Web-based communication and networking: an opportunity to break the glass ceiling?' Paper presented at the 11th International Conference on Diversity in Organizations, Communities and Nations, Cape Town, South Africa, 20th–22nd June.

Stogdill, R.M. (1974) *Handbook of Leadership: A Survey of Theory and Research.* New York: Free Press.

Tannenbaum, R. and Schmidt, W.H. (1958) 'How to choose a leadership pattern'. *Harvard Business Review*, March/April, pp. 95–102.

Witenberg-Cox, A. (2009) 'Diverse and decisive'. *Financial Times*, 22nd June.

Organizational processes 7

*Since management decision-making is a **political** process, **change** is inevitably suffused with organizational politics. In major decisions, whoever is powerful among the decision group will determine the **outcomes**.* (ANDREW PETTIGREW, in PUGH and HICKSON 2007: 193)

CHAPTER OBJECTIVES

By the end of this chapter you will understand:

* the importance of communication in organizations

* different approaches to employee voice

* the concepts of power and politics in organizations and their importance

* the role of management control and different approaches to control

* the significance of conflict in organizations and the range of conflict-handling techniques.

7.1 Introduction

This chapter examines organizational processes. It starts with a review of communication, a process that is of crucial importance for organizations. Everything of significance that happens in organizations involves communication in some way, and managers spend a significant amount of their time and effort communicating. Communication can be analysed at both an interpersonal level – the process of sending and receiving messages between individuals – and an organizational level. One aspect of communication is that of employee voice.

Although issues of power and politics may not be discussed much in organizations, they are also of great importance, and key to our understanding of managers' jobs and how organizations work. The chapter examines different sources of power, and differing perspectives on the topic of power and organizational politics.

Finally, the chapter reviews issues of management control as well as conflict in organizations, and conflict-handling techniques, including negotiation, conciliation, mediation and arbitration.

7.2 Communication

Communication is of crucial importance for organizations. Everything of significance that happens in an organization involves communication in some way. The majority of managers spend a significant amount of their time communicating: talking and listening generally, in meetings, networking and negotiating. Poor communication, or lack of sufficient communication, can be a cause of conflict.

> **Communication:** the process by which information and views are exchanged.

KEY TERM

Interpersonal communication

Interpersonal communication is that which is on an individual level. In simple terms, it involves the transmitter or source, the message and the receiver. This process is set out in Figure 7.1.

FIGURE 7.1 The communication process

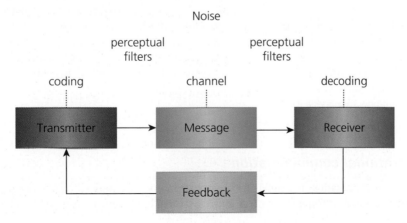

The transmitting person has something that he or she wishes to communicate to the receiving person. The next step is **encoding**, the process of translating an idea or thought into a meaningful form of expression. This could be using written, verbal and/or non-verbal signals and symbols. The **message** is what is communicated. The **channel** is the medium through which the message is sent, such as face to face, telephone or email. The **receiver** is the recipient of the message. To successfully complete the process, the recipient needs to **decode** the message – for example, if it is in a foreign language, the recipient will need to translate it in order to understand it, or if it is in the form of a Microsoft° Word attachment in an email, but the recipient has an older version of Word, he or she will need to reconfigure it.

The communication process will be affected and influenced by the emotions, perceptions and attitudes of both the transmitting person and the receiver. The transmitter may communicate in a manner that is not understood by the receiver, or the receiver may misinterpret the message. There may also be factors that interfere in the process, which are termed **noise**. This may refer to actual noise, such as trying to have a telephone conversation while workmen are busy digging up the street outside, but it also refers to a range of other interferences, including perceptual filters of the recipient, anxiety, pressures, stress and excitement.

Non-verbal communication, or body language, is that part of face-to-face communication that is expressed through our gestures, expressions, mannerisms and signals. It can play an important part in the sending and receiving of messages.

ACTIVITY

Give examples of 'noise' in communication and how it can disrupt effective communication.

CASE STUDY Neurolinguistic programming

Neurolinguistic programming (NLP) looks at how each of us makes sense of the world. NLP practitioners argue that, by implementing it, we can also make our world how we want it to be. It is argued that NLP can make a big difference in how we communicate, motivate, influence, negotiate, lead, empower and manage.

Neuro refers to our neurological system, the way we use our senses of sight, hearing, touch, taste and smell to translate our experiences into thought processes, both conscious and unconscious. It relates to physiology as well as the mind, and to how these function. Much of NLP is about increasing our awareness of our neurological system and learning how to manage it.

Linguistic refers to how we use language to make sense of our experience and how we communicate that experience to ourselves and others. Our language patterns are an expression of who we are and how we think.

Programming refers to the coding of experience. Programming is a series of steps designed to achieve a specific result. The results we achieve and the effects each of us creates in ourselves and in others are the consequence of our personal programmes. There is a sequence of behaviour and thinking patterns that results in our experience.

(Adapted from Knight 1995: 4)

Organizational communication

Effective communication is crucial to organizational performance, yet it is often felt to be an area in need of improvement. A study by the Chartered Institute of Personnel and

Development (CIPD) (Cannell 2007), for example, found that only just over 50 per cent of employees felt that they were being informed about what the company was doing. Good communication is therefore an organizational issue as well as a personal one.

Organizations use a variety of communication methods, which can be one-way (top-down) or two-way. Examples of methods include: regular meetings, cascading information down the hierarchy, in-house magazines, company intranet, team briefings, email, blogs and podcasts, suggestion schemes, appraisal schemes and attitude surveys.

The CIPD outlines key steps towards developing an effective communication strategy:

1 | Convince top management of the importance of communication.

2 | Build alliances across the organization to support initiatives.

3 | Recognize that no single method will be effective.

4 | Use a mix of approaches and use all available channels where relevant (written, face to face, web-based, moving images).

5 | Target the form(s) of communication to the audience.

6 | Respect cultural diversity and vary approaches accordingly.

7 | Make sure that messages are consistent, over time and between audiences.

8 | Ensure clarity of message and keep things as simple as possible.

9 | Train managers in communication skills and ensure that they understand the importance of communication.

10 | Seek wherever possible to develop and sustain two-way communication, dialogue and feedback.

11 | Ask yourself whether employees feel that the culture of the organization is such that they can say what they think without discomfort; if this is not the case, think about how that culture can be changed.

12 | Consider whether communication is built into the planning stages of all activities.

Review communication initiatives to check what has worked, what has not worked, and why.

(Based on CIPD 2010a: 3)

CASE STUDY Communication and technology – Virgin Active

Dominic Boon is an example of a new generation of leaders who embrace technology as a means of communicating with employees. He also uses it as a means of bringing head office and the fitness clubs closer together, and as part of a culture change programme.

❝ I'm always looking for positive things that I can tweet about when I'm out and about visiting our clubs. It is a good way to reach out to all our employees across the country, share news and recognize great performance. My tweets also appear on my LinkedIn page, so it's a way to promote our clubs to my network as well. In the past, we have posted employee recognition award ceremonies on YouTube, which include the People Team in fancy dress! I also send an email in the style of a 'blog' to the full People

Team every Friday, talking about where I have been during the week, what the week's news is and our latest customer satisfaction figures. I end it with a personal touch, such as what I may be up to at the weekend.

While Dominic was slightly worried at first about how his team might respond to his Friday emails, the feedback has been positive.

(Adapted from CIPD 2010a: 13)

Q   Give examples of how technology can be used to facilitate organizational communication.

 ## 7.3 Employee voice

It was pointed out in Section 7.2 that organizational communication can be one-way (top-down from management to employees) or two-way. Mechanisms for two-way communication involve giving employees some sort of 'voice'.

KEY TERM

Employee voice: two-way communication between employer and employee. It is the process of the employer communicating to the employee(s), as well as receiving and listening to communication from the employee(s) (CIPD 2010b).

There are a number of drivers for employee voice, including European Union legislation on information and consultation, and the recognition of the importance of such practices in producing a committed workforce. It thus links to concepts such as employee engagement (see Chapter 4).

There are two differing approaches to giving employees a 'voice': employee involvement and employee participation. Employee involvement covers a range of practices, primarily initiated by management and designed to increase employee information about, and commitment to, the organization. It is aimed at the individual employee or team of employees.

Employee participation tends to be seen as focusing on collective or representative arrangements in which employees, often via their representatives, are involved with management in decision-making (Gennard and Judge 2002).

Employee involvement practices can be classified as follows:

- downward communication
    - team briefing
    - staff newsletter
    - cascading information down via chain of management
    - workplace-wide meetings

- upward problem-solving communication
    - suggestion schemes
    - employee attitude surveys
    - group problem-solving

- financial participation
    - profit-related bonus schemes
    - employee shared ownership schemes.

Employee participation practices can take the following forms:

- joint consultative committee
- collective bargaining
- works council
- European Works Council.

In deciding on which type of employee voice practices to implement, management will have to resolve a number of questions, including the following: how far should employees be involved in decision-making? Should the employee voice be direct or via a representative such as a trade union? At what level should employee voice take place? What sorts of issues should be the subject of employee voice?

Reflective question

Outline the difference between employee involvement and participation, and give examples of each.

 ## 7.4 Power in organizations

As outlined in Chapter 2, Weber argued that legitimate authority would predominate in bureaucratic structures, and this is further discussed in Chapter 8 on organizational structure. When the actions and instructions of managers as power-holders are considered legitimate by employees, authority has been exercised. Yet power in organizations can also be exercised in other ways, which may not always necessarily be seen as legitimate. Consider the following definitions of power:

> A capacity that *A* has to influence the behaviour of *B* so that *B* acts in accordance with *A*'s wishes. (Robbins, Judge and Campbell 2010: 372)

> The capacity of individuals to overcome resistance on the part of others, to exert their will, and to produce results consistent with their interests and objectives. (Buchanan and Huczynski 2010: 694)

> At a broad level, power can be interpreted in terms of control or influence over the behaviour of other people witha or without their consent. (Mullins 2010: 675)

It is also suggested that perhaps the most important aspect of power is probably that it is a function of dependency.

> The greater *B*'s dependency on *A*, the greater is *A*'s power in the relationship. (Robbins, Judge and Campbell 2010: 372).

In addition, power may be latent – it may not always be used; it is the fact that it is there that is important.

Although it may not feature much in management textbooks, and may not always be openly discussed in organizations, power is an inherent and important feature of organizational life.

Power: the ability to get other people to do what you want them to do.

KEY TERM

Sources of power in organizations

A number of sources of power have been identified (see, for example, French and Raven 1959):

- **reward power** – one who can distribute rewards that others want, either financial or non-financial, will have power over them
- **coercive power** – based on the ability to punish
- **legitimate power** – comes from one's position in the hierarchy; it is where employees accept the manager and his or her pronouncements because of the authority of the manager's position
- **referent power** – based on the characteristics of the individual and admiration for that person
- **expert power** – originates from the expertise, knowledge and skill of the individual
- **information power** – based on the knowledge and information that the individual has and that is not readily available.

The first three sources of power are examples of formal power, based on the individual's position in the organization. The next three are examples of informal or personal power, which comes from the individual's special characteristics or knowledge, rather than his or her position in the hierarchy.

> ### Reflective question
>
> Give practical organizational examples of each type of power listed above.

We can see that power can be a function of one's position in the hierarchy – for example, the chief executive or managing director will have formal power based on his or her position. But power can also be found in different individuals and located throughout the organization.

CASE STUDY Waiter power

A well-known US politician and former famous basketball player, Bill Bradley, was the guest of honour and after-dinner speaker at a political gathering. During the meal the waiter came round and served him one pat of butter. Bradley asked for two pats, but the waiter refused, saying, 'Sorry, just one pat of butter per person.'

Bradley replied to this, saying, 'I don't think you know who I am, I'm Bill Bradley, Rhodes scholar, ex-basketball world champion and now US senator.'

To which the waiter replied, 'Maybe you don't know who I am, but I'm the guy who's in charge of the butter.'

(Adapted from Kettle 1999, in Buchanan and Huczynski 2010: 695)

Perspectives on power in organizations

How we view the operation of power in an organization, and its legitimacy, will depend on our perspective or viewpoint (see Section 1.5). A **unitary perspective** will stress managers' right to manage and share goals. It is believed therefore that employees will accept the position power of the manager and based on the location of the post in the hierarchy and the authority vested in that position.

Those adopting a **pluralist perspective** are more likely to see power as a mix of position and personal power distributed throughout the organization, leading to political behaviour, negotiation and possibly power struggles.

A **radical** or **labour process perspective** will view the employment relationship as inherently unequal; one in which the balance of power lies firmly with the employers/owners and management as their representatives.

Taking a **postmodern perspective**, Michael Foucault saw power in organizations as being a reflection of power in wider society and as ingrained in the language, or discourse, we use. As Martin and Fellenz (2010) point out, Foucault reminds us that the boundaries that we see and take for granted, such as hierarchical boundaries between management and employees, are in fact social constructions. We are effectively socialized to see things in a certain way and to accept them. Once formed, these constructions can be difficult to change, so a power base is created that resists attempts to form new organizational frameworks or new ways of doing things.

Organizational politics

Buchanan and Badham (2008) argue that, as organizational structures become flatter and the subject of regular change, there is a concomitant reduction in the significance of formal hierarchical authority, and organizational politics become more important. While power can be seen as the ability to get people to do what you want them to do, politics can be seen as the techniques and tactics to do this. Bolman and Deal (1991, in Buchanan and Huczynski 2010) summarize the political view of organizations as one where goals and decisions emerge as a result of negotiation and bargaining and a process of jockeying for position by various individuals and groups, rather than as a result of rational and intellectual decision-making.

> **Political behaviour:** in an organizational context, this can be defined as 'activities that are not required as part of one's formal role in the organization but that influence, or attempt to influence, the distribution of advantages and disadvantages within the organization' (Farrell and Peterson 1982, in Robbins, Judge and Campbell 2010: 381).

KEY TERM

It can be argued that politics is an inescapable part of organizational life. Organizations are made up of collections of individuals with differing beliefs, values and interests. In the organization they combine to form interest groups and collaborations. They will try to push forward the agenda(s) they believe in and derail those in which they do not. The fact that resources are often limited also leads to competition, and hence political behaviour. Thus, although in theory a purely rational and unitary organization without political behaviour is possible, in practice it is unlikely.

In summary, political processes and political behaviour involve individuals engaging in activities to gain, use and retain power in order to achieve their outcomes. As situations and decisions become more unstructured and complex, the less relevant the rules and regulations become. Where there is uncertainty, the more political processes will come into play. As Robbins, Judge and Campbell (2010) point out, those with good political skills will be able to use their power bases effectively.

> **Reflective question**
>
> Give practical organizational examples of each type of power listed above.

 ## 7.5 Management control

As we saw in Chapter 2, Henri Fayol pointed to five key elements of management: to forecast and plan, to organize, to command, to coordinate, and to control. Such traditional classical writers stressed the formal aspects of management, with Taylor and scientific management, for example, representing a form of close and direct management control over workers.

Of course, management needs to exercise some form of control over the behaviour and performance of staff, checking progress and whether objectives have been achieved. Yet, as other writers have pointed out (Johnson and Gill 1993; Mullins 2010), control is not just a function of the formal organization and the hierarchical structure of authority; it is also a feature of organizational behaviour and interpersonal influence. Drummond (2000, in Mullins 2010: 665) argues that 'common sense suggests that control is preferable to anarchy, and more control is preferable to less. While such assumptions are not necessarily wrong, they are not universally correct either.'

Stewart (1991) refers to a classic dilemma underlying the concept of control: that of finding the right balance between order and possible rigidity, on the one hand, and flexibility and possible chaos on the other. It is on this tightrope that managers have to walk. There is thus a trade-off between trying to get predictability, via tight control, and encouraging individual freedom and responsiveness to changing situations through loosening control.

KEY TERM

Organizational control: concerned with the regulation of behaviour and performance towards organizational goals.

KEY THEMES Tom Peters and liberation management

In his books Thriving on Chaos and Liberation Management, Tom Peters argues that new organizations need new management skills. He argues that the old command-and-control approaches should be ditched, and suggests a new era, characterized by 'curiosity, initiative, and the exercise of the imagination'.

In one of his talks to business leaders and managers he asks the question, 'Do you know where your employees are at this moment and what they are doing?' And if not, then good, because maybe, just maybe, they are being creative and coming up with the ideas that the business needs. He thus encourages managers to let go of tight control and allow employees the freedom to innovate and be creative.

Tight control and authoritarian management are likely to lead to resistance on the part of workers. Looser control and more participatory forms of management mean that a manager's task moves from pure control to a greater emphasis on coordination and direction. Various factors can further facilitate this, including appropriate leadership styles (explored in Chapter 6), motivational techniques (Chapter 4) and membership of groups and teams (Chapter 5). This chapter now considers a number of other processes, including negotiation and conflict resolution techniques.

> **Reflective question**
>
> Outline the different approaches to management control that can be adopted.

7.6 Conflict in organizations

As outlined above, organizations are made up of collections of individuals. Each will bring his or her own unique mix of personality, upbringing, attitudes, beliefs and experiences. At work they will form coalitions and interest groups, each of which will attempt to advance their own agendas. In doing so, conflicts are likely to arise.

Note that in the above description the author of this chapter is putting forward a particular view or belief: that of organizations as political systems. In addition, the informal aspects of organization are given importance. If we adopt a different view – for example, seeing organizations as totally rational entities, then all employees will be assumed to share the same goals; power and control will be centralized and based on formal position in the hierarchy; the authority of managers will be unquestioned; and decisions will be made on an orderly, rational basis.

In the former case, viewing organizations as political systems and adopting a pluralist perspective, conflict is seen as natural. This could be conflict between management and workers as a result of differences of interest (see Chapter 1 on the employment relationship), or between different managers or departments, or between different employees. One of the key roles of management will be to *manage* that conflict, via techniques such as communication, consultation, discussion and compromise, negotiation and bargaining. Such efforts may not always be totally successful, and conflict may manifest itself in various ways: on a collective basis in the form of strikes, for example, and on an individual relationship basis in the form of arguments, grievances and so on.

In the latter case, viewing organizations as rational and adopting a unitary perspective, if conflict is manifested it will be seen as indicating a failure, of management or of systems. If everyone in the organization shares the same goals – that is, the success of that organization – and if management authority and prerogative are accepted, then conflict *should not* occur.

Luckily, we do not have to adopt one view or the other; organizations can be viewed as being a mix of the rational and the political.

KEY TERM

Conflict: a process that begins when one party perceives that another party has negatively affected, or is about to negatively affect, something that the first party cares about (Thomas 1992, in Robbins, Judge and Campbell 2010: 400).

It can be argued that conflict is not necessarily a bad thing; rather, it can have both positive and negative outcomes. Positive outcomes may include new ideas and people having to search for new ways of doing things, creativity, clarification of views and standpoints, as well as 'clearing the air'. Less positive outcomes may include individuals feeling unhappy and mistrustful, individuals and groups concentrating on their own narrow self-interests, and resistance, plus manifestations such as employee turnover and industrial action. Irvine (1998, in Mullins 2010: 99) gives the following view on managing conflict:

Perhaps our reluctance to identify, and then directly address, conflict within organizations is based upon the widely held belief that conflict is inevitable, negative and unmanageable. There is a tendency to see conflict as a result of one person's personality. Conflict may be inevitable, but how dramatically situations could be changed if we could also view it as positive and manageable! What if we think of these situations as raising *questions of difference*? What if we were to make a shift away from blaming individuals and their personalities, recognizing instead that it is through normal human interaction that outward expressions of differences are produced?

Irvine suggests that, rather than viewing organizational conflict as somehow pathological, we view it as a natural expression of difference. This links to our discussions on diversity in Chapter 10; diversity focuses on the multiplicity of differences among people and holds that such individual differences are the basis of diversity.

Reflective question

Why is conflict often seen as an inevitable part of organizational life?

Conflict and resistance: the radical frame of reference

Two different perspectives have been outlined above. One, the unitary perspective, views conflict as an aberration, something that should not occur. The other, is pluralist perspective, sees it as a natural outcome of individuals and groups attempting to advance their own agendas within the organization, with such conflicts to be resolved by negotiation and compromise.

Yet as Buchanan and Huczynski (2010) point out, the continuation of organizational problems, such as bullying, harassment, theft, sabotage, go-slows and strikes, is difficult to explain fully from these two perspectives. In contrast, the radical frame of reference (see Chapter 1) views conflict as an inevitable consequence of the capitalist system in which managers, is agents of the owners, will exploit the workers in order to drive down costs and maximize profits. Such endemic conflict cannot from this perspective be resolved through techniques or processes.

Linked to conflict, but less overt, is the concept of **resistance**. Management's attempt to exert power and control over workers may be met by such a response. Such resistance may also be found at different levels of the hierarchy, from shop-floor workers finding techniques to relieve boredom and alienation, to professionals such as academics and doctors attempting to resist the control of management or administrators, right up to senior managers attempting to resist control from the board of directors (Buchanan and Huczynski 2010: 679).

CASE STUDY A perspective on conflict

Consider the following quote relating to conflict at work and its manifestation in strike action.

❝ It is virtually obligatory for any academic writing on an acutely controversial topic to make ritual genuflections in the direction of objectivity. I am sceptical of such moralistics.

As is argued in one of the most intelligent of recent works of sociological theory, 'objectivity is the way one comes to terms and makes peace with the world one does not like but will not oppose; it arises when one is detached from the status *quo but reluctant to be identified with its critics'. I have attempted to indicate, and to present dispassionately, those theories and interpretations which conflict with my own; but I cannot claim to be detached. My commitment to the traditional humanistic goals of freedom and reason colours the treatment of my subject. Where the attempt of men consciously to control their own destinies clashes with social arrangements rooted in ignorance or manipulation, I cannot profess neutrality. And since I consider it more illuminating to view conflict as a natural response to specific social and institutional arrangements in industry, rather than as an outcome of human wilfulness and irrationality, my approach to strikes is scarcely orthodox. (Hyman 1972: Preface)*

7.7 Conflict-handling techniques

Managers may use a variety of techniques to attempt to prevent, handle and resolve conflict.

> **Conflict resolution:** a process that aims to resolve the conflict between the parties involved.

KEY TERM

Thomas (1976) distinguishes between five conflict-resolution approaches, based on (1) how assertive or unassertive each party is in putting forward its concerns, and (2) how cooperative or uncooperative each is in satisfying the concerns of the other. The different approaches are set out in Table 7.1.

TABLE 7.1 A comparison of conflict-resolution approaches

Approach	Characteristic	Objective	Likely outcome
Competing	Assertive and uncooperative	To get your way	You feel vindicated, but the other party feels defeated and possibly humiliated
Avoiding	Unassertive and uncooperative	Avoid having to deal with conflict	Interpersonal problems do not get resolved, causing long-term frustration, which will manifest itself in various ways
Compromising	Middle path	Reach an agreement quickly	Participants go for the easy rather than effective solutions
Accommodating	Unassertive and cooperative	Do not upset the other person	The other person is likely to take advantage
Collaborating	Assertive and cooperative	Solve the problem together	The problem is likely to be resolved. Also both parties are committed to the solution and satisfied that they have been fairly treated

(Adapted from Whetton *et al.* 2000, in Buchanan and Huczynski 2010: 673)

Negotiation and bargaining

Negotiation: the process of two parties coming together to confer, with a view to making a jointly acceptable agreement.

Negotiation is one type of conflict-reduction or resolution technique. It involves two main elements: purposeful persuasion and constructive compromise (Gennard and Judge 2002). Negotiation can take different forms, such as between managers, grievance-handling to resolve an employee complaint, or bargaining between management and trade union to reach a negotiated settlement.

Bargaining: a type of negotiation where each side has a list of demands.

Two types of bargaining strategies can be distinguished:

- **Distributive bargaining** seeks to divide up a fixed cake. It thus operates under zero-sum conditions; what one gains, the other loses. An example would be bargaining between management and trade unions over a pay increase, or any other discussion over the allocation of limited resources.

- **Integrative bargaining** seeks to create a win-win rather than a win-lose situation. A union management example would be if increased productivity and profits were linked to increased wages and benefits.

Define 'negotiation' and give examples of negotiation types.

CASE STUDY Trade union negotiation and bargaining

The following is based on an interview conducted by the author with Ed Blissett, formerly senior organizer and national negotiator for the GMB union between 1997 and 2005, when he was elected regional secretary. He was involved in negotiations in the gas, motor, aviation and food-processing industries, as well as local government.

For the negotiations you were involved in, could you give some background on how the negotiation process worked?

This was different in various industries, depending on the structure of trade unions and management. For example, in the motor industry, such as at Ford, the process was very structured. If an issue arose, it would normally first involve the shop steward, who is the local representative of the union, and the equivalent supervisor or manager. If there was failure to resolve the issue, it would go to the next level of senior steward or convenor on the union side and a more senior manager. If there was still failure to agree, it would then go to the next level of full-time trade union official and a senior manager, and finally to a national officer and the head of industrial relations/HR.

Although the negotiation of most issues, either individual or group, would start at the local level and only move up if there was failure to agree, the negotiation of certain issues would start at a higher level. Thus pay and conditions at Ford, for example, were negotiated at the national level, which would then be applied to all of Ford's then 18 plants in the UK. Such negotiations were very formalized and would involve close to 100 representatives of the different trade unions and an equivalent number of managers, all sitting in one room for the two to three days of the annual pay and conditions negotiation. The communication at such meetings was also formalized, with representatives having to speak through their convenors or national officials on the union side and through the head of industrial relations/HR or head of Ford UK on the management side.

What sorts of issues were typically the subject of negotiations?

At a national level, negotiations sought to reach agreement on pay and conditions, including such things as pensions and holidays. How these agreements were then applied in the various plants would be negotiated at a more local level. Rules and procedures that governed the staff and managers would also be negotiated. Individual or group grievances, in addition to a whole host of issues to do with the production line, such as the time allowed to finish a certain job, for example, or the timing of breaks, would be negotiated at a local level.

What are the key skills of successful negotiation?

You need to be able to put your case across clearly and succinctly, to your own side as well as to management. The ability to prioritize is also necessary. You also need to be able to marshal your own thoughts and think on your feet – for example, if management make an offer or contradict something they had said before. You need to be able to get across the strength of feeling that the members have about a particular issue. It is important that you appear competent and are able to persuade your own side as to what is a reasonable offer, as well as to manage expectations. In addition to these, good public-speaking skills are a requirement and the confidence to be able to address a large gathering. Finally, if it is a high-profile negotiation, the ability to manage the press and other media.

Conciliation, mediation and arbitration

If two parties, such as trade union and management, cannot reach agreement, there are a number of mechanisms available to them. The first step could be to refer the matter to an internal disputes procedure, which sets out the steps to be followed in such a situation. If the issue is still unresolved, the procedure may have as a final stage the taking of the matter to a third party, such as the Advisory, Conciliation and Arbitration Service (ACAS).

In **conciliation**, the role of the third party is to encourage the two sides to keep talking; it also facilitates the passing of information from one to the other.

A **mediator** listens to the arguments from both sides and then makes recommendations as to how they might be resolved. The parties are free to accept or reject these recommendations.

Arbitration removes the control over the settlement from the parties involved. The arbitrator listens to the arguments put forward and decides on a solution to the parties' differences.

KEY THEMES The management and resolution of conflict in the workplace

Conflict can be defined as the discontent arising from a perceived clash of interests (Dix, Forth and Sisson 2008). Dix, Forth and Sisson further indicate that conflict arises from two situations: collective disputes and individual disputes. In practice, collective disputes are resolved through negotiation; and where this fails, through conciliation or arbitration. Individual disputes arise from grievances or the disciplinary process, where the root cause is sometimes clouded or ambiguous.

A CIPD (2007) Survey Report showed that general behaviour and conduct issues were rated as the most common causes of disputes at work, followed by conflicts over performance, sickness absence and attendance, and relationships between colleagues. A further CIPD (2011) report found that the scale of workplace conflict has increased remarkably. Of those who had used each method of dealing with workplace conflict, nearly half said that their organizations had increased the use of disciplinary action, grievance procedures and mediation. The other methods for dealing with workplace conflict indicated were arbitration, neutral evaluation, training of line managers and troubleshooting by the HR department.

Following the Gibbons (2007) review and the Employment Act 2008 that followed it, there arose the need for organizations to place greater significance within their human resource management processes for managing and resolving conflict more effectively. To do this, it helps if the methods of dealing with conflict are written into the relevant procedures. Organizations are urged to use 'informal' means in advance of, or as part of, the 'formal' grievance and disciplinary procedures.

Mediation (which is a form of alternative dispute resolution, or ADR) is an 'informal' method of resolving disputes. Mediation is a way of resolving disputes without going to court. It is a flexible process that is used to settle disputes in a range of situations, such as consumer and contract disputes, family and neighbourhood disputes, and workplace disputes. It involves a neutral third party bringing two sides together with the aim of reaching mutual agreement. *The Acas Guide* (ACAS 2011) reinforces the use of mediation in the workplace.

These ADR interventions, such as mediation, negotiation, conciliation and arbitration, demand specialist skills. Even investigations, which are a crucial part of the formal grievance and disciplinary processes, require very specific skills. Companies may train their own staff with these skills, or equip them merely with the basic skills to enable them to respond quickly and resolve matters early, and leave the more complex situations to external practitioners who have undergone a programme of professional training, assessment and practice, and who are more neutral and objective. Whatever a company chooses to do, it is important to articulate the process within its procedures to enable managers and staff to deal with the issue more effectively.

(Based on an interview conducted by the author with Len Ryder, University of Hertfordshire Business School. Len Ryder is a business and management lecturer at the University of Hertfordshire Business School, with research interests in conflict resolution. For nearly ten years he was the co-owner/director of a company that provided the specialist professional services of mediation, investigations, policy and training to many major organizations. He continues to be a specialist consultant in this field.)

7.8 Summary

This chapter began by looking at the crucial role of communication in organizations, before considering the issues of power, organizational politics and conflict. Although sometimes seen as aberrations, it is argued that these are an inherent part of the employment relationship and of organizational life, and thus are areas that managers need an appreciation of. Management control and attempts by management to overcome resistance can be viewed as being on a spectrum from formal and authoritarian to more facilitative and encouraging.

This links to aspects covered in previous chapters, including leadership style, approaches to motivation and the importance of team-working. The chapter concluded with a review of some key conflict-handling techniques.

Key ideas

Introduction:

- Communication, power and politics, control and conflict are important organizational processes.

Communication:

- Everything of significance that happens in organizations involves communication in some way.
- Interpersonal communication involves transmission and receiving of a message and can be affected by 'noise'.
- Organizations have a range of possible communication methods.

Employee voice:

- Employee voice describes two-way communication between employer and employee.
- There are two main approaches to employee voice: involvement and participation.

Power in organizations:

- An appreciation of power and politics in organizations is important to managers.
- There are a number of possible sources of power in organizations.
- Power can be viewed from a number of different perspectives.
- Politics can be seen as the techniques and tactics used to implement power.

Management control:

- Control in organizations is concerned with the regulation of behaviour and performance towards organizational goals.
- Control can vary from tight to loose approaches.
- Control can engender employee resistance.

Conflict in organizations:

- There are differing perspectives on conflict: some see it as natural and inevitable, others as something that should be avoided.
- It can be argued that conflict can have positive as well as negative outcomes.
- Conflict can manifest itself in various ways, both individual (labour turnover, grievances, sabotage) and collective (strikes and go-slows).

Conflict-handling techniques:

- Conflict resolution aims to resolve the conflict between two parties.
- There are various possible approaches to conflict resolution that a manager can choose from.
- Negotiation involves purposeful persuasion and constructive compromise.
- Conciliation, mediation and arbitration are third-party interventions when two parties cannot agree.

Review questions

1. Outline the key methods of organizational communication.
2. What are the possible negative and positive outcomes of conflict in organizations?
3. What is meant by the term 'resistance' in organizations? What forms can such resistance take?
4. Outline Thomas' (1976) five key conflict-resolution approaches.
5. Compare and contrast 'mediation' and 'arbitration'.
6. What are the key methods for giving employees 'voice'?

Recommended reading

Argenti, P.A. (2007) *Corporate Communication* (4th edn). London: Irwin/McGraw-Hill.

Braverman, H. (1974) *Labor and Monopoly Capital*. London: Monthly Review Press.

Knights, D. and Willmott, H. (2007) *Introducing Organizational Behaviour*. London: Thomson Learning.

Murton, A., Inman, M. and O'Sullivan, N. (2010) *Unlocking Human Resource Management*. London: Hodder Education.

Useful websites

www.acas.co.uk – access to free, impartial, confidential advice on employment matters with guides to good employment practice

www.cipd.co.uk – free printable factsheets and survey reports on communication, disputes and conflict-handling

www.hrmguide.co.uk/relations – access to information on trade unions, negotiation and collective bargaining

References

ACAS (2011) *The Acas Guide: Discipline and Grievances at Work*. London: Advisory, Conciliation and Arbitration Service.

Buchanan, D.A. and Badham, R.J. (2008) *Power, Politics and Organizational Change: Winning the Turf Game* (2nd edn). London: Sage Publications.

Buchanan, D.A. and Huczynski, A.A. (2010) *Organizational Behaviour* (7th edn). Harlow: Pearson Education.

Cannell, M. (2007) *Employee Communication*. London: Chartered Institute of Personnel and Development.

CIPD (2007) *Managing Conflict at Work*. CIPD Survey Report. London: Chartered Institute of Personnel and Development.

CIPD (2010a) *Harnessing the Power of Employee Communication*. London: Chartered Institute of Personnel and Development.

CIPD (2010b) *Employee Voice Fact Sheet*. London: Chartered Institute of Personnel and Development.

CIPD (2011) *Conflict Management*. London: Chartered Institute of Personnel and Development.

Dix, G., Forth, J. and Sisson, K. (2008) *Conflict at Work: The Pattern of Disputes in Britain since 1980*. NIESR Discussion Paper 316. London: National Institute of Economic and Social Research.

French, J.P. and Raven, B. (1959) 'The bases of social power'. In Cartwright, D. and Zander, A.F. (eds.) *Group Dynamics: Research and Theory*. London: Tavistock, pp. 150–67.

Gennard, J. and Judge, G. (2002) *Employee Relations* (3rd edn). London: Chartered Institute of Personnel and Development.

Gibbons, M. (2007) *Better Dispute Resolution: A Review of Employment Dispute Resolution in Great Britain*. London: Department of Business, Enterprise and Regulatory Reform.

Hyman, R. (1972) *Strikes*. London: Fontana.

Johnson, P. and Gill, J. (1993) *Management Control and Organizational Behaviour*. London: Paul Chapman Publishing.

Knight, S. (1995) *NLP at Work: The Difference that Makes a Difference in Business*. London: Nicholas Brealey Publishing.

Martin, J. and Fellenz, M. (2010) *Organizational Behaviour and Management* (4th edn). Andover: Cengage Learning.

Mullins, L.J. (2010) *Management and Organizational Behaviour* (9th edn). Harlow: Pearson Education.

Pugh, D.S. and Hickson, D.J. (2007) *Writers on Organizations*. London: Penguin Books.

Robbins, S.P., Judge, T.A. and Campbell, T.T. (2010) *Organizational Behaviour*. Harlow: Pearson Education.

Stewart, R. (1991) *Managing Today and Tomorrow*. Basingstoke: Macmillan.

Thomas, K.W. (1976) 'Conflict and conflict management'. In Dunette, M.D. (ed.) *Handbook of Industrial and Organizational Psychology*. Chicago, IL: Rand McNally, pp. 889–935.

Organizational design and structure

8

*The **organization** of offices follows the principle of **hierarchy**; that is each lower office is under the control and supervision of a higher one.* (MAX WEBER)

*In practically all our activities we seem to suffer from the **inertia** resulting from our great size. There are so many people involved and it requires such a tremendous effort to put something into effect that a **new idea** is likely to be considered insignificant in comparison with the effort that it takes to put it across ... Sometimes I am almost forced to the conclusion that General Motors is so large and its inertia so great that it is impossible for us to be leaders.* (ALFRED P. SLOAN)

CHAPTER OUTLINE

1 Introduction
2 Structure: definitions and importance
3 Early approaches to organizational design
4 Key elements of organizational structure
5 Types of structure
6 Organizational relationships
7 A continuum of organizational forms
8 Contingency approach to organizational structure
9 Trends and issues in organizational structure
10 Summary

CHAPTER OBJECTIVES

By the end of this chapter you will understand:

● the meaning and importance of organizational structure

● the different approaches to organizational design

● the different elements and range of types of organizational structure

● the contingency approach to organizational structure and its application

● the key issues and trends in organizational structure.

8.1 Introduction

As introduced in Chapter 1, the study of organizational behaviour involves two key elements: an understanding of work organizations and the behaviour of individuals and groups within them. A third element can be added to this: how the design, culture and functioning of organizations influence and affect people, and, in turn, how people influence organizations.

Organizations can be viewed as collections of people brought together to achieve certain goals, which could include to design things, manufacture them, provide a service, educate people and so on. To do this, activities and tasks are divided up among different individuals and groups. The larger the organization, the more complex this differentiation becomes. There is therefore a need to coordinate and integrate these various activities. This is what structure does: organizational structure is the way in which the organization divides up tasks and coordinates the resulting activities. The structure will determine how activities are grouped together, who does what, and how staff are coordinated and managed. This chapter looks at the different elements of structure, some key types of structure, and some of the key developments, issues and trends in organizational structure.

Reflective question

What is meant by the 'structure' of an organization?

8.2 Structure: definitions and importance

CASE STUDY Ceramics Limited

Eli made pottery in the converted garage of her home. She made pots, bowls and plates. Each of these involved a number of stages: working the clay, forming the pots, tooling them when semi-dry, applying the glaze and then firing the pots in the kiln. Eli did all these tasks herself.

She started to sell her creations in a local craft shop and at market stalls. Her products were in demand and sold well, so Eli hired an assistant, Sue, to help out. The tasks were now divided between them: Sue would work the clay and prepare the glazes, as well as doing various other odd jobs, and Eli would be responsible for the other stages. Co-ordination was easy, as they both worked in the workshop and could easily communicate with each other to sort out any problems as they occurred.

The arrangement worked well and demand for the products continued to grow. Several local shops now stocked their pottery. Soon they were swamped with orders. Three assistants were hired from the local art school, and then two more. A national retail store signed them up to sell their products across the country and by mail order. Co-ordination problems started to occur. Seven people working in the small workshop led to breakages and mistakes, so Eli found new, larger premises to rent. Eli, as managing director of Ceramics Limited, also found that she was spending more and more time with customers, so she appointed Sue production supervisor. The production of pottery was also streamlined, with each employee focusing on one of the key stages.

Two years later the company had again outgrown the premises and moved to a new site on a local business park, with Eli employing 25 staff. The firm had now diversified into other products, including ceramic tiles and garden pots and ornaments. They opened their first dedicated shop and also had a thriving Internet sales site. A second premises was rented to deal with mail-order deliveries. They now employed a variety of people, including a warehouse operator, a travelling salesperson and a marketing assistant.

(Adapted from Mintzberg 1979: 1–2)

The case study above serves to illustrate a key point concerning organizations: every organized human activity, from making and selling pottery to educating people in a university, to manufacturing cars, gives rise to two basic requirements: how to divide up the tasks and how to coordinate the activities. When Eli first started her business this was simple: she did all the tasks herself and coordinated all the activities. But as the business grew, different people started to specialize in different tasks: the design, different elements of production, the selling and so on. Both Eli, as managing director, and Sue, as supervisor, had to coordinate these activities.

Definitions

KEY TERM

> **Organization:** a social arrangement for achieving controlled performance in pursuit of collective goals (Buchanan and Huczynski 2010: 8).

Mintzberg (1979: 2) defines organizational structure as follows:

> The structure of an organization can be defined simply as the sum total of the ways in which it divides its labour into distinct tasks and then achieves co-ordination among them.

This echoes the point above concerning organized human activity consisting of division of tasks and coordination of the resulting activities.

Another definition of structure is as follows:

> The formal system of task and reporting relationships that control, co-ordinate and motivate employees to work together to achieve organizational goals. (Buchanan and Huczynski 2010: 453)

This tells us more about the *purpose* of structure – that is, to achieve the goals of the organization – as well as telling us more about how this might be achieved: by providing managers with a formal system in which to control, coordinate and motivate employees.

KEY TERM

> **Organizational structure:** the formal system of dividing up work tasks, coordinating the resultant activities of employees, and specifying reporting relationships to enable the achievement of organizational goals.

Importance of structure

The importance of structure is summed up in the following two quotes:

> Organizations are collections of people brought together for a purpose. To achieve this purpose successfully, people need to be organized within the best possible structure. Decisions on structure are primary strategic decisions. Structure can make or break an organization. (Lundy and Cowling 1996: 141)

> Good organization structure does not by itself produce good performance. But a poor organization structure makes good performance impossible, no matter how good the individual managers may be. To improve organization structure … will therefore always improve performance. (Drucker 1989: 223)

But what makes a 'good' or appropriate structure for any particular organization? This question will be explored more fully later in this chapter, after a consideration of early approaches and the key elements of organizational structure.

Reflective question

Why is the structure of an organization considered important?

 ## 8.3 Early approaches to organizational design

As Buchanan and Huczynski (2010: 489) point out, organizational design refers to the process by which various dimensions and components of organizational structure are selected and managed so that organizational goals are met. They also pose, and then answer, the question: why study early approaches to organizational design? One important theme of this book is that history matters, and ideas generated in the past still have relevance today. This is not to say that nothing changes, but many current ideas have their basis in former ones, and many older ideas still have relevance now, as long as they are suitably modified to take into account contextual changes.

Bureaucracy

As outlined in Chapter 2, Max Weber was a German sociologist writing in the early part of the 20th century. He was interested in issues of power and authority; from studying societies over history, he identified three different authority types: traditional, charismatic and legitimate. Weber argued that, with the emergence and then dominance of rationalization in modern society (see below), legitimate authority would predominate, with its associated form of structure: bureaucracy.

KEY THEMES The Enlightenment and rationality

The German philosopher Immanuel Kant (1724–1804) described the Enlightenment as 'man's release from his self-inflicted immaturity', meaning that people should use their reason without seeking direction. Such writers sought to replace superstition, tyranny and injustice with reason, tolerance and legal equality. Such ideas spread across Europe and beyond during the 18th century, and saw advances in science as well as a change in how people thought about government and society. Three English philosophers can be seen as formulating key ideas in this context: Francis Bacon (1561–1626), for his development of scientific method based on experiment and observation; John Locke (1632–1704), for his political theory and empiricism (acceptance of knowledge based only on direct experience); and Isaac Newton (1642–1727), for his discoveries and unifying scientific laws. From the middle of the 18th century, such philosophies and the resulting scientific progress led to the Industrial Revolution, with new forms of mechanization and transport leading to an age of industry and manufacturing.

Although Enlightenment ideas were widespread by the second half of the 18th century, there was also a backlash in the form of the 19th-century Romantic movement, which emphasized emotion, imagination and a love of nature over reason and industrial progress.

(Adapted from *History: The Definitive Visual Guide* 2007)

2 | **Hierarchy:** should there be many levels in the structure (tall hierarchy) or few levels (flat), and what are the implications of these for communication, decision-making and employee motivation?

3 | **Span of control:** how many subordinates should one manager or supervisor be responsible for – many (wide span of control) or few (narrow span of control)?

4 | **Chain of command:** to whom should any given employee report in terms of his or her work responsibilities?

5 | **Formalization:** should formal written rules and regulations be used to cover most aspects of the organization (high formalization) or should such rules be kept to a minimum (low formalization)?

6 | **Centralization:** should the majority of the decisions be made by managers at the top of the organization (centralized) or should decision-making be delegated downwards (decentralized)?

In any particular situation, managers need to make decisions in each of these categories. Should work be specialized or broad? Should there be many levels in the hierarchy or few? And so on. This will depend on the circumstances faced by the organization. For example, a small start-up firm is likely to adopt a fairly flat informal structure. This is explored further in Section 8.7.

FIGURE 8.1 Tall and flat organizational structures

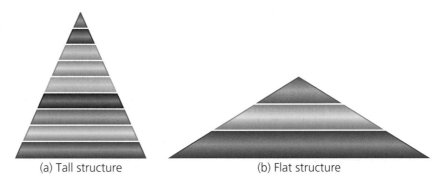

(a) Tall structure   (b) Flat structure

Figure 8.1 shows a tall hierarchical organizational structure – one with many levels and narrow span of control – and a flatter structure – one with few levels and wide span of control.

Reflective question

Outline the relative advantages and disadvantages of a tall and a flat organizational structure.

 8.5 Types of structure

As mentioned above, within the structure of a work organization, work tasks need to be divided up and activities coordinated. Jobs can be grouped together in different ways, the chief of which are as follows:

- **By function:** in which activities are grouped together according to specialization or expertise into departments or sections, such as production, Sales, HR, marketing or finance, as illustrated in Figure 8.2.

FIGURE 8.2 Functional organization structure

- **By product or service:** where different specialists are grouped together according to a particular product group or service (see Figure 8.3). An example would be in a hospital where medical and support staff are grouped together in different units, such as accident and emergency, orthopaedic or maternity.

FIGURE 8.3 Product or service-based structure

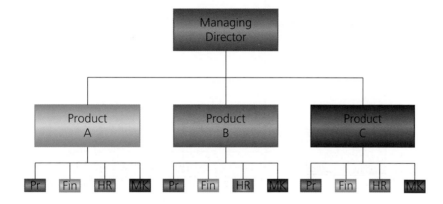

- **By geographical location:** in which the organization is subdivided and activities grouped regionally, as in Figure 8.4. Thus a firm may have a northern, eastern and southern division in the UK, as well as a European branch.

FIGURE 8.4 Geographically based structure

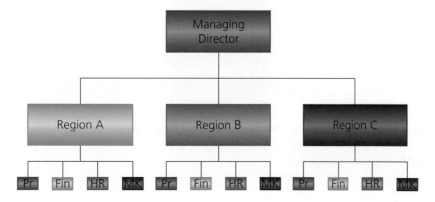

- **Mixed structures:** with the increasing size and complexity of organizations, many will demonstrate a combination of the above types. Thus in a **divisionalized** structure, the organization is divided up into divisions based on product, service or geographical region, with each being operated on a functional basis, but with some strategic elements centralized at head office.

   Another example of a mixed structure is the **matrix** form (see Figure 8.5). Such a structure usually combines a functional form with a project- or product-based form, which can result in greater flexibility, though it may also bring co-ordination problems.

FIGURE 8.5 Matrix structure

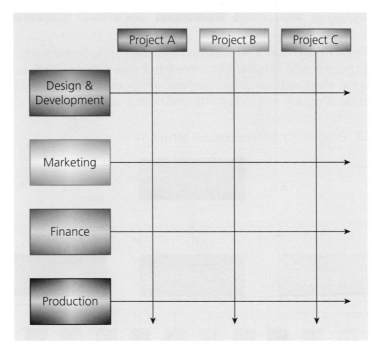

Reflective question

Think of an organization you are familiar with. Which of the above classifications does it resemble most closely? (For a large, complex organization, you may find that it encompasses two or more of the above.)

CASE STUDY Organizational structure

A major confectioner has a strategic objective to design novel and innovative products to expand its share of the market. The current organizational structure comprises large organizational lines, each representing one of the discipline areas required to contribute to new product design, as shown in Figure 8.6.

FIGURE 8.6 Current structure

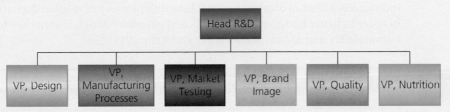

As head of R&D you understand that the current structure has delivered poor productivity in the past, and teams aligned to specific new products seem to progress slowly and with a lack of focus on the end goal, which is to develop products for sale. The paradox is that the people working in the organizational lines illustrated in Figure 8.6, and seconded to product development teams, are well qualified, experienced and highly motivated to achieve.

A recent employee survey commissioned to explore the poor productivity highlighted the following issues:

- A lack of empowerment of product development teams to progress a project. Teams report that the time taken to get approval from the different lines slowed them down and required multiple presentations and lobbying of senior people.

- A lack of focus on delivery because of the way project ownership passed from one line to another, and the constant movements of people in and out of the product development team.

- A lack of direct accountability for delivery, as people often worked on many different product development teams, with no clear prioritization of the work.

You know that you have good people in the organization, and believe that it may be the organizational structure that is holding productivity back. You believe that the organizational structure illustrated in Figure 8.7 may address the productivity issue.

FIGURE 8.7 Proposed structure

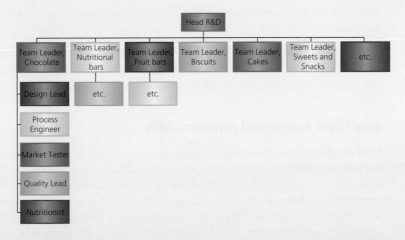

Q 1 **What would be your rationale for moving to the new organizational structure illustrated in Figure 8.7? How could this improve the productivity of the company?**

2 **What would be the major barriers to its implementation?**

3 **Over time (two to three years), what might be some of the issues that could arise as a result of this organizational change, and how might you deal with them?**

4 **As head of R&D, how would you need to lead differently in order to make this new organizational structure successful?**

8.6 Organizational relationships

Individuals within an organization will have different formal relationships with one another. In order to better understand these, it is first necessary to define some key terms: authority, responsibility and accountability (Cole and Kelly 2011: 259).

> **KEY TERM**
>
> **Authority:** the right to make certain decisions and to exercise control over resources.

> **KEY TERM**
>
> **Responsibility:** an obligation placed on a person who occupies a certain position in the organization to perform a task or function.

> **KEY TERM**
>
> **Accountability:** the ultimate responsibility that a manager has and cannot delegate. While managers may delegate authority to others, they themselves remain accountable for the actions of their subordinates.

Line relationships

Within an organization, formal authority is vested in a particular position or managerial post, not in the individual post holder. Authority is accepted by subordinates because it is seen as legitimate. In **line relationships**, authority flows down the hierarchy vertically, following the formal chain of command – for example, from the managing director to senior managers, from senior managers to middle managers, and down to managers and supervisors. Thus this is the direct relationship between manager and subordinate, with each subordinate directly responsible only to one person, their line manager.

The line relationship provides a mechanism for coordinating and controlling the work of employees and links the different parts of the organization together. It also provides channels of communication, both downwards and upwards.

Staff and functional relationships

Staff employees are those who occupy advisory positions and provide line managers with support and specialist advice. One way to provide this is via an assistant to the line manager, who can then delegate tasks and activities to the assistant. The assistant can then provide support and advice to other line managers. Because the assistant is not in a line relationship with these line managers, they do not constitute a level in the hierarchy. In terms of the organizational chart, they are often depicted as being off to one side (see Figure 8.8). Such relationships are known as **staff relationships**. The line managers can choose whether or not to follow the advice given.

A further way to provide support and advice to line managers is via a specialist department, such as HR or IT. Generally, employees in these support functions will have a staff relationship with other line managers in that the support and advice can be accepted or not. But in certain areas these support functions may be given the authority over certain areas for the whole organization by senior management – for example, the HR function may have responsibility for health and safety compliance. The HR manager will then have a **functional relationship** with line managers. Although he or she will not have a direct relationship or line authority over these other managers, he or she will have authority based on his or her functional expertise (see Figure 8.8).

FIGURE 8.8 Organizational chart showing line, staff and functional relationships

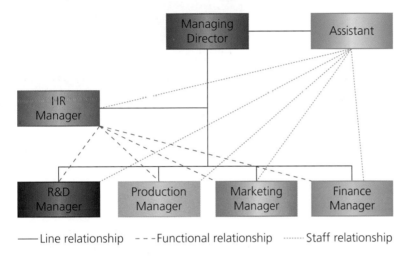

——Line relationship   – – –Functional relationship   ⋯⋯Staff relationship

The formal and the informal organization

The line, staff and functional relationships set out above are those of the **formal organization**. They will be set out in writing in job descriptions and other documentation, and will be depicted in organizational charts. Such charts show the structure and reporting relationships: job titles, seniority, which post reports to which. The **formal organization** refers to the planned, documented processes and relationships, as designed by management, to designate tasks and coordinate activities for the achievement of organizational goals.

Alongside the formal organization, however, there will be an **informal** one (Figure 8.9). This arises from the day-to-day and spontaneous relationships between employees as they interact with each other in the course of carrying out their jobs. Individual employees have psychological and social needs – for example, for social contact and interaction. They also bring their out-of-work experiences with them each day, their hopes and fears, triumphs and disappointments. Employees develop friendships at work, as well as animosities. Informal leaders emerge as well as group norms. Gossip and grapevines can provide important sources of information. The **informal organization** is not planned by management, nor is it formally documented, yet it has an important influence on the workings of the organization and the experience of working there. It can work against the formal organizational goals as set out by management or it can help to achieve these; it can have a negative effect on people's work lives or it can enhance them. Managers need to understand the workings of both the formal and the informal organization.

FIGURE 8.9 The formal and the informal organization (adapted from Gray and Strake, in Mullins 2010: 612)

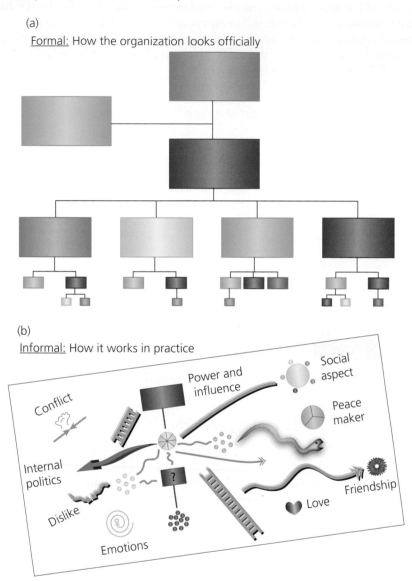

(a)

Formal: How the organization looks officially

(b)

Informal: How it works in practice

Reflective question

Why is an appreciation of the informal organization important to managers?

⟨ 8.7 A continuum of organizational forms

Early approaches to organizational design were outlined in Section 8.3. These stressed formality, standardization and order. Weber argued that the bureaucratic form of organizational structure would maximize efficiency. This may have been true of the time when Weber was writing, but since then there have been a number of criticisms of bureaucracy as an ideal structure, as well as of classical management ideas more generally, particularly in relation to their focus on formality, standardization, hierarchy and command and control. What, then, are the alternatives?

Gareth Morgan (1989) outlines a continuum of different organizational structures, ranging from the traditional bureaucratic at one end of the spectrum, through to flexible forms of structure at the other end. The flexible organic forms are characterized by few rules, little task specialization and high levels of individual responsibility, with day-to-day decision-making delegated to lower levels (see Figure 8.10). Morgan argues that a bureaucracy would, over time, probably evolve from number 1 in the diagram to number 3, or even perhaps to number 4, but to move to number 5 or 6 would require a major transformation, involving not just structural change, but a cultural one as well (see Chapter 9).

FIGURE 8.10 A continuum of organizational structure (adapted from Morgan 1989: 66)

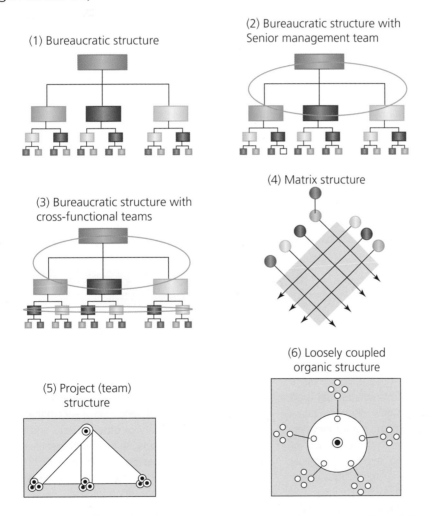

(1) Bureaucratic structure

(2) Bureaucratic structure with Senior management team

(3) Bureaucratic structure with cross-functional teams

(4) Matrix structure

(5) Project (team) structure

(6) Loosely coupled organic structure

Number 1 in the diagram is Weber's classic bureaucracy, with a pyramid-shaped hierarchy and clear lines of responsibility. It is argued that such a structure would suit a very stable environment, since it emphasizes order and predictability. An organization with such a structure, however, would not be able to respond quickly to change or to non-routine situations.

In number 2, the bureaucratic structure is augmented by a senior management team that meets regularly to deal with any non-routine problems or novel issues that arise. This is extended in number 3 to include lower-level staff in cross-functional teams. This allows for more flexibility than the traditional bureaucracy, although it retains many elements of the bureaucratic structure.

The matrix structure illustrated in number 4 (see also Section 8.5) gives equal weighting to projects or customer groups as to functional departments. It brings together teams for particular projects. An extension of this is number 5, the project or team-based structure. Here the majority of the key activities are carried out through project teams. Functional departments either do not exist or are very much in the background. Such an organization would be much better at responding quickly to change than traditional forms, and would provide an environment where creativity and ideas could be developed. It would be less suitable, however, if consistency and standardization were key requirements.

The structure illustrated in number 6 takes flexibility a stage further. The organization consists of a relatively small core of staff. This part of the organization is then loosely coupled with a number of others using a variety of relationships, including outsourcing and subcontracting.

ACTIVITY

Which of the organizational forms explored above would best suit the following organizations? Clearly justify your choice in each case.

1 | A local authority or council.
2 | An advertising agency.
3 | A firm that specializes in long-term scientific research and development projects.
4 | A small creative computer games design and development firm.
5 | A national health service.

KEY THEMES The virtual organization

The structure depicted in number 6 of the continuum of organizational structures raises questions as to what constitutes 'the organization', or where an organization begins and ends. The combination of outsourcing and subcontracting of activities with new electronic communication methods (information communication technologies, or ICTs) gives rise to the possibility of organizations with very little in terms of physical presence, and has led to the term 'the virtual organization'.

Writers such as Castells explore such trends, suggesting that a 'new economy', in tandem with new technologies, has important implications for the structuring of organizations. He characterizes the new economy as being knowledge-based, global and networked, and suggests that organizations are affected by similar trends. Networked organizations will be decentralized and will make use of subcontractors, freelancers and a variety of other flexible and non-standard types of workers. In any such organization, a worker will be connected to the network of that particular organization, but is also likely to be part of other networks and other organizations.

(Based on Castells 2001; Mullins 2010)

8.8 Contingency approach to organizational structure

The traditional approaches to organizational design, such as those outlined in Section 8.3, emphasized a 'one best way' to organizational structure and management. In Section 8.7 it was suggested that organizations can take a variety of forms, and that these will change and develop over time. In this section, some of the influences or determinants of organizational structure are explored.

Organization size

Various studies, including those of the Aston programme (Pugh and Hickson 1976), have shown that larger organizations – for example, those employing more than 2,000 people – tend to have more specialization, more departmentalization, more vertical levels and more rules and regulations. In other words, they tend to be more bureaucratic. But as Robbins, Judge and Campbell (2010) point out, the trend is not linear; once the organization achieves a certain size, further increases in size do not have a proportionate increase in formality, probably because they are fairly bureaucratic already.

Organization strategy

Definitions of organizational structure include reference to the fact that it involves co-ordination of activities to achieve organizational goals. These goals will be determined by the strategy of the organization, indicating a clear link between strategy and structure. It has therefore been suggested that if the management of the organization makes significant changes to its strategy, this is likely to have implications for the structure. Robbins, Judge and Campbell (2010: 442) make reference to Miles and Snow and other authors on strategic types. A typical approach is to categorize firms in terms of whether they primarily have an innovation, cost minimization or imitation strategy, and then to suggest suitable structural types to match.

An **innovation strategy** focuses on exploring new opportunities and creating new products or services. A **cost minimization strategy** seeks to tightly control costs and keep prices low. Organizations taking an **imitation strategy** fall somewhere in between these two. They move into new products or markets only after the innovator firms have proved them to be viable.

TABLE 8.2 The relationship between strategy and structure

Strategy	Suggested structure
Innovation	Organic, loose structure: decentralized, low specialization, low formalization
Cost minimization	Mechanistic, tight control: centralized, high work specialization, high formalization
Imitation	Mechanistic and organic, mix of loose and tight properties: tight control over established activities, looser controls over new undertakings

Adapted from Robbins, Judge and Campbell 2010: 443

KEY THEMES Alfred Chandler

Chandler was a business historian who observed that the organizational structures of organizations such as General Motors, Du Pont and Standard Oil were driven by the changing demands and pressures of the marketplace. This saw moves from rigid functional organizational forms to more loosely coupled divisional structures. Chandler was influential in the decentralization of companies in the 1960s and 1970s.

Chandler defined strategy as 'the determination of the long-term goals and objectives of an enterprise and the adoption of courses of action and the allocation of resources necessary for carrying out those goals'. He argued that organizations, having identified their strategy, could then determine the most appropriate organizational structure in order to achieve this.

Various authors have questioned Chandler's view that structure follows strategy. Thus Tom Peters has argued that it is the structure of an organization that will determine, over time, the choice of markets it chooses to attack. Others have suggested that the link between strategy and structure is more complex than Chandler suggests.

Gary Hamel has offered a more positive view of Chandler's thesis:

> *Of course, strategy and structure are inextricably intertwined. Chandler's point was that new challenges give rise to new structures. The challenges of size and complexity, coupled with advances in communications and techniques of management control, produced divisionalization and decentralization. These same forces, several generations on, are now driving us towards new structural solutions – the federated organization, the multi-company coalition, and the virtual company. Few historians are prescient. Chandler was.*

(Adapted from Crainer and Dearlove 2003; quotation from p. 32)

Q   To what extent does structure follow strategy?

Technology

Technology can be defined as how the organization transfers its inputs into its outputs (Robbins, Judge and Campbell 2010: 443). A car manufacturer, such as Ford, uses production lines to manufacture its vehicles. On the other hand, a university may use a variety of teaching technologies – some traditional, such as the lecture or seminar, and others more modern, such as the case study and a virtual learning environment.

It is suggested that the type of technology has an important influence on the organizational structure. Studies point to the **degree of routineness** as being a key aspect in this. Technologies lie on a continuum from the standardized, routine and automated through to the non-routine and customized. Much of large-scale production-line manufacturing would be an example of the former, while furniture restoring, custom shoemaking and medical research would be examples of the latter. Although the link between routines and structure is a complex one, studies have found a clear association between routineness and formalization: organizations with routine technologies tend to have greater formalization, in terms of rules, regulations, job descriptions and documentation. Routine technologies also tend to be associated with taller and more departmentalized structures.

Environment

Various studies have shown a link between the structure and management of an organization and the external environment within which the firm operates, specifically in relation to the degree of uncertainty and change in the environment.

Burns and Stalker (1961) studied a number of UK firms in different industries and their settings. They characterized these settings or environments into five types, ranging from stable to unpredictable. Two main types of structure and management practice were also identified: the mechanistic and the organic. The mechanistic structure was one with a high degree of task specialization and formalization, tight specification of individual responsibility and authority, centralized decision-making and formal rules and procedures. It can be likened to Weber's bureaucratic structure. The organic structure possessed little task specialization, a low degree of formalization, delegated decision-making and a high degree of individual responsibility.

KEY TERM

Mechanistic structures: organizational structures that show a high degree of task specialization and formalization, tight specification of individual responsibility, clear rules and regulations and centralized decision-making.

Neither form of organizational structure was viewed as being better than the other; what was suggested was that either could be the most appropriate and efficient, depending on the circumstances. Thus in their study, for a textile mill facing a stable and predictable environment, the mechanistic structure was found to be most suitable, while for an electronics firm operating in an unpredictable and rapidly changing environment, the organic structure suited it best.

KEY TERM

Organic structures: organizational structures that have low task specialization and formalization, where individual responsibility is not tightly specified, there are few formal rules and decision-making is delegated downwards.

An assessment of contingency approaches

Contingency approaches to organizational structure have the advantage over 'one best way' approaches in that they allow for a variety of possible structures, depending on circumstances. They have been subject to a number of criticisms, however: one is that of contingent determinism – that is, they specify which structure will be the most suitable in a particular situation. This would mean that all organizations faced with the same environment should have the same structure, yet this is not the case. Even within the constraints of a particular situation, management may exercise some degree of choice. John Child (1972) has argued against the notion that structures are *determined* by their contingent factors; rather, he argues, they *influence* the structure, but leaders and managers still have an important part to play. Thus he stressed the importance of management choice.

Another issue is that organizations are likely to face multiple contingencies (size, technology, environment and so on); how these combine and the effect they may have on the resultant structure could be complex and difficult to predict.

Overall, however, despite these limitations, it can be argued that contingency approaches help managers to gain a deeper understanding of complex situations affecting organizations and their structure.

8.9 Trends and issues in organizational structure

Organizational structure and individual behaviour

In Chapter 1 it was suggested that the subject of organizational behaviour involves the study of organizations and their design and functioning, as well as the behaviour of individuals and groups within them. These two elements will interact; thus not only is it people who design and run organizations, but the design and structure of organizations will influence the people within them.

In attempting to assess the influence of different forms and aspects of organizational structure on people, although some general trends can be discerned, we have to be careful about over-generalizing these; it very much depends on the particular individual and his or her preferences. Although some people will prefer the relative freedom and creativity of an organic organization, others will favour the relative order and predictability of mechanistic structures. This is what makes management both tricky and fascinating! We need to understand what makes each individual 'tick'.

We can illustrate the above with reference to two dimensions of structure: specialization and centralization. In general, evidence suggests that work *specialization* (assuming that a job is capable of being easily subdivided into discrete sub-elements or tasks) leads to higher productivity and lower job satisfaction (Robbins, Judge and Campbell 2010). Yet there are two provisos to this: if specialization is taken to such extremes that the job becomes boring and repetitive, then productivity is likely to suffer. Secondly, although the majority of people may prefer varied work, particularly as the workforce has become more educated and people seek work that is intrinsically satisfying (see Chapter 4 on motivation and engagement), there may well still be some individuals who prefer the repetitive nature of more routine jobs.

In addition, although there is evidence that organizations that are less centralized lead to workers having more autonomy and freedom, and this is positively linked to job satisfaction, there will still be individual differences in this, in that some individuals may find such environments ambiguous and confusing, and thus prefer the regularity and predictability of more centralized organizational structures.

> ### Reflective question
>
> How can the structure of an organization affect individual behaviour?

National culture and organizational structure

The work of authors such as Hofstede (1980) and Trompenaars and Hampden-Taylor (1999) has suggested that national culture makes an important contribution to organization and management. In terms of organizational structure, a study of 15 western European countries by the European Commission (quoted in Robbins, Judge and Campbell 2010: 447) found that in all the countries, apart from Greece, organic structures were more favoured than mechanistic ones. However, within this there were significant national variations: the Netherlands and Denmark had a particularly high preference for organic structures, whereas this was less the case for Portugal, Italy and Greece. Despite this variability, however, it was suggested that all were moving in the same direction in terms of structure, and that strategy, size, environment and technology were more important contingent factors than national culture.

Robbins, Judge and Campbell (2010) also point to studies that suggest national cultural differences in preferences with regard to structure. Thus people in countries with high power distance (Hofstede 1980), such as France, Greece and Latin America, are more accepting of mechanistic structures and hierarchy than those in countries with low power distance (see Section 10.7).

CASE STUDY The Aston studies 50 years on

On the 25th anniversary of the British Academy of Management Conference (13th–15th September 2011) at Aston Business School, Birmingham, some of the original researchers of the Aston studies held a symposium on learning from these studies. The ideas of two of the researchers, Derek Pugh and John Child, are outlined below.

Derek Pugh highlighted a fundamental lesson learned to be that of taking the structure seriously using a contingency approach, in contrast to institutional theorists, who suggest that all organizations in a particular sector will be very similar. He then outlined three key dilemmas or tensions of structure that organizations had to face:

1   The dilemma of centralization – or hierarchy versus participation. A clear hierarchy means that decision-making will be concentrated at the top, but this can result in what is actually put into practice lower down the organization being very different from the message given at the top. On the other hand, greater participation can lead to decision inertia – that is, decisions can be slow and difficult to reach because of the need to consult throughout the organization.

2   The dilemma of standardization – or standard routines versus encouraging personal ideas and contribution. The former gives predictability and consistency but may stifle initiative, while the latter may lead to wayward decisions and actions.

3   The dilemma of specialization – or specialist expertise versus common goals. Having a high degree of unit specialization can lead to units and departments each developing their own goals rather than pulling together, while stressing common goals and reducing unit specialization may result in 'groupthink', with everyone thinking along the same lines.

In deciding on the appropriateness of a particular structure, managers need to balance these tensions, and as the context changes, so does the point of balance. This leads to what is termed 'Pugh's paradox': 'All organizations have the weaknesses of their strengths' and 'All organizations have the strengths of their weaknesses' (as long as they are recognized as weaknesses).

In conclusion, Pugh suggests the need for a detailed analysis of the organization and its context, which will lead to determination of the best structure.

In his presentation, **John Child** reminded us of how organizations affect every aspect of our lives in some way. Most of us are born in an organization, educated and work in them, are affected as consumers and members of our communities by them, and ultimately are buried by them. This stresses the importance of organizations in and to society. Thus organizations and the study of them do matter, not just for reasons of management efficiency, but for wider societal reasons.

The key lesson Child pointed to was that one of the most consistent findings of the Aston studies was the strong association between size of organization, measured by total employment, and the number of levels of its hierarchy. This was found to be the case across a range of sectors: manufacturing, service and public agencies. Hierarchy thus appears to be difficult to avoid as organizations grow. Yet this association raises troubling questions in view of the socially and psychologically negative consequences of hierarchy.

The organizational dysfunctions of hierarchy have been well documented (see Section 8.3 on bureaucracy and classical management approaches, for example), yet there is less awareness of the negative social consequences of hierarchy. Child points to the recent riots in inner cities as just one manifestation of this. The remoteness of decision-making and growing income inequalities that tend to mirror one's position in the hierarchy (or, of course, outside of the organizational hierarchy altogether in direct terms in the case of the unemployed), Child argues, have had a negative effect on well-being and have led to a decline in the perceived legitimacy of social institutions and a decline in trust in our leaders, including our political leaders. This has led some to suggest a seemingly inevitable slide towards a post-democratic age.

Child quotes E.F. Schumacher, author of *Small is Beautiful*, in asking how we can seek to achieve smallness within large-scale organizations and thus mitigate the negative social effects of hierarchy, either directly, via delayering and downsizing, or indirectly, by developments such as employee ownership and partnerships, as in the case of John Lewis. Such direct and indirect forms may allow hierarchies, and thus organizations, to be brought within the ambit of society.

(Adapted from BAM 2011)

8.10 Summary

This chapter began by outlining what is meant by organizational structure, as well as reviewing the importance of structure in terms of the coordination of activities to achieve organizational goals. Early approaches to organizational design stressed formality and hierarchy, and bureaucracy was seen as the most efficient structure. Contingency approaches move away from a 'one best way' and suggest that the most effective structure will be determined by consideration of a number of important variables, including strategy, technology, size and environment. However, authors such as John Child have argued that, while such variables will influence structure, there is still room for management choice. The chapter also considered key elements and types of organizational structure, as well as relationships. Key trends and issues were also reviewed.

Key ideas

Organizational structure:

- Organizational structure can be defined as the way that work is divided and activities coordinated to achieve organizational goals.
- It provides managers with a formal system in which to control, coordinate and motivate employees.
- An appropriate structure makes good performance possible.

Approaches:

- Early approaches to organizational design stressed formality, hierarchy and rules.
- Bureaucracy was seen as the most efficient form of structure.
- Contingency approaches moved away from such ideas and suggested that the most effective structure could be determined by consideration of a number of key variables, including strategy, size, technology and environment.
- Some authors have argued that, while such variables will have an important *influence* on organizational structure, they will not *determine* it, and that there is still room for management choice in any particular set of circumstances.

Key elements, types and relationships:

- Key elements of structure are: division of work, hierarchy, span of control, chain of command, degree of formalization and centralization.

- Managers need to make decisions about each of these elements, based on the characteristics of the organization and the particular circumstances faced.
- Work tasks need to be divided up and activities co-ordinated. Jobs can be grouped together in various ways to result in different structural types, the chief of which are: by function, by product or service, and by geographical location.
- Real-world complexities mean that most large organizations will have mixed structures, examples being divisionalized and matrix structures.
- The main formal relationships in a structure are: line, staff and functional.
- Key aspects in terms of formal relationships are: authority, responsibility and accountability.
- These relationships relate to the formal aspects; alongside this there will be informal organizational relationships as well.

Trends and issues:

- Changes in the external environment have meant that organizations have had to be more flexible and able to make quicker decisions.
- This has led to more flexible organizational structures, including the use of project teams and loosely coupled organic structures.
- Structure has an important influence on individual employees.
- Although certain general tendencies can be discerned, in terms of which structural types will be preferred, there will still be individual differences in such preferences.
- Studies have shown that national culture has an influence on structure and on individual preferences in terms of structure.

Review questions

1. Why is a consideration of structure important to managers?
2. Outline the key characteristics of bureaucracy.
3. What is the relevance to managers today of early approaches to organizational design, such as those of Weber?
4. What is meant by 'span of control'?
5. What are the possible advantages and disadvantages of the matrix structure?
6. Outline the difference between *line* and *staff* relationships and give examples of each.
7. What is meant by the term 'the virtual organization'?
8. Compare and contrast 'mechanistic' and 'organic' organizations.
9. How and why will structure affect individual behaviour?
10. What were the key findings of the Aston studies in relation to structure?

Recommended reading

Grey, C. (2009) *A Very Short, Fairly Interesting and Reasonably Cheap Book About Studying Organizations* (2nd edn). London: Sage Publications.

Handy, C.B. (1999) *Understanding Organizations* (4th edn). Harmondsworth: Penguin Books.

Pugh, D.S. (1997) *Organization Theory: Selected Readings* (4th edn). Harmondsworth: Penguin Books.

Pugh, D.S. and Hickson, D.J. (2007) *Writers on Organizations* (6th edn). London: Penguin Books.

Useful websites

www.bam.ac.uk – provides information on events, conferences and journals of the British Academy of Management

www.derekpugh.com – Derek Pugh's website, includes the Pugh OD Matrix

References

BAM (2011) Conference Proceedings, 13th–15th September. London: British Academy of Management.

Buchanan, D.A. and Huczynski, A.A. (2010) *Organizational Behaviour* (7th edn). Harlow: Pearson Education.

Burns, T. and Stalker, G.M. (1961) *The Management of Innovation*. London: Tavistock Publications.

Castells, M. (2001) *The Internet Galaxy*. Oxford: Oxford University Press.

Child, J. (1972) 'Organizational structure, environment and performance: the role of strategic choice'. *Sociology*, 6(1), pp. 1–22.

Cole, G.A. and Kelly, P. (2011) *Management Theory and Practice* (7th edn). Andover: Cengage Learning.

Crainer, S. and Dearlove, D. (2003) *The Ultimate Business Guru Book*. Oxford: Capstone Publishing.

Drucker, P.F. (1989) *The Practice of Management*. Oxford: Heinemann Professional.

History: The Definitive Visual Guide (2007). London: Dorling Kindersley.

Hofstede, G. (1980) *Culture's Consequences: International Differences in Work-related Values*. London: Sage Publications.

Lundy, O. and Cowling, A. (1996) *Strategic Human Resource Management*. London: Routledge.

Mintzberg, H. (1979) *The Structuring of Organization*. London: Prentice-Hall.

Morgan, G. (1989) *Creative Organization Theory*. London: Sage Publications.

Mullins, L.J. (2010) *Management and Organizational Behaviour* (9th edn). Harlow: Pearson Education.

Pugh, D.S. and Hickson, D.J. (1976) *Organization Structure in its Context: The Aston Programme 1*. Farnborough: Gower.

Pugh, D.S. and Hickson, D.J. (2007) *Writers on Organizations* (6th edn). London: Penguin Books.

Robbins, S.P., Judge, T.A. and Campbell, T.T. (2010) *Organizational Behaviour*. Harlow: Pearson Education.

Trompenaars, F. and Hampden-Taylor, C. (1999) *Riding the Waves of Culture* (2nd edn). London: Nicholas Brealey Publishing.

9 Organizational culture and change

*I believe that the real difference between **success** and failure in a **corporation** can very often be traced to the question of how well the organization brings out the great **talents** of its people. What does it do to help these people find common cause with each other? And how can it sustain this common cause and sense of **direction** through the many changes which take place from one generation to another?* (THOMAS WATSON JR)

My starting point has always been 'change'. (ALVIN TOFFLER)

CHAPTER OUTLINE

1   Introduction

2   How is organizational culture defined?

3   Typologies of organizational culture

4   Change in organizations

5   Change models

6   Changing organizational culture

7   Summary

CHAPTER OBJECTIVES

By the end of this chapter you will understand:

- how to explain and define the meaning of the term 'organizational culture'

- the hidden and less visible aspects of culture

- the different types of and varying perspectives on culture

- the reasons why organizations may need to change, and the external and internal triggers driving change

- the process of achieving cultural change in organizations.

9.1 Introduction

Organizational culture: the shared values, norms and behaviours that guide how employees work within an organization and act as a cohesive force.

For many years, anthropologists have studied the norms, values and belief systems that emerge within groups of people living in the same country, region and society. These studies have demonstrated that such shared ways of behaving and thinking will also impact on the way that formal business organizations operate, and the communications and relationships of employees.

One of the most well-established studies of culture was that conducted by Geert Hofstede in the 1980s. His research identified that there were common belief systems in different countries around the world. In the same way that such systems emerge within a society or country, when people come together as employees to work within an organization, over time, patterns of behaving, common attitudes and norms become established. These patterns can clearly impact on the performance of organizations and they have provided a focus for many academic research studies since the 1980s. The popular book *In Search of Excellence* by Peters and Waterman (1982) explored the connection between the 'culture' of an organization and its performance, in an effort to find out what made organizations 'excellent'. They identified that the common features of a number of 'excellent' or highly successful organizations were related to cultural factors – the way people worked together and with their internal and external customers. Although this research attempted to put forward a 'recipe for success', it attracted many critics, particularly in relation to the research methodology employed and the fact that many of the companies identified as 'excellent' suffered a dip in performance not long after the publication of the book. These critics pointed out that having a fixed culture that cannot change was clearly a problem, and we will return to this aspect of change later in the chapter. What Peters and Waterman's research did achieve, however, was to raise awareness about the importance of the attitudes, behaviours and values of employees within the organization.

ACTIVITY

Organizational culture and you

To get us into thinking about the concept of **organizational culture**, imagine that you are starting work as an employee for a company and it is your first week. You will typically take part in an induction process, which will inform you of the ways of working within the organization. As the week progresses, you will begin to assimilate, through interaction with other employees, the accepted ways of working and behaving within the company. This can be as simple as the way you dress, the way you answer the phone, the way that you communicate with others and whether employees take a lunch break. Over the first few weeks you will begin to be more aware of the established norms – for example, whether employees come in early and stay late and the values that the company adheres to. New starters soon learn whether they can fit in and feel comfortable with the way of operating; if everything continues to feel strange for the new employee, an 'induction crisis' can occur, when they may choose to exit the organization very quickly. This experience fits into the domain of organizational culture.

9.2 How is organizational culture defined?

A classic definition is provided by Deal and Kennedy (1982), who suggest that culture is 'the way we do things around here'. This definition captures the concept, as organizational culture is all about attitudes, values and beliefs that employees share. Although the focus of Hofstede's (1984) work was the wider culture in society, his definition of national culture highlights the critical aspect of 'learning' in relation to culture: 'a body of learned behaviour, a collection of beliefs, habits and traditions, shared by a group of people and learned by people'. New recruits to an organization have to 'learn' the ways of behaving and must partially accept this or leave.

Culture is sometimes seen as something that binds people together – for example, 'organizational culture can be thought of as glue that holds an organization together through a sharing of patterns of meaning. The culture focuses on the values, beliefs, and expectations that members come to share' (Siehl and Martin 1984, cited in Butler and Rose 2011: 353).

Culture has a vital role to play in organizations, as it moulds and shapes the way that people behave, both internally and with the external environment, which includes customers and stakeholders. Yet culture is difficult to explain because it is rather like jelly – it is moulded and set, but it is a struggle to grasp it. Another complication with the concept is that organizations do not employ people to become automatons and all act the same, but they do expect employees to conform.

In summary, culture is a vehicle through which an organization's identity emerges in terms of what it stands for, how employees should behave and what it believes in.

Another way to think about organization culture has been put forward by Schein (1992, cited in Knights and Willmott 2007), in the form of an iceberg, which has only a relatively small part of its total mass visible above the water. Using this metaphor, some elements of culture can be seen and are easily accessible. Other elements of culture are hidden beneath the surface, often not written down and become apparent only once an employee is socialized into the way of working.

Some of the **visible aspects** are:

- the uniform or style of dress
- the products and services offered
- the stated vision and mission of the organization
- the structure and hierarchy, the atmosphere and physical environment
- formal communications and policies and procedures
- mottoes and stories, language and jargon.

Hidden elements include:

- power and politics
- informal subcultures
- leadership style
- values, attitudes and beliefs.

To illustrate some of these aspects of visible and hidden culture, it is useful to consider some company examples.

TABLE 9.1 Culture in action

Company	Culture
John Lewis	Has a motto of 'never knowingly undersold' (**www.johnlewis.com**).
Nando's	Every restaurant manager is known as a 'patraos', Portuguese for head of the family (Evans 2010).
White Stuff	This retailer refers to benefits and perks as 'benny' and 'perky' (*Sunday Times* Best Companies to Work For 2011: 41).
Innocent	The office of the drinks company Innocent is set on a field of AstroTurf with huge parasols. The open-plan office is designed to give the feel of an English village fair, and is furnished with picnic benches, table football and a red phone box. People can socialize in the beer garden and the environment reflects the slightly quirky approach to business. The head office is known as Fruit Towers. There are hanging basket chairs and sofas in a chill-out area for employees to have a quiet break. 'To keep things open, mix people up and keep them close to each other, but also give them space to escape. Every six months there is a desk reshuffle to encourage bonding of staff and the sharing of knowledge and ideas. A fundamental concept driving the culture at Innocent is "collaboration" in order to create innovation' (Evans 2010).
Lush	An ethical cosmetics company with the mission statement 'We believe in happy people, making happy soap, putting our faces on our products and making our mums proud'. Founder and 'guardian' of the brand, Mark Constantine, operates the company on a set of strong values and moral principles. A fundamental belief is that products will NOT be tested on animals, only humans. The company adopts a strong ethical stance in terms of charity work and helping the communities that supply its ingredients. The products are virtually preservative-free and unpackaged. There is a very strong environmental agenda with a 'recognition' culture in that Lush acknowledges staff who have gone the extra mile in different ways, including a 'star of the day' award, and a prize shelf of gifts and products in every store to choose from. (adapted from *Sunday Times* Best Companies to Work For 2011: 58).

Some examples of organizational values in practice

If we take a further look at **Innocent**, it provides an interesting example of the underlying organizational values on which the company is based.

Our purpose: to make natural, delicious food and drink, that helps people live well and die old.

Our long-term vision: the earth's favourite food company.

We have one core principle around which we base all our decisions: create a business we can be proud of. We have broken this down into five simple values, each reflecting what we are, how we do things, and where we increasingly want to be:

- Be natural
  We want to make 100% natural, delicious, healthy stuff, 100% of the time.
- Be entrepreneurial
  We chase every opportunity … We want to be creative and challenge the status quo.

- | Be responsible
    We have to be conscious of the consequences of our actions, in both the short and the long term.
- | Be commercial
    Creating growth and profit for us and our customers is central.
- | Be generous
    With our feedback for others … with rewards when people deliver, and with our charitable support.

(**www.innocentdrinks.co.uk/careers/business/purpose/**)

Often the values are more difficult to access unless you work for an organization and become socialized into the ways of working. The following two quotes are taken from the websites of Marks & Spencer and B&Q. While these are clearly going to be presented as positive, they do give some flavour of what it is like to work for each organization.

The following quote is from an employee of **Marks & Spencer**.

> There is a definite culture to stay once you're part of the team, and you get a sense that people are very loyal to the company. A lot of that has to do with the fact there are so many opportunities to develop new skills and progress within the business. Plus Marks & Spencer works very hard to offer its people a good work/life balance, no matter what level they're at.
>
> For once in my life I can truly say that I enjoy going to work every day, and I really like the buzz you feel all around the store. And because Marks & Spencer really believes its people are its most valued asset, this creates an environment where everyone enjoys coming to work. (**http://corporate.marksandspencer.com/mscareers/opportunities/store_roles/retail_management**)

The following quote is from an employee of **B&Q**.

> B&Q's culture is the best I've experienced yet. It is made up of a combination of down-to-earth and personable people, with approachable and friendly managers who are genuinely proud to be a part of B&Q. This really makes you feel welcome and part of the team from day one. Seeing people's enthusiasm is brilliant and I've been very impressed by the culture at B&Q. (**www.diy.com/diy/jsp/corporate/content/careers/our_people/stories.jsp**).

ACTIVITY

In small groups, consider the aspects of culture provided in the company examples above and show where they fit on Schein's iceberg model. Now think about the culture of your university/college, and list some of the visible aspects of culture and what you consider to be the more hidden, underlying values and beliefs that exist. In your group, instead of using an iceberg to illustrate organizational culture, create your own visual image to represent your version of culture.

Identify some of the limitations of taking the published aspects of culture provided above as a 'true' indication of the culture of these organizations. What other questions might you want to ask to find out more?

From the discussion above and work conducted within your group, you will begin to see that organizational culture is a complex concept, with observable, accessible aspects and hidden, deeper elements that are often 'taken for granted' and therefore more difficult to identify. It would also be too simplistic to believe that if we were to interview all employees within one organization they would say the same thing about what it is like to work there, or that there is one dominant culture in every organization. Rather, as in any society, it is more likely that within one organization there will be several subcultures that employees perceive and identify with, depending on the position and status of the individual.

In addition, there is an interesting debate about culture within academic circles. For example, some view organizational culture as something that can be managed, adapted and changed by senior management, in an effort to become more competitive. Culture, from this perspective, is often viewed as 'corporate culture'. (For a further insight into this view, take a look at the work of Kotter and Heskett 1992; Deal and Kennedy 1982.) Others see organizational culture as emerging and growing as the company develops, and the norms, attitudes and values become established as part of the history, past actions and successes of the organization. Taking this view of organizational culture would mean that it would be very difficult to change from the top down, as it is so enmeshed within the roots of the organization. (For an interesting explanation of these approaches, and to explore this aspect of organizational culture in more depth, review the work of Smircich 1983; Martin 1992.)

While we do not intend to discuss this aspect further in this chapter, it is worth recalling that in Chapter 1 we did indicate that this book has adopted a more managerial viewpoint, and as such culture is viewed as something that can be changed. This is discussed later.

9.3 Typologies of organizational culture

Typology: a classification system, or a way of grouping together different cultures, to provide a framework for reviewing culture.

Even though there might be several cultures in operation within one organization, it can be helpful to broadly classify the type of culture that predominates. There are many different typologies or classification systems describing organizational culture. A well-established typology is that presented by Handy (1993). He drew on the work of Harrison (1972) and presented four different types of culture deriving from the way that the organization was structured.

TABLE 9.2 Handy's typologies of culture

Typology of culture	Description
Power culture	Often found in small organizations with central control by a limited number of key individuals. Few rules, procedures and systems. Face-to-face communications and fast decision-making. For example, a small family business.
Role culture	Typical of bureaucratic organizations. Lots of rules and regulations in place to control how employees operate. Power is allocated according to level in the hierarchy. People work to a job description and their position in the organization is their source of power. For example, a local council, government departments.

Typology of culture	Description
Task culture	Often depicted as a matrix organization where people work in teams to achieve projects. Task is key rather than the individual. Knowledge and expertise are more important than position in a hierarchy. The organization can be viewed as a network where there is freedom and flexibility to move between teams and tasks. For example, management consultants.
Person culture	This occurs in few organizations. Individuals are the central focus and the structure is designed around them. For example, a group of architects who join together in a practice, where they might share office space and administration, but all operate individually in their own area of specialism; a chamber of barristers.

The link that Handy made to the type of culture and the way that the organization is structured points to the possibility that culture might be dependent on the different context of an organization, with large public sector organizations needing more in the way of rules and bureaucracy than a small private sector family business, for example. Handy also implied that there may be signs of the four different types in existence within one organization.

ACTIVITY

Think of an organization where you have worked and try to use Handy's typology to describe the culture. Does the organization clearly fit into one type of culture, or have you found that there are examples of other types of culture in existence? Compare what you have found with another student. What conclusions can you draw from this exercise?

Reflecting on the last activity, you may have found that culture can be a unifying experience or an unsettling one, with conflicts and clashes between subcultures in an organization. A deeper perspective of culture, demonstrating the complexity surrounding the concept, is put forward by Martin (2006, cited in Matthew and Ogbonna 2009). Martin proposes the 'three perspective framework' of culture, which 'simultaneously captures the unifying aspects of culture, the sub-cultural themes, as well as the contradictions in organizational life' (Martin 2006, cited in Matthew and Ogbonna 2009: 658). The three perspectives are:

- **integration perspective** – the shared beliefs, values and attitudes holding the organization together
- **differentiation perspective** – the differences in the way people behave and think in an organization, particularly within subgroups, and the conflicts and clashes that can exist as people interpret prevailing norms in different ways
- **fragmentation perspective** – portrayed as when there is ambiguity, a lack of clarity and therefore confusion as to how to behave and act within an organization. So employees will drift between subcultures and can feel left out and confused as to what the accepted norms are.

To summarize organizational culture, it is a multifaceted concept, with varying levels of complexity, making culture a constant challenge for organizations to tackle. Yet we know that a major focus for change within organizations often involves cultural transformation.

9.4 Change in organizations

Since the economic downturn in 2007/8 and the 'credit crunch', if we were to summarize what is happening within the world of business, the main aspect would be about 'change'. Organizations have had to restructure, reduce in size, make employees redundant or merge with other companies to increase their chance of success, and change their product range and the services they offer to keep providing what their customers demand. Just watch the news every morning for one week and you will note that many companies have to adapt what they do to keep afloat. The rising cost of fuel, increasing restrictions on bank lending, increased global competition, lack of skills in the labour market, problems with the euro, and so on have all had a dramatic impact on how organizations operate. Those organizations with the ability to change and adapt quickly are more likely to be able to survive in this turbulent climate. Changes required by organizations that are driven by external forces are often not planned for, but the organization that deals effectively with such pressures is likely to survive.

On the other hand, as organizations become established, grow and develop, the top management team may deliberately and strategically plan that certain internal changes are necessary to ensure that the business remains successful. These proactive changes require careful implementation to ensure that employees are 'on board'.

ACTIVITY

In small groups, list all the reasons why an organization may need to change. Organize your list into **external** factors creating the need to change, and **internal** factors driving the need to change.

Some of the reasons your group might have highlighted in the last activity are:

- changes in global markets (external)
- tough trading conditions because of the economy (external)
- changes in technology (external)
- customer pressure (external)
- new legislation (external)
- high level of labour turnover (internal)
- increasing number of accidents (internal)
- need to learn new skills (internal).

(Adapted from CIPD 2010)

Separating external factors from internal triggers for change may be artificial. Hughes (2006) discusses the lack of consensus about what triggers change and suggests that this will differ according to the context. For example, the demands by the UK government and media on tackling the growing obesity problem is an external driver for companies making chocolate, which have to respond by considering internal change, such as the production of reduced-size chocolate bars and altering the ingredients.

If we consider all the changes listed above, many of them relate to changing people and their attitudes and behaviours, which, according to Balogen and Hope Hailey (2008: 2), often requires a 'significant investment in terms of managerial time and energy as well as financial investment'. From our discussion of culture, we know that people act and behave in an organization in set ways, forming the cultural 'glue' that establishes how things are done, but in these dynamic and uncertain times, this glue sometimes needs to be loosened to allow the organization to do things in a different way and respond to changing market conditions.

The *Managing Change Survey* conducted by IRS Employment Review (2010) asked 114 different organizations what type of change they were implementing. Interestingly, 80 per cent of respondents were embarking on cultural change programmes in an effort to change cultural values and leadership. Research by the CIPD (2010), however, suggests that less than 60 per cent of change initiatives involving restructuring the organization achieved the anticipated outcomes. Much has been written about the management of change, and in the next section we will explore some of the academic change models and company practices to illustrate the sorts of challenges that are faced.

 ## 9.5 Change models

> **Change models:** these are frameworks designed to allow a systematic analysis of a change situation.

KEY TERM

Two famous, but much criticized, models of change were put forward by the psychologist Kurt Lewin (1890–1947) in 1947. Lewin was particularly interested in how people responded to change, and how patterns of attitudes and behaviours required attention during the change process. One model that he proposed was the **three-step model of change** (see Table 9.3):

TABLE 9.3 Lewin's three-step model of change

1. Unfreeze	2. Move	3. Refreeze
Establish a clear reason for the need to change. Ensure that the driving forces of change outweigh the restraining and negative elements (see Lewin's force field analysis model, which follows).	Make the changes through altering, reconfiguring tasks and processes, and changing the actions and behaviours of people and technology.	Reinforce the behaviours through recognition and reward. Review results and make modifications where necessary.

Lewin recommended that those managing change should be aware of the process that successful change involves. He suggested that unless there is clarity about the need for and the benefits of the change, and the required outcome, change initiatives can often fail to deliver. His force field analysis model is also well established, and is used in conjunction with his three-step model.

Lewin designed the **force field analysis model** (see Table 9.4) as a management tool to help analyse the need for change.

The model can be used to identify the factors that support the reason for change, thus helping those involved to think about why it is necessary and what the benefits will be. The restraining forces provide a framework for identifying what the barriers might be to achieving change in practice.

TABLE 9.4 Lewin's force field analysis model

Driving forces pushing change	Restraining forces against change
Clear management goals	Individual and group employee resistance
Stable employee relations	Structural issues
Clear vision and objectives for change	Leadership weaknesses
Available resources	Systems, processes and habits
External pressures – competition	Entrenched interests of stakeholders
Employee adaptability	Lack of resources
Economies of scale	Threat to power bases
Clearer management control	Organizational culture

CASE STUDY   Change in action

The authors interviewed a sales team who worked for an organization that was relocating from three different geographical areas to one central location. This was the story they told.

The change was communicated by senior management and the HR director 18 months prior to the move. A 'relocation champion' was assigned to each department, tasked with identifying any concerns that the staff within that department had and communicating them to the team managing the relocation. Regular updates were announced as the changes progressed.

Initially, there was much resistance to the change, as many staff did not see why the move was necessary, and rumours began to spread that there would be no parking spaces at the new central location, where parking charges within the town were very high. This caused anger and frustration with many staff, and some started to look for new jobs elsewhere.

Within one month of the move taking place, having lost several highly skilled members of staff already, the organization announced that the employees affected by the move were to be offered an incentive in the form of a contribution to their additional mileage and travel costs that they would be entitled to claim for one year following the move. In addition, just two or three weeks prior to the move taking place, an announcement was made that there were more parking spaces available for staff than originally thought, and that all permanent staff could apply for a space for a small annual charge. This announcement caused much relief and staff began to pack up their offices and embrace the change.

Following several prearranged tours of the new location for groups of staff to familiarize themselves with their new offices and working environment, the move took place smoothly and employees settled in well.

Q 1 Using Lewin's force field analysis model, identify the possible factors driving this change and the restraining forces.

2 Plot the stages of the move along the *three-step model* and identify some ideas about how this change could have been handled differently to avoid staff losses.

The case study illustrates how a relatively straightforward change such as relocation can be impeded by staff anxieties and fears. The intentions of senior management were clearly that there should be open communication throughout, but concerns over transport and travel costs and parking (the **hygiene** factors that were discussed in Chapter 4) created a dissatisfied and disgruntled workforce. Figure 9.1 shows Elisabeth Kubler-Ross's change curve, which she produced in 1969 in her book *On Death and Dying*, on handling grief. It helps to explain the emotional stages that employees went through during this change initiative.

FIGURE 9.1 Elisabeth Kubler-Ross's change curve

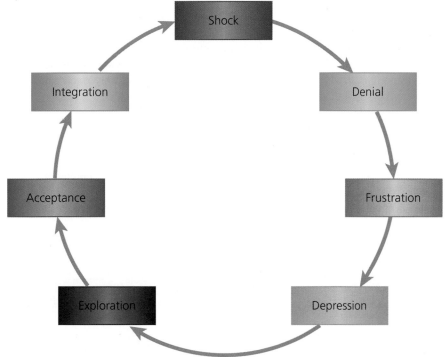

 ## 9.6 Changing organizational culture

While the last case study illustrates a relatively straightforward physical change of location, it was clear that, despite the good intentions of senior management, the human factor had been underestimated. With more complex change initiatives, such as efforts to change the culture of an organization, the attitudes, norms and behaviours of employees will be the fundamental aspects that require change. Some of the strategies used to overcome resistance to change include:

- education and communication – involving employees by gaining their ideas and sharing the senior team's views
- training and development – running workshops to establish new ways of working
- facilitation – through coaching and policies that make the change more palatable
- consultation and negotiation – working with trade unions or established representative groups, using employee attitude surveys to gain an insight into current thinking
- coercion and discipline – forcing the change through, threats to job security and using changes to contracts of employment.

The following company examples illustrate how cultural change was achieved in practice. In reading these, try to identify some of the approaches listed above in the way that each company went about cultural change.

CASE STUDY   Cultural change in action at Novo Nordisk

Novo Nordisk was featured in an article in *People Management* in September 2011, which explored how the company had taken action to reinforce the corporate culture and generate a commitment to business ethics and environmental responsibility (Smedley 2011). The company had grown rapidly over the past ten years, with 30,000 employees operating in 81 countries, and as it expanded senior management were determined to 'develop and maintain' what they described as their 'special culture'.

To reaffirm the 'Novo Nordisk way', the CEO embarked on a 'talking tour' of the company, in which he captured the essence of what this meant to employees through face-to-face interviews and asked employees how they saw the company in the future. A concise and accessible document was published to illustrate what the 'Novo Nordisk way' means in practice, and every three years an internal team audits how closely each unit acts according to these values and principles.

Such efforts have helped to create what the company describes as a 'unified' culture as it expands. Novo Nordisk clearly manages its culture rather than leaves it to chance. The executive vice president for corporate relations, Lise Kingo, comments: 'You could say that we handle company culture just as concretely as we handle financial performance.'

CASE STUDY   Cultural change in action at Bombardier

Bombardier has concentrated on building a world-class culture. It has transformed its culture from one 'driven by engineering and manufacturing goals, with deep cultural divisions, to one focused on customers, an engaged work force and continuous improvement'. An interview carried out by McKinsey reveals some of the ways that this was achieved (Simpson 2011).

The company established through an employee survey that there was a mismatch between customer expectations and employee priorities. It was also clear that there was a gap in perceptions about strategic plans, goals and what the company valued. Managers revealed a blame culture and a lot of subcultures, with a strong task focus and minimal teamwork.

The company acknowledged that with 30,000 employees worldwide, culture change was going to take time. They identified some small 'quick win' projects, to demonstrate the changes needed; these were managed by project champions who had been trained in the new ways of working. The successes of these projects helped to persuade the doubters. Communication was key throughout, as well as training employees in new ways of working, and coaching and supporting them.

The company aimed to blend the technical hard skills with a soft people focus, encouraging people to work in teams in order to implement improvements in the organization to achieve their goal of becoming 'world class'.

 ## 9.7 Summary

From the discussion presented it can be seen that culture is a critical aspect of organizational life, yet it is difficult to define and control. Culture pervades every organization and influences people's attitudes and behaviours at work and the way they perform their daily activities. Given a continually changing environment, organizations need to ensure that they are capable of adapting and responding, and cultural transformation has become a key strategic tool to achieve this. Academic research into culture and culture change highlights the challenges facing organizations when trying to change deeply embedded attitudes, values and beliefs. The company examples provided in this chapter illustrate how some organizations have attempted to transform ways of working and control and manage culture, but every employee is a complex individual, and such change is difficult to achieve and sustain.

Key ideas

- Culture is a body of beliefs, habits, norms, attitudes and values shared and learned by people and providing a template for behaving in an organization.

- It is argued that there are visible aspects of culture that are easily accessible, and other aspects that are hidden and harder to uncover.

- Typologies of culture suggest that cultures can be classified by their specific characteristics.

- Some writers argue that there are different lenses through which culture can be viewed. This can be from a harmonious viewpoint (integration perspective), or through the subcultures in an organization (differentiation perspective), or from the point of view of ambiguity (fragmentation perspective).

- Reasons for change can be considered by reviewing the internal/external triggers driving the need to do things differently.

- Lewin's models on change provide a framework and analytical tools by which the process of change can be reviewed.

- Strategies for changing culture include clear communication, consultation, training and development, along with more negative approaches that can involve coercion and discipline.

Review questions

1. Culture is defined by Deal and Kennedy (1982) as 'the way we do things around here'. If this is the case, what do you think this means in practice?

2. Differentiate between the visible aspects of culture and the hidden elements of organizational culture.

3. Some argue that culture can be managed by an organization, while others suggest that culture emerges as the organization grows and develops. What do you think, and why?

4. Using Handy's typology, consider the advantages and drawbacks of working in an organization classified as having a role culture.

5. The current economic downturn is requiring many organizations to cut costs and operate more effectively and efficiently with less. Identify some of the ways in which an organization could achieve this.

6. When organizations introduce change, why might individual employees be hostile?

Recommended reading

Evans, R. (2010) 'Wish you worked here'. *People Management*, 17th June.

Simpson, B. (2011) 'Flying people not planes'. The CEO of Bombardier on building a world-class culture. *McKinsey Quarterly*, March. (Available at www.mckinseyquarterly.com)

Smedley, T. (2011) 'On my agenda'. *People Management*, September, pp. 30–3.

Useful websites

www.personneltoday.com – provides access to related online articles covering subjects such as employment, training and legal issues

www.thetimes100.co.uk – provides company examples of good practice and case studies that show how organizations attempt to manage and develop their culture and what impact this can have on people at work

References

Balogen, J. and Hope Hailey, V. (2008) *Exploring Strategic Change*. Harlow: FT Prentice Hall.

Butler, M. and Rose, E. (eds.) (2011) *Introduction to Organizational Behaviour*. London: Chartered Institute of Personnel and Development.

CIPD (2010) 'Change management'. Factsheet. London: Chartered Institute of Personnel and Development. (Available at www.cipd.co.uk)

Deal, T. and Kennedy, A. (1982) *Corporate Culture*. Reading: Addison-Wesley.

Evans, R. (2010) 'Wish you worked here'. *People Management*, 17th June, pp. 18–22.

Handy, C.B. (1993) *Understanding Organizations* (4th edn). London: Penguin.

Harrison, R. (1972) 'Understanding your organization's character'. *Harvard Business Review*, May/June, pp. 119–28.

Hofstede, G. (1984) *Culture's Consequences: International Differences in Work-related Values*. London: Sage.

Hofstede, G. (2001) *Culture's Consequences* (2nd edn). Thousand Oaks, CA: Sage.

Hughes, M. (2006) *Change Management: A Critical Perspective*. London: Chartered Institute of Personnel and Development.

IRS Employment Review (2010) *Managing Change Survey 2010: The Role of HR*. (Available at www.xperthr.co.uk/article/104626/.aspx)

Knights, D. and Willmott, H. (2007) *Introducing Organizational Behaviour and Management*. London: Thomson Learning.

Kotter, J.P. and Heskett, J.L. (1992) *Corporate Culture and Performance*. New York: Free Press.

Kubler-Ross, E. (1969) *On Death and Dying*. New York: Touchstone.

Lewin, K. (1947) 'Frontiers in group dynamics'. In Cartwright, D. (ed.) (1952) *Field Theory in Social Sciences*. London: Social Science Paperbacks.

Martin, J. (1992) *Cultures in Organizations: Three Perspectives*. New York: Oxford University Press.

Matthew, J. and Ogbonna, E. (2009) 'Organizational culture and commitment: a study of an Indian software organization'. *International Journal of Human Resource Management*, 20(3), March, pp. 654–75.

Peters, T.J. and Waterman, R.H. (1982) *In Search of Excellence: Lessons from America's Best-run Companies*. New York: Harper & Row.

Simpson, B. (2011) 'Flying people not planes'. The CEO of Bombardier on building a world-class culture. *McKinsey Quarterly*, March. (Available at www.mckinseyquarterly.com)

Smedley, T. (2011) 'On my agenda'. *People Management*, September, pp. 30–3.

Smircich, L. (1983) 'Concepts of culture and organizational analysis'. *Administrative Science Quarterly*, 28(3), pp. 339–58.

Sunday Times Best Companies to Work For 2011 (ed. McCall, A.) *Sunday Times*, 6th March. (Available at www.thetimes100.co.uk)

Contemporary trends and developments in organizational behaviour 10

*People, especially the **best educated** and **most skilled**, increasingly see themselves as sole proprietors of their skills and abilities – free agents.* (BRUCE TULGAN)

Although companies are fond of saying 'people are our most important asset', when it comes to backing those words with action, few do. (JEFFREY PFEFFER)

***Creativity**, not capital, is now the principal constraint in **business** formation.* (THOMAS PETZINGER JR)

I'm finding that, especially in management studies and business, people are often too quick to promote the rational over the emotional. (IAN MITROFF)

CHAPTER OBJECTIVES

By the end of this chapter you will understand:

● emerging issues impacting on organizational behaviour

● the debates surrounding these issues

● the latest thinking and trends that may influence the individual in the workplace.

10.1 Introduction

Each chapter of this book has raised a number of key issues in organizational behaviour, some new and some ongoing. Topics have included emotional intelligence and employee engagement, transformational and distributed leadership, new technologies and the virtual organization. Some major themes emerge, including change and continuity, learning from the past in order to better tackle current and future issues, global interconnectedness and ethical considerations.

Work is a crucial part of life, and the relationship that individuals have with work is established as society develops and grows. In challenging economic times, work takes on a different perspective, particularly for those who have lost their jobs or been made redundant. Having the opportunity for paid work is critical for sustaining an economy, and for the self-esteem and confidence of individuals living within society. Also, for those surviving downsizing or organizational restructuring, the nature of individual job roles often changes. We spend a sizeable proportion of our waking hours at work, and with changes in the Default Retirement Age 2011 introduced in the UK recently, it seems that in the future we will be working for longer. This chapter explores some new perspectives on work and organizational life, and provides some insights into the changing face of work.

 ## 10.2 Work/life balance

> **KEY TERM**
>
> **Work/life balance:** the equilibrium that an individual may seek to achieve between work and non-work commitments.

Changes in the workplace have created a growing interest in the notion of work/life balance. This concept is widely recognized and embraces the idea of employees having some control over how, when and where they work, in order for them to juggle work demands with their non-work lives. A classic definition is provided by Clutterbuck (2003):

Work/life balance is about:

- being aware of different demands on time and energy
- having the ability to make choices in the allocation of time and energy
- knowing what values to apply to choices
- making choices.

The driving forces compelling organizations to pay attention to work/life balance include the following:

- **The changing profile of the workforce** – for example, with more women in the labour market and an ageing population, it is increasingly common for workers to have caring responsibilities outside the workplace. The CIPD (2010) highlights the fact that there are more women in the labour market, 68 per cent of whom have dependent children. In addition, there is what is termed the 'sandwich generation', who also have dependent care challenges – eldercare, people with disabilities and long-term illnesses. Currently there are 20 million people aged 50 and over in the UK, and by 2030 this figure is expected to reach 27 million, representing a 37 per cent increase (**www.acas.org.uk**).
- **Full-time mothers** – in the past 20 years, more full-time mothers have gone back to work, and they potentially have a greater need for a good work/life balance. This is

confirmed by a 2011 survey by the BBC (2011a), showing that 88 per cent of mothers feel guilty about their work/life balance and how much time they can give their children.

- **Dual earners and single parents** – Chang, McDonald and Burton (2010) suggest that there are greater numbers of 'dual-earners' in the workplace and single parents requiring workplace flexibility.

- **Increasing work intensification** – it has been found that approximately one in six workers works over 60 hours a week, while 29 per cent of employees with high stress levels work ten hours over the contracted amount every week (**www.unison.org.uk**).

- **The expectations of new generations** – Generation Y (those born between 1977 and 1991) make up over 25 per cent of the UK workforce, and research into their expectations suggests that they 'don't live for work … they work to live' (Anushka 2008). Hewlett (2011) reported that 60 per cent of employees regard work/life balance as one of the most important aspects when considering a role. In an article by the Institute of Leadership and Management, McAllister (2011) suggests that the standard working day of nine to five will no longer exist in the future, as flexibility becomes the norm.

- **Changing legislation** – in April 2003, the government introduced the 'right to request flexible working'. This originally gave parents with a child aged under six (or parents of a disabled child under the age of 18) the right to request flexible working arrangements from their employer. This right to request has been extended, from April 2007, to the carers of certain categories of adults; and from April 2009 to the parents of children under 17 years of age. In April 2010, similar procedures were introduced to enable employees to request some flexibility with time off work, to enable them to undertake study or training (CIPD 2011).

- **Employers' perspective** – work/life balance initiatives are a valuable recruitment and retention tool. Utilizing a flexible labour force has enabled employers to extend their service delivery to customers, to meet the demands of a 24/7 society.

- **Global economic downturn** – some organizations have used more flexible working opportunities to save on wage costs and have offered part-time working arrangements or sabbaticals as a means of avoiding or minimizing redundancies.

- **Technological changes** – the changing face of technology allows people to work from home, but still remain connected to the workplace, for example.

The drivers discussed above present organizations with new challenges and opportunities for organizing work and rethinking behaviour patterns, beyond the traditional nine-to-five routine. In addition, employers have had to rethink the employer–employee relationship, in order to achieve the best level of performance.

CASE STUDY   An insight into company practice

Google offers 'time away from the office', which enables employees to take time off in times of need; 'supporting families', which enables extended maternity and paternity leave; and 'giving and being green', which enables employees to take time off work to volunteer (**www.google.ca/jobs/lifeatgoogle/benefits**).

PricewaterhouseCoopers (PwC) was listed as the best employer for 2010 by *The Times* (**www.thetimes100.co.uk**). In order to maximize flexibility, the company offers 'PwC Lifestyle', which enables employees to cope with life events such as caring and parenting, work/life integration, health and fitness, finances, and managing time and stress.

Tesco offers lifestyle breaks, study support, foster care support, fertility treatment breaks, child care vouchers and flexible working options, for example (IDS HR Studies 2008).

In return for offering more work/life balance initiatives and flexibility, there is no doubt that organizations expect a return on their investment. Research confirms that offering work/life balance schemes can change behaviour at work in a positive way. For example, organizations have experienced reduced levels of absenteeism, higher levels of productivity, better customer service and increased retention of staff. An employee survey carried out for CIPD in conjunction with the London School of Economics, the University of Surrey, the University of London and Kingston University in 2010 found that workers on flexible contracts tend to be more engaged than others, in relation to both the extent and the frequency of engagement.

A clear debate exists, however, between the positive implications of adopting work/life balance initiatives in the workplace and the counterarguments that such practices can create tensions in the workplace. Some of these debates are outlined below:

- Taylor (2010) suggests that variations between different employee terms and conditions can result in tensions and disintegration into subcultures. An example would be complaints from 'singletons' left holding the fort!

- Budd and Mumford (2006, cited in Heywood, Siebert and Wei 2010) make it clear that firms can provide 'family-friendly benefits but actually discourage their use'. So opportunities may exist, but are not meaningful in terms of actual practice.

- Do work/life balance opportunities exist for everyone? It is argued that work/life balance appears to be a privilege of the highly educated in top jobs, who have the option to choose where they work. In contrast, many employees working in low-paid and low-status jobs do not have such an option (Torrington *et al.* 2011).

- Mullins (2010) notes problems such as family-friendly schemes still being perceived as concessions to women.

- Line managers often have fears about reorganizing work and understaffing (Torrington *et al.* 2011).

CASE STUDY Is work/life balance for women only?

The literature on work/life balance often refers to 'family-friendly policies', and many initiatives appear to be centred on family responsibilities. Interestingly, Centrica (2009) reported that:

- 53 per cent of its flexible workers are male
- 60 per cent of employees work flexibly, including senior managers
- 57 per cent of employees sacrificing part of their salary for child care vouchers were male.

Q In a labour market where males and females have almost equal representation, identify some ways that organizations can encourage a wider take-up of work/life balance initiatives.

In summary, the debate on the advantages and challenges of work/life balance will continue. Some academics, such as Gregory and Milner (2009), suggest that there is a trade-off between work and life, and argue that the term 'balance' would be better replaced with the term 'integration'. There is concern in the literature that the term 'balance' suggests that we are all able to achieve equilibrium between work and life domains (Campbell-Clark 2000). In practice, others argue, work/family conflict would provide a more realistic focus, as work often creates conflict or interference with family and vice versa (Greenhaus and Powell 2006).

An interesting interpretation to emerge is that of 'work/life culture', which can be defined in a similar way to the concept of organizational culture, relating to a set of shared behaviours that is shaped through the way the organization supports and values the integration of employees' work and family lives (Chang, McDonald and Burton 2010).

It is clear that the boundary between work and home life has become blurred. As organizations face the growing need of employees to harmonize their home and work domains, they will need to be proactive in developing strategies to support employees in their quest.

10.3 Happiness at work

Happiness and unhappiness have become popular topics for discussion, with TV programmes and magazine articles covering themes such as 'how married people can stay happy', 'be happy during the credit crunch' or 'eat your way to happiness' (Warr and Clapperton 2010: 7). At a national level, Richard Layard, an economist at the London School of Economics, has advised the government on societal happiness and well-being. Such advisers and policymakers not only want to raise the rate of employment in the economy, they want to raise the rate of enjoyment as well (*The Economist* 2006). Yet we find little coverage dealing with how to be happy in your job, even though many of us spend more than a third of our waking hours at work.

At first glance, work does not appear to provide particularly fertile ground as a route to happiness. Dictionary definitions of work include reference to 'what a person has to do', 'action involving effort or exertion directed to a definite end, especially as a means of gaining one's livelihood; labour, toil', while economics traditionally views work as a chore: people sell their labour at the expense of their leisure time. This mirrors the ancient Greeks' view of work, in the sense of providing the basic necessities of life, as a degrading activity that was to be allocated to the lowest orders of social life, especially to slaves. They gave primacy to leisure activities over work. Such views are summed up well in a line by the poet Philip Larkin (1922–85): 'Why should I let the toad work squat on my life?'

Yet historically there are also more positive conceptions of work as a means to happiness. Thomas Carlyle (1588–1679) stated that 'work is good; it truly is a motive for life', and Martin Luther (1436–1546) claimed that a human being is created to work as the bird is to fly. Luther was instrumental in forming the protestant work ethic, based on the idea that hard work will get you to heaven, as well as making you wealthy here on earth.

Warr (2007: 10) points out the difficulties in nailing down the concept of happiness; his general definition is 'a state of feeling good'. Argyle (2001) suggests three components of happiness: a state of joy or other positive emotion, satisfaction with life, and absence of depression, anxiety or other negative emotion. Work studies have tended to focus on the last two elements – for example, looking at the causes of job satisfaction and the negative outcomes of stress at work. It is also suggested that, although employers and managers are very interested in their own and their family's happiness, they are not so sure whether they should be concerned with their employees' happiness. Many consider it 'none of their business'. They may also view happiness at work as being a rather 'wishy-washy' subject, and not one that is in line with the financial success of the business (Warr and Clapperton 2010: 42). This may be changing, however, as managers become more aware of studies seeking to link human resource practices and line management competence to positive employee outcomes and organizational performance (Guest *et al.* 2000). Interest in employee engagement, commitment and the psychological contract has also put the concept of happiness at work generally more centre stage.

Several studies have suggested that people in certain jobs will be happier than those in others. Thus, in the UK, Rose (2003) found that individuals who worked as gardeners, hairdressers or care assistants were the most satisfied, while job dissatisfaction was highest among bus drivers, postal workers and assembly-line workers. Warr (2007; Warr and Clapperton 2010) suggests a 'vitamin model', 12 job features that most affect happiness and unhappiness at work, as well as ways of measuring the happiness of employees:

1. **Personal influence** – having some discretion, independence or opportunity to make your own decisions.
2. **Using your abilities** – having the opportunity to apply skill or expertise.
3. **Demands and goals** – job outcomes that are suitably challenging.
4. **Variety** – variation in activity and/or place.
5. **Clear requirements and outlooks** – knowing expectations and what might happen in the future.
6. **Social contacts** – interaction with other people.
7. **Money** – being paid well for what you do.
8. **Adequate physical setting** – acceptable physical working conditions.
9. **A valued role** – being in a job that is personally significant to you.
10. **Supportive supervision** – having bosses who support your welfare.
11. **Good career outlook** – being able to look forward to a good future.
12. **Fair treatment** – being part of an organization that treats others fairly.

(Adapted from Warr and Clapperton 2010: 72)

> ### Reflective question
>
> Review the list above. Is there anything you would add in terms of features leading to happiness at work?
>
> Warr does add that there will be other factors at play, including the social situation, cultural and demographic factors, and individual personality differences.

10.4 Soft skills in the workplace

> **Soft skills:** these are non-technical attributes that an individual possesses and are highly prized by organizations as complementary to technical expertise; they are said to contribute to high levels of performance.

KEY TERM

We have discussed in earlier chapters (on motivation, team-working, leadership and personality, for example) that individual employees are not passive recipients of organizational or managerial policies and practices. Individual employees are complex and they have different life experiences, different social and cultural backgrounds, different educational qualifications and different personalities, and when employees are at work it is these complexities and capabilities that create the dynamics of an organization. Individuals also bring with them their expectations, beliefs and attitudes, and these help to shape the collective organizational culture, creating a rich mix of shared norms and behaviours.

Research into this employment relationship highlights the growing trend among employers to search for employees with the right mix of attitudes and skills, in an effort to enrich organizational culture and, ultimately, organizational performance. Soft skills, such as emotional intelligence, communication, self-motivation, team-working, resilience, sensitivity to others and self-awareness, are being acknowledged as of equal importance as technical skills by those seeking new employees. New recruits are increasingly required to work closely in teams, and leadership qualities are expected to emerge throughout the organization, not just from the top.

As the patterns and nature of employment change, so has our understanding of what skills are important; it is now recognized that while knowledge and technical skills are of value, people skills, including emotional and social intelligence, are critical to organizational success. 'Soft skills count – they are vital to the success not only of individuals (personally and professionally) and organizations (locally and globally), but to the competitiveness of nations' (CIPD 2010).

Reporting in *The Guardian*, Tims (2011) states: 'In simpler times, relevant know-how and a clean shirt could secure you a job. That was before soft skills were invented.' The article also comments on the saying that hard skills will help to land the interview, but to get the job you will need to exhibit soft skills.

The rise in interest in soft skills has also emerged in response to the dissatisfaction of employers with the qualities and skills of new graduates, who appear to be lacking in soft skills, which was reported by the Association of Graduate Recruiters (2007).

Reflective question

What is meant by 'soft skills' and why are they considered important in the workplace?

KEY THEMES Lack of skills in the labour market

Below are some of the statistics highlighting the skills gap in the UK.

- Even with millions out of work, 75 per cent of employers are struggling to find candidates with the right skills to fill the places they have available (Tyler 2011).

- Today, over 70 per cent of our 2020 workforce have already completed their compulsory education, so there is a need to embed into the culture of the UK a desire to continue to learn and develop.

- UK employers were voicing serious concerns as early as 2006 about the lack of soft skills (CIPD 2010).

- In response to these alarms about skills, universities and colleges are putting a stronger emphasis on embedding employability and lifelong learning into the curriculum.

- In a survey of 1,000 IT professionals (Williams 2011), 84 per cent of respondents believed that employers should offer more training in soft skills, such as business and people management skills. Almost all of those surveyed (93 per cent) felt that they would be more valuable to businesses with further training.

Research by the Institute of Leadership and Management (2010) suggests that what is needed from leaders is changing. Historically, it may have been about charisma and commanding and controlling others, but today a more rounded individual is needed – that is, 'the whole package'. The Institute's research confirms that personal characteristics, such as the ability to motivate others, emotional intelligence, being a good communicator and being self-aware, are the foundations of being 'the complete leader'.

This fits with our earlier discussion of behavioural competencies, which some employers have now established as a mechanism for selecting leaders of the future.

An interesting dimension that also needs to be considered is the concept of human intuition as a factor in decision-making. Bonabeau (2003) discusses the contribution that intuition, or 'trusting your gut instinct', can make to the way that you behave and make decisions in the workplace. As Einstein recognized, 'The intellect has little to do on the road to discovery. There comes a leap in consciousness, call it intuition or what you will, and the solution comes to you, and you don't know how or why.' This has been further identified as 'intuitive intelligence', which Lieberman (2000) puts forward as the **two minds model**.

TABLE 10.1 The two minds model

Analytical mind	Intuitive mind
Narrow 'bandwidth' (serial processor)	Broad bandwidth (parallel processor)
Controlled processing	Automatic processing – 'gut reaction'
Step by step	Whole pattern recognition
Conscious	Non-conscious – comes from within
'Talks' in language of words	'Talks' in language of feelings
Fast formation (learns quickly)	Slow formation (learns slowly, through experience)
Slow operation	Fast operation

(Adapted from Lieberman 2000)

CASE STUDY Research insight

The authors were the academic supervisors for a Knowledge Transfer Partnership project exploring the skills and competences of individuals working in sales, who regularly hit or exceeded their sales targets in an IT sales-based company. The data collected highlighted that one of the key differentiators repeatedly referred to in the research interviews with the top performers was 'intuition'. This was articulated, for example, as a 'gut feel about a customer', or 'I could just tell that this client was going to buy'.

Q   Think about times when you have used your intuition to make a decision. What did you base your decision on and was it effective? Think about a time when your intuition has let you down and why this might have been.

From the discussion above, it seems to be the case that when we go to work we are not only required to provide our professional and technical skills, but there is also a need to engage our social and emotional talents. Soft skills are now acknowledged as important contributors to success at work, and increasingly employers are searching for a wider range of skills than just technical competence. As the CIPD (2010) points out, today is more about 'using the head and heart at work'.

10.5 Diversity and women at work

> **Diversity:** a term used to describe the mix of skills, abilities, genders, ages, cultures, ethnic groups and so on relating to a workforce.

More women are participating in the labour market than ever before. This is combined with an ageing working population, global labour markets and a multicultural society in Britain, resulting in an increasingly diverse workforce. The particular issues that women face include what is reported as the 'gender pay gap', with women typically earning less than their male counterparts. The BBC (2011b) reported that there had been a widening of the pay gap between male and female managers of £500, to £10,546 in the past year. Average earnings of female managers were £31,895, compared with £42,441 for men doing the same job. The Chartered Management Institute (2011) claims it would take '98 years to gain parity at the same rates'. On a positive note, junior female managers are earning more than males for the first time, a total of £602 more.

In debates about patterns of female employment there is also much discussion centred on the 'glass ceiling', perceived to be an invisible barrier that many women find hard to break through to reach more senior levels. Another term is the 'glass escalator', which relates to males in employment enjoying speedier acceleration to more senior positions, particularly in industries dominated by women (Williams 1992, cited in CIPD 2007). In addition, the term 'glass cliff' has emerged as one suggesting that gender may have an impact on bottom-line performance, and in a financial downturn, companies with females on the board could attract negative publicity, further damaging company performance (Judge 2003).

Research by Cranfield University (Vinnicombe *et al.* 2010) found that out of the FTSE 250 companies, 52.4 per cent have no women on their boards. The report also shows a three-year plateau in the percentage of women on FTSE 100 boards at 12.5 per cent. Yet there is some evidence of women reaching top levels, provided in the 2010 ranking, where Burberry reaches the top position, with three out of eight female board members (37.5 per cent), and Diageo plc comes in second, with a total of four out of 11 board members being female (36.4 per cent).

Recently, the coalition government in England and bodies such as the Confederation of British Industries have debated bringing in direct quotas, or setting a timeline to tackle the under-representation of women at board level. In Norway, for example, the government set a target in 2002, with an initial deadline of 2005, for the proportion of women making it to board level to reach 40 per cent – this was achieved by 2009.

> ### *Reflective questions*
>
> In relation to achieving a more diverse workforce, to what extent would you support the imposition of targets? What do you think would be the advantages and some of the barriers?

There is much research evidence as to why few women make it to senior management positions. Some of the key arguments are set out in Table 10.2.

The position of women in the labour market is complex, with occupational segregation still in existence, yet female participation in the labour market has expanded, with women making up just over 50 per cent of the workforce in 2011. The more recent focus has been on female representation at senior management/board level. The barriers are clearly identified, yet Mullins (2010) points out that the situation is even more blurred, with several more issues needing consideration. Some of the points that he raises are that women and men are viewed as homogeneous groups, ignoring individual differences; that the differences themselves can be as much within gender as between genders; that little attention has been paid to differences based on social class, race and age, for example; and that much of the research into women at work has been undertaken by white, middle-class women, which could lead to distortion, as they impose their own values and perceptions on the research.

TABLE 10.2 Why there are few women in senior management

Issue	Explanation
Occupational segregation	Women tend to be concentrated in lower-paid and often peripheral roles that do not offer career progression, such as catering, hairdressing, cleaning.
Stereotypes	Some jobs are perceived to be more suited to men or women, and this influences younger generations in their career choices (Daniels and Macdonald 2005).
Women's own attitudes and beliefs	Some argue that women's self-concept of their worth and place in society limits their ability and confidence to compete on an equal footing with men (Dixon 2011).
Legislation	While equality legislation exists, it still has a long way to go in order to drive through equal treatment at work. Discrimination still exists in the workplace.
Role models	Two aspects – one is the influence of parental role models, with children often following in the footsteps of their parents, with limited exposure to any alternatives. The second is the absence of female role models in senior positions in organizations, which may lower the aspirations of junior managers.
Equality – who wants it?	According to Daniels and Parkes (2008), many women find the traditional role of mother and homemaker very rewarding and do not place a value on a career and making it to the top.
Timeline differences	With women still predominantly absorbing responsibility for child care, they often have gaps in their work life, so do not have the same length of job experience as their male counterparts. Women often make the choice to take time out in order to raise a family, while males continue to build their careers (Smith 2011). 'One of the problems often cited in securing women onto boards is the lack of a pipeline of senior women with the type of leadership and management experience that counts in the selection process' (Dixon 2011).

10.6 Technology and work

When the authors of this book started work, computers filled vast rooms, fax machines were used to speed up communications, and email was unheard of. Information came to us via the television, radio, newspapers, letters, and published books and journals, and much time was taken in searching for the crucial evidence to back up a proposal to make a change in a business or to support a business decision. To analyse data often meant a day trip to a centrally based computer to download card reader data and feed this into a huge processing machine, and then wait for days for the analysis to be completed.

Technology has advanced dramatically in the past 20 years, changing the way that organizations carry out their business and altering the nature and speed of work. Mobile phones, laptops and Internet-based conferencing facilities have all contributed to creating a fast-paced, 24/7 society, where work and non-work become blurred. The speed at which information can be accessed, analysed and produced has had a major impact on how people carry out their work.

In this section we are keen to present a snapshot of some of the ideas relating to the way technology has impacted on people at work.

New technology and social networking sites, for example, have changed the way that some organizations handle their new recruits. For example, T-Mobile recently set up a Graduate Forum online, connecting all newly recruited graduates, and this helped the company to retain 100 per cent of its new recruits over the summer period before they started work. The Royal Opera House created six 50-second videos on YouTube to show different careers within the organization, and this attracted a 22 per cent increase in applications for jobs (CIPD 2008).

BlackBerry, the makers of smartphones, carried out a survey of users and found that they could save 60 minutes per day by being able to access, read and deal with emails while they were away from their desks (Crush 2011). On the other hand, Seeley (2011), in her research into the use of BlackBerrys, found that 'more than 60 per cent of the business users … felt that they must stay tethered 24x7x365 to their BlackBerry or similar device (even on Christmas day, driving and in the bedroom). When asked why, most confess that it is self-imposed, rather than their boss's (and clients') expectation'.

The 'Web 2.0 in the workplace' report (Clearswift 2010) identified that many respondents remained connected to their mobile technology, never switching off from either their work or home life. They described them as the 'generation standby' (socially and technologically never disconnected). An interesting trend appears to be emerging in that alongside the job offer, candidates appear to be expecting to be able to access social networking sites, such as Twitter and Facebook, and personal email at work. The survey found that in return for working harder and longer hours, there appears to be a shift in the 'deal' at work, and an expectation is that there is some 'give' in return for increased work pressure. So, being able to check personal email, shop online and check or make social arrangements on Facebook may come to form part of the 'deal', and become an integral part of the new 'psychological contract' discussed earlier in the book. This shift raises some interesting issues for organizational behaviour and culture, and how employees are managed, in that a key ingredient will rest on the level of trust and the degree of control that an employer hands over.

The possible misuse of technology at work, with employees using contracted work time to sort out their private lives, is acknowledged as an issue for attention, with some employers banning the use of social networking sites during work time, others restricting the time spent to lunchtime sessions only, and others allowing free access as long as work targets are met.

CASE STUDY The impact of technology on the pace of work

Alison works in the administration office of a large university and at different times during the academic year receives in excess of 500 emails per day, which creates tremendous pressure for her as an employee. To add to the pressure from this barrage of communications, the university has a target of replying to emails within 24 hours, to ensure that queries are dealt with promptly. One of Alison's appraisal objectives last year was to manage her emails and respond as quickly as possible, to ensure that students are assisted. To further increase the pressure, many of these emails are not written clearly, some appear to be written in text speak and often they appear to be unnecessary, as some students do not seem to be following clearly presented instructions published on the main university website.

Q **List the advantages and drawbacks of using email as a communication tool. What could Alison do to ensure that she is able to cope with the pressure during these busy times of the year?**

Emerging benefits of mobile technology appear to be related to creating more opportunities for collaborative working.

CASE STUDY Enhancing collaboration through technology – company practice

It appears that new technology can be the key to enabling greater collaboration in the workplace. The examples below provide an indication of how this can be achieved.

Philips has introduced new ways of working through technology, in an effort to generate more creativity and innovation. The company offers hot-desking and mobile communications, and has set up virtual private networks, enabling employees to work flexibly. Over 55,000 employees will eventually be connected, but the system has already improved communications and generated a more collaborative culture.

West Yorkshire Fire and Rescue Service has implemented a new digital information hub, to allow 24/7 access to policies and procedures. Technology has impacted on the ways of working through mobile devices as well as computers, and the sharing of resources such as the expertise of specialist staff.

Smart working is being achieved at GlaxoSmithKline through the reorganization of office spaces, so that employees can work flexibly between collaborative and quiet work spaces. Mobile technologies are influencing changes in employee behaviour, and allowing freedom of choice in terms of work area, as fixed desks and telephones are no longer the norm (Dodds 2011).

PricewaterhouseCoopers (2010) has predicted that technology will create new opportunities for working and generate new shapes for organizations (e.g. 'guilds'), but that key to the future is increased connectivity through technology and collaborative behaviours.

Cloud technology (a way of working where individuals use applications through a web browser, rather than having software installed on their computer system) is another development that it is argued will help employees work 'faster and smarter by increasing access to information, regardless of who created it, what format it's in, or where it lives' (Brown 2011, cited in Dodds 2011: 35).

CASE STUDY Cloud technology in action

The authors conducted an interview with the IT director of a financial services organization currently using cloud technology. The concept was explained as follows:

> *Cloud computing refers to the ability to use computing resources as a utility, so this means someone else provides the computing infrastructure and hardware and you pay for what you use, like gas and electricity. The term 'cloud' comes from the fact that all computer connections to the outside world are generally shown as Computer A talking to Computer B on the other side, with a wavy circular line between them, which resembles the telephone network but looks like a fluffy cloud!*
>
> *Amazon has a cloud or 'Compute Farm' model where you can buy computing resources on a short-term basis; they have all the machines in the cloud and give you access to as many as you need and can provide a new machine online in less than an hour. The Amazon offering is 'Amazon EC2'.*
>
> *We use cloud computing at work for our flexible benefits system and the recruitment system, and one of our software suppliers provides development and test machines for us via a cloud. A number of firms in the financial services sector use cloud computing for risk purposes, as this requires intensive calculations using lots of machines, and use of the cloud means they need to buy and maintain less equipment in their own data centres.*

Technology enables workers to base themselves at a distance from the fixed office location. This is often known as 'remote working'. BT has thousands of employees working remotely from home, working flexibly or on the move. The benefits that this has brought for the company are many, including:

- travel cost savings of 39 million euros per year
- property estate cost savings of 750 million euros per year
- 1,800 years of commuting time (the equivalent of 1.5 million return journeys) were saved through BT conferencing technology
- reduction in fuel consumption of 12 million litres per year (equivalent to 55,000 tonnes less CO_2)
- employees accessible 24/7
- employees able to access customer records from any location
- operational effectiveness is maintained even in adverse weather conditions and during transport strikes and so on
- flexible employees are 20 per cent more productive than their office-based counterparts
- absenteeism reduced by 63 per cent among flexible employees
- 58 per cent of BT customers claim their approach to corporate social responsibility influences their buying and partnering decisions.

(Adapted from **www.bt.com**)

It is clear that technology has produced some cost savings, and faster and more efficient ways of working, with instant access to information allowing quicker decision-making and better communications. However, there are potentially some negative implications for the longer-term future of how people work and the behaviours expected, which Gratton (2010) discusses in her recent article. She suggests that because the dramatic revolution in technology is changing how people are organized at work, the classic role of the middle manager could be under threat and eventually not be needed. She argues that now that technology can monitor performance more closely, provide instant feedback and replace some of the more repetitive tasks, the role of the middle manager will change.

Malone, Laubacher and Johns (2011) suggest that the work of the future will be broken down into smaller component parts, with many workers doing small elements of what is regarded as a single job today. They paint a picture of jobs being broken down into pieces and sent to remote workers to achieve cost savings and speed, while keeping control of quality. They call this 'hyperspecialization', which is facilitated through technology, but has overtones of Taylorism and scientific management principles – that is, tasks broken down into their simplest component parts and becoming routine and repetitive, with 'digital sweatshops' becoming a workplace of the future. On the other hand, they cite some of the advantages as being that employees have a degree of choice over the hours and tasks that they carry out; companies can rapidly expand or contract capacity to suit customer demands; and some of the lower-level tasks can be contracted out through technology on a global basis. Pfizer, for example, found that many of its highly trained staff were spending up to 40 per cent of their time on routine tasks like data entry and web research. Hyperspecialization – that is, breaking these jobs down into separate activities – allowed them to connect through technology with other companies to perform these tasks, releasing the key knowledge workers to complete more value-adding activities.

There is no doubt that technology has changed the way that we work and communicate. Our behaviour patterns have changed in response to the rapid transformation of mobile communications and technology. While there appear to be some significant advantages, which offer more creative and innovative ways of working and collaborating with others, the dark side of technology suggests an increasing pace and pressure of work and the dilution of face-to-face interaction. As technology has transformed itself within the last 20 years, we can only imagine what the jobs of the future might look like, along with changes in the patterns of work as technological innovation continues.

10.7 Managing in a global context

In Chapter 2 it was suggested that one of the key current challenges for managers is that of global interconnectedness. Life in general, and business in particular, is increasingly interconnected and linked – a process known as globalization. Modern transportation and communication technologies, combined with international competition and free trade agreements, have made the international dimension of business increasingly important. While this creates challenges for managers and organizations, it also results in opportunities – for trade, new markets and growth.

KEY THEMES Internationalization of production

Hollinshead (2010) points out that many household products are now assembled and delivered as part of a 'global production chain'. Consider the following example:

> When one typical US car was examined to see how 'American' it was, it turned out that nine countries were involved in some aspect of its production or sale. Roughly 30 per cent of the car's value went to South Korea for assembly, 17.5 per cent to Japan for components and advanced technology, 7.5 per cent to Germany for design, 4 per cent to Taiwan and Singapore for minor parts, 2.5 per cent to the UK for marketing and advertising services, and 1.5 per cent to Ireland and Barbados for data processing. Only 17 per cent of the car's marketing value was generated in the USA.
> (PILGER, quoted in HOLLINSHEAD 2010: 13)

It is also pointed out that such practices are common in other sectors, including clothing, footwear, computing and electronics. More recently, service-sector organizations have mirrored this trend, with work being offshored to other countries – for example, UK banking and finance, with call centres in India.

Global culture and labour market

In Chapter 9, on organizational culture, the work of Geert Hofstede (1980) was discussed briefly with regard to his research into national cultural differences. The research that Hofstede carried out was one of the largest studies of its kind, and his findings remain the foundation for many studies focusing on cross-cultural management. His sample of 116,000 respondents was made up of employees working for the multinational company IBM, and represented the attitudes and opinions of employees working in 40 different countries. By doing this, Hofstede argued that he was keeping the study restricted to one organization, thus keeping organizational culture constant, and that any differences identified would therefore be measuring differences in national culture. Despite much criticism of his methodology, the dimensions of culture that emerged were:

- **Masculinity/femininity** – refers to the division of roles between the sexes. What is seen as a typical role for men or for women can vary from one society to another. Societies can therefore be classified according to whether they try to minimize or maximize sex role divisions.

- **Collectivism/individualism** – this dimension is concerned with the relation between an individual and others. At one end of the spectrum there are societies in which ties are very loose and everyone tends to look after their own self-interest, and at the other end we find societies where the ties between individuals are much tighter.

- **Power distance** – refers to how society deals with the fact that people are unequal. Some let these inequalities grow over time into inequalities of power and wealth, while others strive for greater equality.

- **Uncertainty avoidance** – this dimension is concerned with how societies deal with the fact that the future is uncertain. In some societies, people accept this and are more likely to take risks easily, in others, people will try to create security and avoid risk.

Hofstede suggested that national cultures can be classified on these dimensions, and this has been largely confirmed by later research. He asserted that common values exist within most national cultures and that there was a general tendency to prefer certain states of affairs over others.

Convergence versus divergence

Many authors have argued that globalization has led to a convergence in national cultures – that is, the development of a universal citizenship, with individuals sharing the same norms and behaviours, and the gradual dilution and even elimination of local cultures (Basica 2005). Grint (1998) refers to this as the 'McDonaldization' or 'Microsoftization' of the world. As an example of convergence, Thompson and McHugh (2002) point to the rise of individualism and uncertainty in Russia following the break-up of the Soviet Union, in contrast to the old values of solidarity.

However, it is argued that growing similarity relates more often to production and IT systems, which are likely to converge due to best practice and universal standards. People management and other aspects of management are less likely to converge, due to national institutional frameworks and culturally derived preferences (Mullins 2010: 32). Thus Hollinshead (2010) has identified that national culture influences organizational practices such as organizational structures, recruitment processes, the determinants of pay and the amount of security guaranteed.

Another example, the well-documented experience of Disney in establishing its theme park in France, brought to attention the difficulties that may arise from a clash of cultures. Employees in France did not initially accept a rigid dress and appearance code; customers were not prepared to pay high prices in the restaurants; and the misfit of cultures damaged the business in its infancy. A French commentator, Mnouchkine, condemned the park as a 'cultural Chernobyl', even before it was opened (Rudolf 1991).

ACTIVITY

1 | Create a visual picture of what you think symbolizes 'Britishness'.
2 | Now take another country and do the same thing and compare the results.
3 | Identify the challenges that managing a team made up of individuals from different national cultures might present, and suggest how these challenges could be overcome.

KEY THEMES International differences in management

Landy and Conte (2010: 31) outline the results of a number of research reports on cross-cultural differences in the behaviour of US managers and workers in comparison with other nationalities:

- Compared with US managers, Japanese managers are much more likely to solve a strategic problem cooperatively, making sure that individuals share equally in rewards.

- Japanese managers are much more likely to seek compromise solutions than their US counterparts, who tend to follow win–lose strategies.

- In conflict negotiations, Japanese business leaders are much more likely to use power that flows from status than their US counterparts are.

- US software engineers are likely to provide assistance to a colleague only when they expect to need that colleague's help at some time in the future; Indian software engineers provide help to whoever needs it, without expectation of future reciprocation.

- US workers are less concerned about job insecurity than Chinese workers are.

Today, not only have many organizations gone global and entered new diverse markets, but they are also employing a culturally diverse workforce. In terms of organizational behaviour, this raises some interesting challenges in creating a shared set of values and attitudes to 'glue' the organization together. Employees bring different cultural values and norms to the workplace, all of which need to be managed. PricewaterhouseCoopers (2010) states that 'as companies try to reinforce corporate values, these can often be at odds with cultural values and can present challenges'.

In the UK it is acknowledged that the labour market is one of the most diverse in the western world. Berry's (1997) notion of 'culture shredding' is interesting and pertinent for our study of organizational behaviour. He portrays an image of individuals from different cultures who come into continuous first-hand contact with each other, going into a process of 'acculturation', where their original behavioural repertoire is adapted to the new cultural dimensions that they are exposed to. Individuals often embrace several cultures, which Chao and Moon (2005) have referred to as 'the cultural mosaic'.

10.8 Summary

This chapter has highlighted some key current issues and trends in organizational behaviour, as well as the debates surrounding these. Some of these issues and trends are at least partly driven by changing attitudes on the part of individuals towards work as a part of wider life, such as the desire to seek a balance between work and non-work activities, and recent interest in happiness at work. Societal changes are also an influencing factor, with greater participation rates of women in the labour market and an increasingly diverse workforce. In addition, organizations are having to grapple with global interconnectedness and technological developments. There is also an increased recognition of the importance of softer skills, creativity and intuition at work.

In an earlier chapter of this book it was stated that, arguably, management is about ideas and their application. This book has attempted to draw attention to some of the key ideas concerning people, work and organizations, and to introduce the debates concerning their application.

Key ideas

- In recent years, the concept of work/life balance has grown in importance, as the pressures of work create the need for individuals to juggle competing commitments.

- While happiness in general has become a popular topic for discussion, the issue of happiness at work has not attracted much attention, although this is starting to change.

- Twelve key features have been identified relating to happiness at work.

- Although technical skills are important, the value of soft skills, such as team-working and resilience, has come to the fore and has been recognized as contributing to high levels of performance.

- The issue of diversity is key for organizations today, and the role of women in the labour market has seen many changes and challenges.

- Technology has dramatically changed the way we work, and as it continues to develop it will impact on jobs, pace of work, workloads and behaviours.

- The world is increasingly interconnected – a process known as globalization. This creates both challenges and opportunities for organizations and managers.

Review questions

1. What does the term 'work/life balance' mean and can it ever be achieved in practice?

2. What, in your view, are the important features leading to happiness at work?

3. How could soft skills be assessed as part of a selection process?

4. Given the current data on the position of women in management positions, what can organizations do to achieve a higher representation of women at board level?

5. Home-working has increased through the use of technology. While many advantages have been identified, what do you think the challenges might be?

6. Outline and explain Hofstede's dimensions of national culture.

7. What is meant by the 'convergence/divergence debate', and what are the implications for managers?

Recommended reading

Dodds, S. (2011) 'People, places and technology'. *People Management*, 25th October, p. 35.

Malone, T.W., Laubacher, R.J. and Johns, T. (2011) 'The age of hyper specialization'. *Harvard Business Review*, July/August, 89(7/8), pp. 56–65.

Useful websites

www.pwc.co.uk/eng/issues/managing_tomorrows_people_the_future_of_work_to_2020.html – read this interesting report, 'Managing tomorrow's people: the future of work to 2020', from PricewaterhouseCoopers

www.worklifebalancecentre.org – contains some useful surveys, reports and articles on the latest thinking in relation to flexibility and work/life balance

References

Anushka, A. (2008) 'They don't live for work ... they work to live'. *The Observer*, 25th May.

Argyle, M. (2001) *The Psychology of Happiness* (2nd edn). Hove: Routledge.

Association of Graduate Recruiters Report (2007) 'Many graduates "lack soft skills"'. Report of Bi-Annual Survey of Association of Graduate Recruiters. (Available at http://news.bbc.co.uk/1/hi/education/6311161.stm)

Basica, N. (2005) *International Handbook of Educational Policy* (2nd edn). Dordrecht: Springer Publishing.

BBC (2011a) '1970s and 1980s "were the best time to raise children"'. BBC News, 8th March. (Available at www.bbc.co.uk/news/education-12667107)

BBC (2011b) 'Gender pay gap widens to £10,500 for managers, CMI says'. BBC News, 31st August. (Available at www.bbc.co.uk/news/business-14721839)

Berry, J.W. (1997) 'Immigration, acculturation and adaption'. *International Journal of Applied Psychology*, 46, pp. 5–34.

Bloomberg Business Week (2009) (Available at www.businessweek.com)

Bonabeau, E. (2003) 'Don't trust your gut'. *Harvard Business Review*, 81(5), May, pp. 116–23.

Campbell-Clark, S. (2000) 'Work/family border theory: a new theory of work/family balance'. *Human Relations*, 53(6), June, pp. 747–70.

Centrica (2009) 'Report on top employers for working families'. (Available at www.topemployersforworkingfamilies.org.uk/downloads/company-winner-reports/49_top_employers_for_working_families_2009___centrica_plc.pdf)

Chang, A., McDonald, P. and Burton, P. (2010) 'Methodological choices in work life balance research 1987 to 2006: a critical review'. *International Journal of Human Resource Management*, 21(13), October, pp. 2381–2413.

Chao, G.T. and Moon, H. (2005) 'The cultural mosaic: a metatheory for understanding the complexity of culture'. *Journal of Applied Psychology*, 90, pp. 1128–40.

Chartered Management Institute (2011) 'Happiness is the key'. 23rd September. (Available at www.managers.org.uk)

CIPD (2007) 'Women in the board room: the risks of being at the top'. Change Agenda. London: Chartered Institute of Personnel and Development. (Available at www.cipd.co.uk)

CIPD (2008) 'Podcast on social networking'. London: Chartered Institute of Personnel and Development. (Available at www.cipd.co.uk)

CIPD (2010) 'Using the head and heart at work: a business case for soft skills'. London: Chartered Institute of Personnel and Development. (Available at www.cipd.co.uk)

CIPD (2011) 'Flexible working'. Factsheet, August. London: Chartered Institute of Personnel and Development. (Available at www.cipd.co.uk)

CIPD with the London School of Economics, the University of Surrey, the University of London and Kingston University (2010) 'Creating an engaged workforce'. Research Report, January. London: Chartered Institute of Personnel and Development. (Available at www.cipd.co.uk)

Clearswift (2010) 'Web 2.0 in the workplace'. Report. (Available from www.clearswift.com)

Clutterbuck, D. (2003) *Managing Work–Life Balance: A Guide for HR in Achieving Organizational and Individual Change*. London: Chartered Institute of Personnel and Development.

Crush, P. (2011) 'What happened to our work life balance?' *The Guardian*, 18th June. (Available at www.guardian.co.uk)

Daniels, K. and Macdonald, L. (2005) *Equality, Diversity and Discrimination: A Student Text*. London: Chartered Institute of Personnel and Development.

Daniels, K. and Parkes, C. (2008) *Strategic HRM: Building Research-based Practice*. London: Chartered Institute of Personnel and Development.

Dixon, S. (2011) 'Will quotas get the right women on boards?' 4th June. (Available at http://blogs.brad.ac.uk)

Dodds, S. (2011) 'People, places and technology'. *People Management*, 25th October, p. 35.

Gratton, L. (2010) 'The future of work'. *Business Strategy Review*, 21(3), fall, pp. 16–23.

Greenhaus, J. and Powell, G.N. (2006) 'When work and family are allies: a theory of work–family enrichment'. *Academy of Management Review*, 31(1), June, pp. 72–92.

Gregory, A. and Milner, S. (2009) 'Work life balance: a matter of choice'. *Gender, Work and Organization*, 16(1), January, pp. 1–13.

Grint, K. (1998) *The Sociology of Work* (2nd edn). Cambridge: Polity Press.

Guest, D., Michie, J., Sheehan, M., Conway, N. and Metochi, M. (2000) *Effective People Management: Initial Findings of the Future of Work Study*. London: Chartered Institute of Personnel and Development.

Hewlett, S.A. (2011) 'Ys just wanna have fun (and flexibility)'. Bloomberg, 3rd June. (Available at http://mobile.bloomberg.com/news/2011-06-03/ys-just-wanna-have-fun-and-flexibility-?category=%2Fncws%2Fhewlett%2F)

Heywood, J.S., Siebert, W.S. and Wei, X. (2010) 'Work–life balance: promises made and promises kept'. *International Journal of Human Resource Management*, 21(11), September, pp. 1976–95.

Hofstede, G. (1980) *Culture's Consequences: International Differences in Work-related Values*. London: Sage.

Hollinshead, G. (2010) *International and Comparative Human Resource Management*. Berkshire: McGraw-Hill Education.

IDS HR Studies (2008) *Work Life Balance*, issue 873, July.

Institute of Leadership and Management (2010) 'Failure and adversity are key to leadership potential say UK employers'. 5th October. ILM. (Available at www.i-l-m.com/research-and-comment/9150.aspx)

Judge, E. (2003) 'Women on board: help or hindrance?' *The Times*, 11th November.

Landy, F.J. and Conte, J.M. (2010) *Work in the 21st Century. An Introduction to Industrial and Organizational Psychology*. Hoboken, NJ: John Wiley & Sons.

Lieberman, M.D. (2000) 'Intuition: a social cognitive neuroscience approach'. *Psychological Bulletin*, 126, pp. 109–37.

Malone, T.W., Laubacher, R.J. and Johns, T. (2011) 'The age of hyper specialization'. *Harvard Business Review*, 89(7/8), July/August.

McAllister, M. (2011) 'Working nine to five will be "no way to make a living"'. Institute of Leadership and Management: Newsroom article. (Available at www.i-l-m.com)

Mullins, L.J. (2010) *Management and Organizational Behaviour* (9th edn). Harlow: Pearson Education.

PricewaterhouseCoopers (2010) 'Managing tomorrow's people: the future of work to 2020'. (Available at www.pwc.co.uk)

Rose, M. (2003) 'Good deal, bad deal? Job satisfaction in occupations'. *Work, Employment and Society*, 17, pp. 503–30.

Rudolf, B. (1991) 'Monsieur Mickey: Euro DisneyLand is on schedule but with a distinct French accent'. *Time*, 25th March, p. 48.

Seeley, M. (2011) 'BlackBerry crumble reveals the depth of our email addiction'. 18th October. (Available at www.hrmagazine.co.uk)

Smith, P.E. (2011) 'Web-based communication and networking: an opportunity to break the glass ceiling?' Paper presented at the 11th International Conference on Diversity in Organizations, Communities and Nations, Cape Town, South Africa, 20th–22nd June. Taylor, S. (2010) *People Resourcing and Talent Management* (5th edn). London: Chartered Institute of Personnel and Development.

The Economist (2006) 'Economics discovers its feelings'. 23rd January, pp. 35–7.

Thompson, P. and McHugh, D. (2002) *Work Organizations: A Critical Introduction* (3rd edn). Basingstoke: Palgrave.

Tims, A. (2011) 'The secret to understanding soft skills'. *The Guardian*, 5th March.

Torrington, D., Hall, L., Taylor, S. and Atkinson, C. (2011) *Human Resource Management* (8th edn). Harlow: FT Prentice Hall.

Truss, C., Soane, E. and Edwards, C. (2006) 'Working life: employee attitudes and engagement'. Research Report. London: Chartered Institute of Personnel and Development. (Available at www.cipd.co.uk)

Tyler, R. (2011) 'UK job skills shortage must be taken seriously'. *The Telegraph*, 15th June.

Vinnicombe, S., Sealy, R., Graham, J. and Doldor, E. (2010) *The Female FTSE Board Report 2010: Opening up the Appointment Process*. Cranfield University, School of Management: International Centre for Women Leaders.

Warr, P. (2007) *Work, Happiness and Unhappiness*. London: LEA Publishers.

Warr, P. and Clapperton, G. (2010) *The Joy of Work? Jobs, Happiness and You*. Hove: Routledge.

Williams, J. (2011) 'Lack of soft skills training is curbing IT career progression'. *Computer Weekly*, 26th August. (Available at www.computerweekly.com)

GLOSSARY

Accountability the ultimate responsibility that a manager has and cannot delegate; while managers may delegate authority to others, they themselves remain accountable for the actions of their subordinates

Attitudes beliefs that we hold that influence our approach to the way we work and how we treat others

Authority the right to make certain decisions and to exercise control over resources

Bargaining a type of negotiation where each side has a list of demands

'Big Five' these are the five common personality dimensions that psychologists have agreed appear to form the basis of everyone's personality

Bureaucracy a structure that emphasizes specialization, formalization, rules and regulations, and centralized authority and decision-making

Classical management an approach to management that stresses the formal aspects of organization and structure

Communication the process by which information and views are exchanged

Conflict a process that begins when one party perceives that another party has negatively affected, or is about to negatively affect, something that the first party cares about (Thomas 1992, in Robbins, Judge and Campbell 2010: 400)

Conflict resolution a process that aims to resolve the conflict between the parties involved

Content theories a body of research that suggests that motivation is driven by wants and needs

Contingency theories of leadership the most appropriate approach to leadership will depend on the particular situation

Diversity the mix of skills, abilities, genders, ages, cultures, ethnic groups and so on relating to a workforce

Employee engagement this relatively new concept explores the degree to which an individual forms an attachment to an organization

Employee voice two-way communication between employer and employee; it is the process of the employer communicating to the employee(s), as well as receiving and listening to communication from the employee(s)

Emotional intelligence this refers to the concept of tapping into our emotional awareness and sensitivities to others, and using this to guide our interpersonal behaviour in a more powerful way

Fordism a form of work design that applied scientific management principles to production line work and the introduction of single-purpose machine tools; called after the 19th-century American industrialist Henry Ford

Globalization the process in which organizations extend their activities beyond purely national boundaries to participate and compete around the world

Hawthorne effect the tendency for people to behave differently than they normally would when they are observed or are part of an experiment

Leadership 'a relationship through which one person influences the behaviour or actions of other people' (Mullins 2010: 373)

Mechanistic structures organizational structures that show a high degree of task specialization and formalization, tight specification of individual responsibility, clear rules and regulations and centralized decision-making

Motivation the force that drives individuals to take action

Negotiation the process of two parties coming together to confer, with a view to making a jointly acceptable agreement

Organic structures organizational structures that have low task specialization and formalization, where individual responsibility is not tightly specified, there are few formal rules and decision-making is delegated downwards

Organization 'a social arrangement for achieving controlled performance in pursuit of collective goals' (Buchanan and Huczynski 2010: 8)

Organizational behaviour (OB) can be defined in various ways but, in general, OB is concerned with the behaviour of individuals and groups in an organizational context

Organizational culture the shared values, norms and behaviours that guide how employees work within an organization and act as a cohesive force

Organizational control concerned with the regulation of behaviour and performance towards organizational goals

Organizational dilemma refers to the difficulty that may be experienced in reconciling individual goals with organizational goals

Organizational structure the formal system of dividing up work tasks, co-ordinating the resultant activities of employees, and specifying reporting relationships to enable the achievement of organizational goals

Perception this refers to the process by which we make sense of different stimuli in the environment in order to make judgements and decisions that we then act on

Personality the characteristics of an individual that make the individual unique and shape his or her behaviour

Political behaviour in an organizational context, this can be defined as 'activities that are not required as part of one's formal role in the organization but that influence, or attempt to influence, the distribution of advantages and disadvantages within the organization' (Farrell and Peterson 1982, in Robbins, Judge and Campbell 2010: 381)

Power the ability to persuade other people to do what you want them to do

Process theories the notion that individuals weigh up the value of what they give in return for what they expect to get, so motivation also comprises a rational decision-making process

Psychological contract the mutual and unwritten expectations arising from the people–organization relationship

Responsibility an obligation placed on a person who occupies a certain position in the organization to perform a task or function

Socio-technical system a system made up of both technology and a social organization (the people aspect)

Soft skills non-technical attributes that an individual possesses and which are highly prized by organizations as being complementary to technical expertise; such skills are said to contribute to high levels of performance

Stress experienced when pressure at work turns into a negative experience that an individual is unable to cope with

System a framework that operates through the interdependence of its component parts

Style theories of leadership characterize leadership behaviour patterns in order to identify effective leadership styles

Team a group of people who work together and have shared goals, cooperating and working towards achieving their goals

Team competence an ability, skill or expertise related to working within a team; many organizations today seek evidence of competence in team-working from applicants applying for a job

Team role an individual's preference for a particular style of behaviour or way of contributing in a team situation; the role is usually based on the individual's past experience of team-working

Technology how an organization transfers its inputs into outputs

Trait theories of leadership approaches based on the belief that leaders have certain personality traits and attributes that can be identified

Transformational leaders leaders who have the ability to transform followers to perform beyond their expectations

Virtual team where team members are based in different locations, perhaps around the world, but are connected through technology such as video-conferencing and email

Work/life balance the equilibrium that an individual may seek to achieve between work and non-work commitments

Chapter 1

1. How would you define 'organizational behaviour'?

Organizational Behaviour (OB) can be defined in various ways. In general, OB is concerned with the behaviour of individuals and groups in an organizational context and how these different elements interact and influence each other.

2. Why might the study of OB be considered important?

It is considered important to improve our understanding of organizations and the individuals and groups within them. OB can enable people to be better managers, and to improve organizational effectiveness.

3. Why is the study of relevant theory considered important in OB?

Theory can give a useful guide to practice. Almost any management action or decision (on how best to motivate employees, for example) is based on some sort of idea or model as to what the outcome will be, even if it's just a hunch. The advantage of a manager being aware of the various theories (of motivation, in this case) is that it leads to a more in-depth understanding of the situation and, hopefully, a better decision and outcome. One could, therefore, argue that the test of a good theory is its usefulness, i.e. the extent to which it can be applied in practice.

4. What are the key levels in OB?

These are the individual, group, organization and wider environment.

5. What is meant by the 'organizational dilemma'?

The organizational dilemma refers to the difficulty that may be experienced in reconciling individual goals with organizational goals. For example, the organizational goals of efficiency and performance may conflict with individual desire for self-expression, freedom and autonomy.

6. Why is an appreciation of the external context important to our understanding of OB?

Organizations operate within the wider environment: local, national and global, and this environment will influence both individuals and organizations, as will changes and trends in the wider environment.

7. In the employment relationship, what is meant by the 'balance of power'? And what factors can help shift this balance?

The term 'balance of power' relates to the relative power that each party has over the other. Factors that can shift the balance of power include: the relative rarity of the skills and abilities that the employee, i.e. whether these skills and abilities are in short supply; legislation and trade unions, as well as the general economic situation.

8. **Compare and contrast the unitary, pluralist and radical perspectives.**

   - **Unitary perspective** — stresses common goals and an absence of conflict. This equates with a particular managerial philosophy that seeks to promote a common culture and high commitment.

   - **Pluralist perspective** — suggests a number of different interest groups, each with different goals. Thus, management may have differing goals to employees, and different departments in an organization may also have competing goals. This is seen as natural and inevitable. Conflict is also seen as natural, but to be managed through communication, negotiation and compromise.

   - **Radical or critical perspective** — sees the Capitalist economic system and the work organizations within such systems as leading inevitably to exploitation of employees and their alienation (Bratton *et al.*, 2011).

Chapter 2

1. **List Fayol's five key elements of management.**

   Fayol saw management as comprising five key elements:

   - to forecast and plan
   - to organise
   - to command
   - to coordinate
   - to control.

2. **What is meant by a rational-economic view of motivation?**

   Fayol used this classification to divide up his writings on how to manage.

3. **What is meant by the term 'Fordism'?**

   Fordism is a form of work design that applied scientific management principles to production line work and the introduction of single-purpose machine tools.

4. **What are the chief characteristics of bureaucracy?**

   The main characteristics of bureaucracy are:

   - **Specialization** — applying more to the job than the person undertaking the job. This makes for continuity as the job will usually continue after the current post-holder has left.

   - **Hierarchy of authority** — making for a sharp distinction between management and workers. Within the management ranks there are clearly defined levels of authority. This stratification is particularly marked in the armed services and civil service.

   - **System of rules** — which aims to provide for an efficient and impersonal approach. The system of rules is generally stable, though there may be some modification and updating at times; a knowledge of the rules is essential to holding a job in a bureaucracy.

   - **Impersonality** — meaning that allocation of privileges and the exercise of authority should not be arbitrary, but in accordance with the specified system of rules. In more highly developed bureaucracies there tend to be carefully defined procedures for appealing against certain types of decisions.

5. Outline the key experiments and findings of the Hawthorne studies.

The Hawthorne studies took place in the Hawthorne works of the Western Electric Company near Chicago. They are often associated with Elton Mayo (1880–1949). The studies involved four main phases:

- **The illuminations experiments (1924–1927)** — These set out to measure the effect of changes in lighting on productivity. The results were inconclusive in that no correlation was found between the two (Buchanan and Huczynski, 2010). Production even increased both when the lighting was reduced and in the control group where lighting stayed the same. Clearly, other factors were at work.

- **The relay assembly test room (1927–1933)** — The work here involved assembling telephone relays from small parts. Six women workers were transferred from their normal work stations to a separate area, with a researcher to take notes. Changes were made to hours worked, rest pauses and breaks. The results showed an almost continuous increase in output, this began when rest periods, lunches and early finishing times were introduced, but were maintained when these were withdrawn. It was concluded that the reasons for the increase in output were that the women felt themselves to be a special group and had self-elected; that they had been consulted about the experiments and had built up a good relationship with the supervisor and observer/researcher.

  The improved output due to an increase in attention paid to the workers in the study became known as *The Hawthorne Effect*. People behave differently than they normally would when they are observed or are part of an experiment. The effect of the group seemed very important, which led the researchers to set up an employee-interviewing programme to explore employee attitudes.

- **The interviewing programme (1928–1930)** — The researchers carried out over 20,000 interviews to explore how employees felt about their working conditions and supervision. These interviews can be seen as a precursor of modern employee involvement schemes, attitude surveys and employee counselling. One outcome of the interviews was that informal groups existed in the workplace alongside the formal groups, and this formed the basis of the next study.

- **The bank wiring observation room (1931–1932)** — This involved the study of 14 men. It was found that they formed informal groups with specified 'norms' of behaviour and ways of enforcing these. Although a financial incentive scheme was in operation, the men decided on a level of output that was below what they could have achieved, believing that otherwise management would simply raise the level required. The experiment highlighted that work is a group activity and that people feel the need to be part of a group. Informal groups can have a strong influence on individual behaviour at work and managers need to understand the workings of such groups and to collaborate with them.

These conclusions led to the 'Human Relations Approach' to management, which recognized that work has an important social function for employees and is a group activity, and also that how managers and supervisors behave has an important effect upon employee motivation and productivity.

6. What were the key findings of Trist and his colleagues' investigation into coal-mining?

The idea of viewing an organization as a system emerged from work done at the Tavistock Institute of Human Relations in London. Erik Trist and colleagues at the Institute focused in particular on two components: the technical and the social. Their ideas came from an investigation of the introduction of new technology in the coal-mining industry. Traditionally the miners had worked in small cohesive self-selected groups on one part of the coal face – the 'shortwall' method, with each group having relative independence and autonomy. The introduction of new technology in the form of mechanical coal-cutters and mechanized conveyor belts fundamentally changed this way of working. Shift-working was introduced with each shift specializing in one operation, which was known as the 'long wall' method. The new method led to problems: a lack of cooperation between shifts and dissatisfaction among the miners, which meant that the new technological system was not as efficient as it should have been.

The researchers realized that the introduction of such new technology could not be viewed in isolation, but needed to be considered in conjunction with the effects it would have on the social system, i.e. a socio-technical approach. A 'composite long wall' method was introduced which, while keeping the main elements of the new technology, gave more responsibility to the team and re-introduced multi-skilling and multi-tasking, with a reduction in the degree of specialization evident in the long wall method. This new method proved successful, both economically and in terms of meeting the psychological and social needs of the workers.

7. With reference to organizations, give an example of an 'if-then' contingency relationship.

The contingency approach has been characterized as an 'if-then' relationship. One example of this relates to the size of the organization. *If* an organization is small in size, *then* its structure is likely to be relatively flat and its management systems fairly informal.

8. Summarize the social action approach to organization and management.

Social action can be seen as a sociological approach to the study of organizations. Writers from this tradition attempt to view the organization from the perspective of individual members of that organization, each of whom will have their own goals, beliefs and interpretations. Thus, to understand behaviour at work it is argued that we need to understand the individual's own perceptions of any particular situation.

Chapter 3

1. How would you define personality and why are organizations interested in this concept?

Personality can be defined as the unique characteristics that influence how we behave. Organizations are interested in the concept because personality characteristics are considered to be reasonably stable and can be used to predict how a person may act and respond in the workplace. When we look at Chapters 6 and 9, on leadership and organizational culture and change, we will see that personality dimensions play a significant role.

2. **What are the key characteristics of Type A and Type B personalities, and how will their behaviours be different in the workplace?**

Type A personalities are considered to be competitive, aggressive, impatient, hasty, feel the urgency of time and have a need to control.

Type B personalities, in contrast, are relaxed, less worried about time, less frenetic in their pace of work, have a lesser need to control, and rate themselves in a positive way.

3. **Differentiate between the nomothetic and the idiographic approaches to personality.**

This debate is otherwise known as the 'nature/nurture debate'. Nomothetic psychologists believe that personality is inherited, stable over time and unlikely to change. In contrast, the idiographic school of psychologists (nurture) argues that personality develops over time and is influenced by our environmental and social experiences, as well as our psychological development as we mature.

4. **Researchers have agreed that personality comprises five major dimensions. Consider why these might be a useful foundation for further research into the link between personality and performance at work.**

The 'big five' characteristics include agreeableness and conscientiousness, which might lend themselves to positive workplace behaviours – for example, someone exhibiting these characteristics may see their work through to the end and work well with others.

5. **How would you define emotional intelligence, and why might it be of particular relevance for leadership?**

Emotional intelligence relates to self-awareness, sensitivity to others and using one's feelings at work. It is suggested that effective leaders utilize emotions to achieve high levels of performance by connecting with subordinates and being sensitive to their needs.

6. **How far do you think the psychological contract provides a useful indication of what an employee might expect in the workplace?**

The psychological contract attempts to capture the unwritten expectations that employees have, beyond their written contract of employment. The problem is that it is different for every individual and may change over time.

7. **Explain why attitudes might be resistant to change.**

Attitudes are formed over time and become part of who we are; they are constantly reinforced by the way that we react and respond to different situations. These become firmly established as a means of coping with myriad stimuli and are, therefore, resistant to change. They represent who we are and what we believe, and play a significant role in our lives; as such, we can be hostile to changing our attitudes. Any change tends to be in response to life experience or through strategies used within organizations, such as education and communication programmes, where attitudes can be discussed and confronted.

Chapter 4

1. **How would you define the term 'motivation'?**

   Motivation is a force within that spurs us into action.

2. **Some writers argue that theories such as Maslow's hierarchy of needs and Herzberg's two-factor theory focus more on the satisfaction of needs than on actual motivation. What do you think of this view?**

   Maslow's and Herzberg's theories focus on the satisfaction of human needs. There is a question as to whether satisfying an employee's needs at work will actually lead to better performance. It may be just someone feeling comfortable with what they are doing rather than them delivering high levels of performance.

3. **A criticism of Maslow's work is that needs may change as we progress through life. To what extent do you agree with this point, and why?**

   Research evidence suggests that our needs and wants change over time. Maslow's hierarchy did not consider a time dimension, and the set of needs was presented as a fixed model and so could be interpreted as inflexible.

4. **Process theories suggest that our behaviour is based on rational decision-making, which will drive our motivation. Consider the limitations of this view.**

   Expectancy theory is a process by which an individual will put in effort to perform to a high level based on consideration of the reward. A key limitation of this is that the reward may not be within their control and their effort may be thwarted by their lack of ability and limited resources or peer pressure.

5. **Explain how the notion of employee engagement differs from traditional motivation theories.**

   Employee engagement provides a more holistic explanation of motivation; it goes beyond motivation and job satisfaction through its consideration of cognitive, emotional and behavioural elements. It stresses the significance of the psychological relationship between the employer and the employee.

6. **What is the value to organizations of identifying the needs and expectations of different generational groups?**

   Identifying the needs and expectations of different generational groups may help organizations to respond more appropriately to the changing expectations of different groups; it may also help them to tailor their rewards and benefits packages to what people want and value. In a tight labour market, this may prove an attractive offer and help to retain staff and increase levels of loyalty and commitment.

Chapter 5

1. **Explain why teams are used by organizations.**

   Teams are important to organizations because they provide a sense of connection for individuals and can help to engage them psychologically, socially and emotionally. Teams help to create an extra dynamic within the workplace and help to create a collaborative organizational culture.

2. Why might team-working go wrong?

Teams can go wrong for many reasons, including communication problems, multiple goals within the team, unequal effort, too many ideas, no individual recognition and lack of trust between team members.

3. Teams are said to progress through a series of stages as they develop. Identify the stages and suggest why this categorization might be helpful.

Tuckman argues that teams progress through five discrete stages, which move them from a disparate group of individuals to a high-performing team. The new addition of the 'moving on' stage adds a further realistic dimension. The categorization is helpful to be aware of as a team leader or team member, as it can signal the need for intervention and support.

4. Reflect on your own contribution in a team that you have been part of, and the role that you played. How does this fit with Belbin's research into team roles.

The answer will depend upon your own response and experience of working in teams. The question encourages you to reflect into Belbin's nine team roles and the value of such research.

5. Identify the skills needed for effective team-working.

The skills for effective team-working include listening, questioning, preparing in advance, enthusiasm for the shared goals, willingness to contribute and share ideas, and taking responsibility for your own team tasks.

6. Now that organizations are carefully defining team-working competencies, how might this help them to select the best person for the job and to fit the team?

Organizations have produced behavioural competencies relating to team-working and, as a result, have targeted interview questions to look for evidence of team behaviours and contribution. This is sometimes taken further through the use of an assessment centre, where team capabilities are examined through a range of exercises. Some personality tests have questions related to team-working that provide further information on a candidate. This process helps an organization to identify individuals who are more likely to fit in and adapt to team-working within the organization.

Chapter 6

1. How would you define leadership? What are the common elements of leadership?

There are many different views as to what constitutes 'leadership'. Ball (2007) however suggests that an analysis of these definitions show that three common elements can be discerned:

- goal-setting and achievement
- group activities
- influence upon the behaviour of others.

Although it is difficult to generalize about leadership, Mullins (2010) suggests that, in essence, leadership is: 'a relationship through which one person influences the behavior or actions of other people'.

2. What are seen to be the main differences between leadership and management?

Leadership is normally seen more in terms of providing vision, inspiration and strategy, with *management* seen more in terms of getting things done on a day-to-day basis and ensuring consistency.

3. What are the main shortcomings of trait approaches to leadership?

There are a number of shortcomings to the trait approach to leadership. Firstly, it proved impossible to arrive at a generally agreed list of required characteristics that a leader should have; different people came up with different lists. Secondly, the characteristics listed tended to be rather generalized. Many of the traits are also rather vague. A final shortcoming of the trait approach is that it takes no account of the specific situation, yet in reality what works well in one situation may not work in another.

4. Outline Tannenbaum and Schmidt's continuum of leadership behaviour.

Tannenbaum and Schmidt suggested a continuum from autocratic 'boss-centred leadership' at one end to 'subordinate-centered leadership' at the other. This gave managers a 'tool kit' of styles to choose from, depending on the situation faced. They argued that managers should choose the most relevant approach in any one particular situation based on three inter-related forces or influences:

Characteristics of the manager	personality, values, beliefs, confidence in subordinates
Characteristics of subordinates	need for independence, tolerance of ambiguity, level of knowledge
Characteristics of the situation	organizational customs and norms, size of group, nature of the problem

5. Assess the strengths and weaknesses of contingency approaches to leadership.

The key strength of contingency theories of leadership is that they suggest that different approaches to leadership will be needed, depending on the particular situation. Some of the more basic theories appear rather prescriptive, however, suggesting that in situation 'A', the manager should do 'B'. This sort of 'contingent determinism' is likely to be too simplistic and does not allow for management choice.

On the other hand, the challenge for more sophisticated contingency theories is which variables to focus on. In reality, any one particular situation is likely to be the product of a complex interaction of many variables and, thus, it is difficult for managers to get clear guidance. Another limitation is that the contingency approach tends to concentrate on more conventional middle management or supervisory situations, i.e. when a manager or supervisor is leading a group of subordinates. Arguably, the contingency approach has less to say about leadership at a strategic level, or about leadership as a process amongst members of a group or team, i.e. outside the hierarchical system.

6. What is meant by 'transformational leadership'?

The term 'transformational' was used to describe leaders' ability to transform followers to perform beyond expectations. Transformational leaders are seen as being able to motivate others to:

- view their own work from new perspectives
- have an awareness of the mission and vision of the organization

- attain high levels of ability and potential
- look beyond their own interests to that of the group.

7. Give a practical example of distributed leadership

Distributed leadership involves a number of people acting together in formal and informal roles which may be spontaneous and intuitive. Leadership functions may be shared and the leader role may shift from one person to another as circumstances change. It is argued that distributed leadership has become more important as organizational structures have become flatter and less centralized. Examples would include self-managed teams or an individual informally mentoring or coaching a colleague.

Chapter 7

1. Outline the key methods of organizational communication.

Key methods of organizational communication include:

- regular meetings
- cascading information down the hierarchy
- in-house magazines
- company intranet
- team briefings
- e-mail
- blogs
- podcasts
- suggestion schemes
- employee appraisal scheme
- attitude surveys.

2. What are the possible negative and positive outcomes of conflict in organizations.

Negative outcomes may include individuals feeling unhappy and mistrustful, individuals and groups concentrating on their own narrow self-interests, and resistance, plus manifestations such as employee turnover and industrial action.

Positive outcomes of conflict may include new ideas and people having to search for new ways of doing things, creativity, clarification of views and standpoints, as well as a general 'clearing the air'.

3. What is meant by the term 'resistance' in organizations? What forms can such resistance take?

Management's attempt to exert power and control over workers may be met by resistance, i.e. a reluctance, to do what management wants. Such behaviour may be found at different levels of the hierarchy, from shop-floor workers finding techniques to relieve boredom and alienation, to professionals (such as academics and doctors) attempting to resist the control of management or administrators, right up to senior managers attempting to thwart the control of the board of directors.

4. **Outline Thomas's (1976) five key conflict-resolution approaches.**

   Thomas (1976) distinguishes between five conflict-resolution approaches based upon (a) how assertive or unassertive each party is in putting forward its concerns and (b) how cooperative or uncooperative each is in satisfying the concerns of the other. The different approaches are:

   - competing
   - avoiding
   - compromising
   - accommodating
   - collaborating.

5. **Compare and contrast 'mediation' and 'arbitration'.**

   A *mediator* listens to the arguments from both sides and then makes recommendations as to how they might be resolved; the parties are free to accept or reject these recommendations. *Arbitration* removes the control over the settlement from the parties involved; the arbitrator listens to the arguments put forward, and decides on a solution to the parties' differences.

6. **What are the key methods for giving employees 'voice'?**

   There are two differing approaches to giving employees a 'voice': employee involvement and employee participation. Employee involvement covers a range of practices, primarily initiated by management and designed to increase employee information about, and commitment to, the organization. It is aimed at the individual employee or team of employees. Employee participation tends to be seen as focusing on collective or representative arrangements in which employees, often via their representatives, are involved with management in decision-making (Gennard and Judge, 2002).

Chapter 8

1. **Why is a consideration of structure of importance to managers?**

   Organizational structure is the way in which the organization divides up tasks and coordinates the resultant activities. The structure will determine how activities are grouped together, who does what, and how staff are coordinated and managed. To achieve its purpose an organization needs the best possible structure.

2. **Outline the key characteristics of bureaucracy.**

   The key characteristics of bureaucracy are: work specialization, authority hierarchy, employment and career, recording, rules and procedures, and impersonality and impartiality.

3. **What is the relevance of early approaches to organizational design, such as those of Weber, to managers today?**

   Early approached to organizational design, such as Weber's bureaucracy provide important ideas for managers today. Many large-scale modern organizations still contain features of bureaucracy.

4. **What is meant by 'span of control'?**

   The term 'span of control' refers to how many subordinates one manager or supervisor is directly responsible for. This can be many (wide span of control) or few (narrow span of control).

5. **What are the possible advantages and disadvantages of the matrix structure?**

Matrix structures usually combine a functional form with a project or product-based form, which can result in greater flexibility and encourage creativity and team-work. However, they may also bring coordination and control problems.

6. **Outline the difference between *line* and *staff* relationships and give examples of each.**

In *line relationships* authority flows down the hierarchy vertically along the formal chain of command. An example would be from the managing director to senior managers, from senior managers to middle managers, and on down to managers and supervisors. Thus, this is the direct relationship between manager and subordinate, with each subordinate directly responsible to one person only, i.e. their line manager.

Staff employees are those who occupy advisory positions and provide line managers with support and specialist advice. One way to provide this is via an assistant to the line manager. The assistant can then provide support and advice to other line managers. Because the assistant is not in a line relationship with these line managers, they do not constitute a level in the hierarchy. Such relationships are known as *staff relationships,* the line managers can choose whether to follow the advice given or not.

Another way to provide support and advice to line managers is via a specialist department, such as HR or IT. Generally, employees in these support functions will have a *staff relationship* with other line managers in that the support and advice can be accepted or not.

7. **What is meant by the term 'the virtual organization'?**

The combination of outsourcing and sub-contracting of activities with new electronic communication methods (information communication technologies or ICTs) gives rise to the possibility of organizations with very little in terms of physical presence and has given rise to the term 'the virtual organization'.

8. **Compare and contrast 'mechanistic' with 'organic' organizations.**

An organization with a *mechanistic* structure is one with a high degree of task specialization and formalization, tight specification of individual responsibility and authority, centralized decision-making and formal rules and procedures. It can be likened to Weber's bureaucratic structure. An organization with an *organic* structure possesses little task specialization, low degree of formalization, delegated decision-making and a high degree of individual responsibility.

9. **How and why will structure affect individual behaviour?**

People design and run organizations, but the design and structure of organizations will, in turn, influence the people within them.

In attempting to assess the influence of different forms and aspects of organizational structure on people, some general trends can be discerned, although we should be careful about over-generalizing these — it very much depends on the particular individual and their preferences. Thus, although some people will prefer the relative freedom and creativity of an organic organization, others will prefer the relative order and predictability of mechanistic structures.

10. **What were the key findings of the Aston Studies in relation to structure?**

The Aston Studies suggested taking organizational structure seriously by using a contingency approach. They suggested the need for a detailed analysis of the organization and its context, which will lead to determination of the best structure.

Chapter 9

1. **Culture is defined by Deal and Kennedy (1982) as 'the way we do things around here'. If this is the case, what do you think this means in practice?**

   It is to do with the unwritten beliefs, habits and norms of behaviour that people come to share when they work for an organization.

2. **Differentiate between the visible aspects of culture and the hidden elements of organizational culture.**

   Visible aspects are:

   - the uniform or style of dress
   - the products and services offered
   - the stated vision and mission of the organization
   - the structure and hierarchy, the atmosphere and physical environment
   - formal communications and policies and procedures
   - mottoes and stories, language and jargon.

   Hidden elements include:

   - power and politics
   - informal subcultures
   - leadership style
   - values, attitudes and beliefs.

3. **Some argue that culture can be managed by an organization, while others suggest that culture emerges as the organization grows and develops. What do you think, and why?**

   There is clear evidence that some organizations make strong efforts to manage their culture (as seen in the company examples provided within Chapter 9), but the debate still exists. There is no definite answer, as many still believe that culture cannot be captured and controlled.

4. **Using Handy's typology, consider the advantages and drawbacks of working in an organization classified as having a role culture.**

   The advantages might be the formality — that the rules provide a framework and guidance for people. There would be clear job descriptions, so employees would know what was expected of them; power would be clearly linked to positions held in the organization; a formalized organization structure would differentiate roles and departments and offer clear career progression opportunities. The disadvantages could be a lack of flexibility working within such a formal structure. If there is downsizing, career opportunities will disappear, and it could take time to get decisions agreed, which could lead to frustration and the inability to change quickly.

5. **The current economic downturn is requiring many organizations to cut costs and operate more efficiently and efficiently with less. Identify some of the ways in which an organization could achieve this.**

   Strategies could include:

   - reducing staff levels
   - outsourcing/offshoring some activities

- reducing the working week
- re-locating to cheaper premises
- encouraging staff to work from home to save office accommodation costs
- using technology to speed up processes.

6. **When organizations introduce change, why might individual employees be hostile?**

Individual employees may be hostile for a whole range of reasons, including:

- being concerned about their lack of skills
- having a fear of change
- being comfortable with the status quo
- negative experience of previous change initiatives
- being concerned about job losses
- being concerned about changes to patterns of work and job content
- being concerned about what advantages there are for the individual.

Chapter 10

1. **What does the term 'work/life balance' mean and can it ever be achieved in practice?**

Work/life balance refers to the achievement of a fair split between work and non-work commitments, enabling an individual to feel in control of his or her life. Some organizations offer extensive work/life balance opportunities, which help people to achieve this, but it also relies on the individual having support outside of work. On the other hand, some individuals will choose to work long hours at the expense of their non-work life, as they see work as a central part of their life and who they are.

2. **What, in your view, are the important features leading to happiness at work?**

There are no right or wrong answers to this question; it all depends on the individual. However, authors such as Peter Warr have suggested certain features that they consider are related to happiness at work, such as personal influence, being able to use one's abilities, variety and challenge, clear expectations, reasonable physical environment, a valued role, supportive supervision, good career outlook, fair treatment and being paid well for what you do.

3. **How could soft skills be assessed as part of a selection process?**

Soft skills can be assessed as part of a selection process through the use of behavioural competency-based questions, which can be tailored to seek evidence of contribution as a team-player or sensitivity to others, and so on. The use of an assessment centre provides an opportunity to see soft skills in practice across a range of activities. In the recruitment stage, the application form can also focus on evidence-based questions, seeking confirmation of capability in these areas.

4. **Given the current data on the position of women in management positions, what can organizations do to achieve a higher representation of women at board level?**

Organizations can set targets to improve representation; establish role models and a mentoring system to develop a female talent pipeline; offer work/life balance initiatives and have case examples of senior-level employees who work part-time; offer female-only development opportunities as a means of creating a network of support; revisit the internal promotion criteria, so that women who have taken a career break, for example, can compete on an equal footing.

5. **Home-working has increased through the use of technology. While many advantages have been identified, what do you think the challenges might be?**

The challenges of home-working include the feeling of isolation from colleagues and office gossip; the perception that 'out of sight = out of mind', which may impact on career opportunities; the complexity of managing people at a distance, and setting targets and measuring performance; the need for a high level of self-motivation; communication difficulties and problems with the technology that may impact on the pace of work.

6. **Outline and explain Hofstede's dimensions of national culture.**

Hofstede's key dimensions of national culture are:

- **Masculinity/femininity** – refers to the division of roles between the sexes. What is seen as a typical role for men or for women can vary from one society to another. Societies can therefore be classified according to whether they try to minimise or maximise sex role divisions.

- **Collectivism/individualism** – this dimension is concerned with the relation between an individual and others. At one end of the spectrum there are societies in which ties are very loose and everyone tends to look after their own self-interest, and at the other end we find societies where the ties between individuals are much tighter.

- **Power distance** – refers to how society deals with the fact that people are unequal. Some let these inequalities grow over time into inequalities of power and wealth, while others strive for greater equality.

- **Uncertainty avoidance** – this dimension is concerned with how societies deal with the fact that the future is uncertain. In some societies people accept this and are more likely to take risks easily, while in others people will try to create security and avoid risk.

7. **What is meant by the 'convergence/divergence debate', and what are the implications for management?**

This debate refers to the extent to which cultures in different countries are becoming more similar (convergence) or different (divergence). The implications for managers are that, in the convergence scenario, people will increasingly share the same norms and patterns of behaviour, and therefore standard practices of management can be applied throughout the world. In the divergence scenario, managers will need to be sensitive to national cultural differences.

INDEX

Note: Page numbers in *italics* refer to figures and information contained within tables; page numbers in **bold** refer to keyword definitions.